Democracy Betrayed

DEMOCRACY BETRAYED

A HISTORY OF THE DEMOCRATIC PARTY FROM COTTON PLANTATION TO URBAN PLANTATION

Nelson L. Dawson

Algora Publishing
New York

Library of Congress Cataloging-in-Publication Data

Names: Dawson, Nelson L., author.
Title: Democracy betrayed: a history of the Democratic Party from cotton plantation
to urban plantation/
  Nelson L. Dawson.
Description: New York : Algora Publishing, [2020] | Includes
  bibliographical references and index. | Summary: "The Democratic Party
  is usually extolled as a heroic party of the people, but it has a sordid
  past rooted in slavery, segregation, and cynical exploitation of African
  Americans. This book traces the Party from its origins in the political
  philosophy of Thomas Jefferson to the end of Reconstruction and LBJ's
  Great Society"— Provided by publisher.
Identifiers: LCCN 2020038770 (print) | LCCN 2020038771 (ebook) | ISBN
  9781628944259 (trade paperback) | ISBN 9781628944266 (hardcover) | ISBN
  9781628944273 (pdf)
Subjects: LCSH: Democratic Party (U.S.)—History—19th century.
Classification: LCC JK2316 .D42 2020 (print) | LCC JK2316 (ebook) | DDC
  324.273609/034—dc23
LC record available at https://lccn.loc.gov/2020038770
LC ebook record available at https://lccn.loc.gov/2020038771

Front Cover: An 1827 lithograph published by H. R. Robinson, N.Y.
THE FIRST APPEARANCE OF THE DEMOCRATIC DONKEY. Jackson rides it, Van
Buren follows it. The distribution of the surplus in "pet banks" had far-reaching effects,
particularly in the western part of the country. The new banks issued "wildcat" currency,
and with the inflated money, speculation in land was booming. To stop it, Jackson issued
a Super Circular, which demanded hard currency — gold or silver — for payments on land
from the public reserves.

Printed in the United States

Acknowledgments

I would like to express my profound gratitude to my wife Susan Holman Dawson of Louisville, Kentucky, and to my son Christopher Lloyd Dawson of Columbus, Ohio, for their invaluable contributions in editing and proofreading the manuscript. My son Matthew Jarvis Dawson of Tampa, Florida, and his wife Jamie along with our grandchildren Nathaniel, Clara, Jeremy, and Wesley have helped sustain me with their love and support.

Table of Contents

Introduction: We Are All Cleons Now

The Democratic Party is such an ongoing disaster for the United States that it seems fitting to organize this introduction using the triad of slogans adopted by the dystopia of George Orwell's *1984*.

War is Peace

The antebellum Democratic Party was the party of slavery; until well into the twentieth century, it was the party of racism. The contemporary Democratic Party consists of affluent elites who have created urban plantations of dependents by their social, educational, and economic policies. These dependents then vote Democratic to ensure a cornucopia of government bounty—at the expense of middle-class Americans. This plan is brilliant for short-term political success but deadly for long-term national survival. The Democratic Party is waging war on the America of the Founders. Has it become the vehicle by which skepticism about democracy will be validated?[1]

---

[1] The title is a rephrasing of "We are all Keynesians now," attributed variously to Milton Friedman and Richard Nixon in acknowledgement of the dominance of the economic philosophy of John Maynard Keynes (1883–1946).

This is the working mantra of the Democratic Party.

Cleon (d. 422 B.C.) was an Athenian demagogue who exploited democratic rhetoric and class conflict as a means to power.

John Adams observed that "Democracy never lasts long. It soon wastes, exhausts, and murders itself. There never was a Democracy yet that did not commit suicide." John Adams to John Taylor, December 17, 1814. https://founders.archives.gov/documents/Adams/000-02-02-6371.

Winston Churchill observed that democracy is the worst form of government—except all the others that have ever been tried.[2] Democracy has always been a fragile plant, requiring delicately balanced conditions to survive. The experience of the ancients reflected this. Athens, the fountainhead of western democracy, quickly stumbled from the statesman Pericles to the demagogue Cleon, and its democracy never recovered. A flourishing Roman Republic experienced a similar, though more protracted, descent into demagoguery, civil war, and emperors.

Our democracy has been cited to refute this skepticism. But we are now witnessing a variant of Freud's return of the repressed; the vulnerability of democracy, seemingly thwarted by American political genius, has returned in force.[3] The Democratic Party is the product of a devolution which reflects all the politically correct distortions of common political sense. It is difficult to write such a book as this without looking like one of those stereotypical eccentrics with sandwich boards at busy intersections warning that the end is near. But what counts is not signs but evidence not that we are doomed, but that we are in grave peril.

An iconic moment occurred at the Democratic National Convention of 2012.[4] The party platform had omitted any mention of God and failed to affirm Jerusalem as the capital of Israel.[5] Criticized by Mitt Romney and other Republicans, President Obama intervened to order the politically expedient affirmations. But then came the chaos of the raucous voice-vote in which the nays clearly dominated the ayes. But by fiat, the changes were declared approved to the accompaniment of boos.

At this point, a backward look is necessary. "I belong to no organized political party," Will Rogers asserted, "I am a Democrat." Most of us smile wanly at this old quip. The statement is true of most complex human institutions. A Democrat—but of which Democratic Party? The Democratic Party of Thomas Jefferson who believed in small government, an agrarian America

---

[2] The International Churchill Society, http://winstonchurchill.org/resources/quotes.

[3] The great bulwark of our democracy is our Constitution. It is predictable that leftists want to replace it with a "living Constitution" which translates into "let's just do whatever we want." See Ruth Bader Ginsburg's musings on undermining the very document it is her job to uphold. "Ginsburg to Egyptians: I Wouldn't Use U.S. Constitution as a Model," *Fox News*, February 6, 2012.

[4] Much has happened since 2012. The Brett Kavanaugh fiasco of 2018 reveals a party increasingly complicit with mob behavior. Chronicling Democratic misbehavior is an unending task.

[5] See Josh Lederman and Julie Pace, "Democrats Change Platform to Add God, Jerusalem," *Yahoo News*, September 5, 2012. The aspect of American society which most disgusts leftists—religious commitment—is precisely that which has always been central to our democratic life. This is a major theme of Alexis de Tocqueville's *Democracy in America* (1835).

with little taxation and slavery? The Democratic Party of Andrew Jackson who harried the Cherokee from their land, believed in hanging traitors, and defended slavery? The Democratic Party of James Buchanan who did nothing while the country fell apart because his fellow Democrats in the South were preparing to defend slavery by rebellion? The Democratic Party of Grover Cleveland anchored by political bosses in the cities of the East and Midwest? The Democratic Party of Franklin D. Roosevelt which embraced dramatic growth in the size and power of the Federal government?

It is tempting to throw up one's hands and see the Democratic Party as a series of parties with no common core. Its history would be a history of Democratic parties. But this is inadequate, for there is one constant amid all the vagaries and policy shifts—a consistent determination to benefit from the prevailing selfishness of the evolving democratic ethos. This is an abstract thesis; the purpose of this book is to elucidate it in the unfolding historical narrative.[6] A corollary to this thesis is that this tendency has been present in the Democratic Party from its inception. It has generally worked out well politically, but it is reaching its final stage in our own time. Reform is always a possibility, but it will not come easily.

The initial failure of the Democrats to mention God in their 2012 party platform is an indication of the inroads of an increasingly aggressive secularism. President Obama's contemptuous remark about his fellow Americans clinging to guns and religion is another indication. All the Founders, Christian or Deist, believed that religion is necessary for the long-run viability of democracy.[7] For us, the long-run is running out. A secularized society obsessed with effortless gratification as an entitlement detached from foresight and sacrifice is the sociological base for the blandishments of demagoguery. The Democratic Party functions in a synergistic relationship to a welfare society, both by helping create it and then by benefitting from its constant expansion. However, the strategy will work only as long as there is enough of other people's money to redistribute. The Democratic Party is at war with the America of the Founders.

---

[6] One caveat is essential. All political parties in democratic societies must accommodate themselves to prevailing sentiments to some degree or die. There is a point, however, at which a difference in degree becomes a difference in kind.

[7] John Adams again: "Our Constitution was made only for a moral and religious people. It is wholly inadequate to the government of any other kind." President John Adams to the Officers of the First Brigade of the Third Division of the Militia of Massachusetts, 1798, Adams, *Works*, 9:229.

Ignorance is Strength

This sociological base encompasses an expanding pool of poverty-stricken voters. But where do such voters come from? For the most part from our public-school system.[8] And who controls the public schools? The teachers' unions. And which party is mainlining the political contributions of the teachers' unions? And which first black president let black students languish in failed inner-city schools rather than cross the teachers' unions over the issues of vouchers and charter schools? The Democratic Party has a vested interest in ignorance.

The implementation of these policies is being enabled by a media establishment which also has a vested interest in ignorance. Proving that a stiflingly pervasive leftist media bias exists is like another breathless announcement of the proof of the Pythagorean Theorem.[9] The function of the Democratic Party apparatchiks masquerading as journalists is to provide cover for Democrats. Never have so many been lied to by so few about so much. One might expect historians to fight in academic trenches for objective standards and honest evaluation. Some do—and often at great personal cost. But it is also true that the prevailing ethos is undeniably leftist. Many historians function as if their chief role in life is to provide historiographical absolution in one form or another for the catastrophes the Democratic Party leaves in its wake.

The most egregious example of propaganda as history is Howard Zinn's *A People's History of the United States, 1492–Present* (1980). It has gone through five editions and multiple printings, sold more than a million copies, and been assigned in thousands of college classes. Michael Kazin, editor of *Dissent* and a man very much of the left, has written a powerful indictment of the book and by implication of the multitude of college professors who have assigned

---

[8] The stance of the Democratic Party on this issue is disastrous because of its direct impact on disadvantaged children. An honorable Democratic dissenter is Eva Moskowitz, an eloquent champion of charter schools in New York. Matthew Kaminski, "Eva Moskowitz: Teachers Union Enemy No. 1," *Wall Street Journal*, February 16, 2014. For the ongoing leftward movement of teachers' unions, see https://www.insidesources.com/liberal-politics-teachers-unions/.

[9] Media bias is also reflected by the bias in books about the media. Robert A. Rutland's history of journalism *The Newsmongers: Journalism in the Life of the Nation, 1690–1972* (1973) is an example The *New York Times* has sixty-four citations; the *Wall Street Journal* is mentioned only once. One of the greatest scandals in the history of American journalism is the pro-Soviet propaganda by the Pulitzer-Prize-winning *New York Times* reporter Walter Duranty, particularly his cover-up of the Ukrainian famine. Yet Rutland mentions him only in connection with his coverage of World War I. Rutland devotes several pages to unfavorable commentary on Joseph McCarthy but does not mention Alger Hiss. Yet he assures us that: "To tell the truth is still the highest calling in politics, in medicine, in law, and, above all, in journalism" (390).

it. He concludes that Zinn's book is "quite unworthy of such fame and influence." It is a "bad history, albeit gilded with virtuous intentions" (the ever-reliable road to hell). The premise—that the American people have always been governed and manipulated by "a tiny band of rulers whose wiles match their wits"—is "better suited to a conspiracy-mongers Web site than to a work of scholarship."[10] Richard N. Current, an eminent historian of an earlier generation, issued a timely admonition in 1990: "Those who rewrite the past to serve a present cause, no matter how worthy the cause, are engaged in the very essence of mythmaking."[11]

Many books—Howard Zinn's among them—deserve to be forgotten, but among those now forgotten which deserve to be remembered is Julien Benda's *La Trahison des Clercs* (*The Treason of the Intellectuals*). Written in 1927 in the aftermath of the orgy of nationalism which ignited World War I, Benda denounced the French and German intellectuals of the nineteenth and twentieth centuries for their abandonment of dispassionate universalist discourse in favor of nationalism, warmongering, and racism. Benda begins with a quotation by Charles Bernard Renouvier: "The world is suffering from lack of faith in a transcendental truth" and with the assertion that "our age is indeed the age of the intellectual organization of political hatreds."[12] This is even more valid at present when everything has become political. Benda was committed to a civilizational mission as a proponent of a balance of classical civilization and the Christian faith. The abandonment of the quest for truth, love, and beauty for obsession with race, class, and gender justifies a modification of the classic Pogo dictum: "We have met the barbarian and he is us."[13]

Freedom is Slavery

In surveying the history of the Democratic Party, perhaps the bitterest irony of all consists of its very name. In 1897, President Grover Cleveland vetoed a bill to appropriate ten thousand dollars for the aid of drought-stricken Texas farmers, commenting that "though the people support the

---

[10] See Michael Kazin's review "Howard Zinn's History Lessons," *Dissent* (online), Spring 2004; https://www.dissentmagazine.org/article/howard-zinns-history-lessons. See also Mary Grabar, *Debunking Howard Zinn: Exposing a Fake History That Turned a Generation Against America* (2019).

[11] Quoted by Patrick Riddleberger in his review of *The Historian's Lincoln* (1990) by Gabor S. Boritt in the *Journal of American History* 70 (1990): 1270.

[12] Julien Benda, *The Treason of the Intellectuals* (1927). Renouvier quote, frontispiece; intellectual hatreds, 27.

[13] See https://humorinamerica.wordpress.com/2014/05/19/the-morphology-of-a-humorous-phrase/

government, the government should not support the people."[14] The obvious point is the incongruity of the quote in the context of the evolution of the Democratic Party in the pre-FDR era. Read another way, however, it is eerily prophetic of the emergence of an elitist Democratic political class which, in redistributing the earned wealth of productive citizens, is actually supporting itself.

This fundamentally unjust system is increasingly compelled to rely on power. The program of the Democratic Party today is buttressed by a panoply of coercion. Leftists do not care what you do as long as it is mandatory. A good, though dismal, example is the implementation of Obamacare. Pounded by fair means or foul through a reluctant Congress, consistently rejected by large majorities of Americans, subject to website fiascos, and lawlessly modified by delays, waivers, and exemptions, this monstrosity has fundamentally degraded healthcare. But no matter, it is still good medicine for us because they say so. Notice how this works on social issues. We can kill millions of babies, but children are expelled from school for pointing a finger and saying "bang." The right to privacy justifies abortion, but middle-school boys who feel like girls on any given day can have access to girls' restrooms. The list goes on and on, but the underlying principle is simple: zero tolerance for what leftists do not like and absolute license for what they do. Civility is great unless we are talking about racist, sexist, homophobic, guns-and-religion-clinging Americans. What we really need right now is zero tolerance for zero tolerance. Perhaps the most obvious symptom of this metastasizing authoritarianism is the steady substitution of vituperation for argument. After years of liberal handwringing over the prospective emergence of a right-wing theocracy, we get a left-wing theocracy in which the science is always settled, the results are always conclusive, and the Christian faith is always heresy.

On January 17, 2014, New York governor Andrew Cuomo hammered the views of "extreme" Republicans who, he said, "have no place in the state of New York because that is not who New Yorkers are." He graciously conceded that moderate Republicans could stay—for now anyway. The extremists are the anti-gay, pro-gun, right-to-lifers. The conclusion is that anyone belonging to any of these forbidden categories are enemies who do not belong in New York.[15] They are heretics. Theocracy anyone? Cardinal Francis George, who retired as bishop of Chicago in 2012, once predicted that he would die in

---

[14] George F. Parker, ed., *The Writings and Speeches of Grover Cleveland* (1892; repr., 1970), 450.
[15] See https://nypost.com/2014/01/18/gov-cuomo-to-conservatives-leave-ny/ In the face of strong pushback, the governor fell back predictably on the I-was-misquoted defense; see https://townhall.com/columnists/calthomas/2014/01/23/cuomo-to-conservatives-leave-new-york-n1783146.

his bed, his successor would die in prison, his successor would be martyred, and his successor would help rebuild a shattered civilization.[16] No one can possibly know if things will turn out like this; the cardinal himself claimed no special revelation. However, it is a grim testimony to our current leftist mindset that his extrapolation is not intrinsically inconceivable.

How did we come to this? Why does this history of the Democratic Party begin with the American Revolution rather than with Martin Van Buren and Andrew Jackson? The party has existed as a formal political organization only since the 1820s. Nevertheless, the political debates regarding the nature of the American Revolution and the emerging American Republic, conducted by the Founders themselves, provide a necessary context for understanding subsequent political evolution. The explicit ideological framework of the Democratic Party has existed since Thomas Jefferson and his disciples embraced the French Revolution, Jacobins and all. An exploration of this ideology is essential for an understanding of the political environment which shaped the essential identity of the Democratic Party.

---

[16] See Religious News Service for the quote and his obituary, April 17, 2015 and https://religionnews.com/2015/04/17/chicago-cardinal-francis-george-dies-78-icon-conservatism-suddenly-favor/

CHAPTER ONE: THE GLORIOUS CAUSE OR A KIND OF REVOLUTION? 1776–1783

Was it a revolution? Jacques Barzun defines revolution as "the violent transfer of power and property in the name of an idea."[17] Yet he believed that the leaders of the "American War of Independence" wanted only a return to the "good old days."[18] Samuel Eliot Morison also stressed the narrow range and limited goals of the Revolutionary War in which American leaders engaged in a "constant struggle. . . to keep innovation within reasonable bounds and avoid anarchy and steer clear of the rocks of dissolution."[19] Other historians have asserted that the American Revolution was a social movement, mainly concerned with internal reform—the issue being, as Carl Becker put it, not only home rule but "who should rule at home."[20] These

---

[17] Chapter title

The phrase "Glorious Cause" is, appropriately, from George Washington who used it on a number of occasions. See, for example, "Acceptance of Appointment as General and Commander in Chief," June 16, 1775, in *Writings of George Washington from Original Manuscript Sources, 1745–1799*, edited by John C. Fitzpatrick (1931–1944), 39 vols., vol. 3, 203. "A Kind of Revolution" is the dismissive title of chapter five of Howard Zinn's *A People's History*, dealing with the American Revolution and Constitution. For him, the revolution is just another dismal example of the same old story of the rich exploiting, deceiving, and coercing the poor for their own selfish purposes. Robert Middlekauff, however, comments that the revolutionaries "believed that their cause was glorious—and so do I." See *The Glorious Cause, The American Revolution, 1763–1789* (1982), vii; he revisits this theme throughout the book, especially, 463-64, 508, 549, and 581.

Jacques Barzun, *From Dawn to Decadence: 500 Years of Western Cultural Life* (2000), 3.
[18] Barzun, *Dawn*, 397.
[19] Samuel Eliot Morison, *The Conservative American Revolution* (1976), 3-4.
[20] Carl L. Becker, *The History of Political Parties in the Province of New York* (1909; repr., 1968), 22. The classic exposition of the social-reform perspective is J. Franklin Jameson, *The*

quotations introduce an important contrast which runs through the revolutionary era—the contrast between intention and result. What did the revolutionaries *intend* and what did they actually *do*? The American Revolution was a complex, unfolding drama from the initial tensions in 1763 until the ratification of the Constitution in 1789. It is important to delineate the founding principles by which the political evolution of the Democratic Party can be evaluated.

With regard to revolutions in general, the most powerful engine of social change is a people's need for immediate relief of social and economic distress. Societies live long, while individuals die soon.[21] A man who sees his children malnourished because of his low wages is not interested in the long run, and revolutions promise quick results. But there are costs. Revolution is at best a high-risk affair which can easily go wrong. Most revolutions do go wrong, according to a distinct historical pattern. Crane Brinton provides a revolutionary fever chart.[22] Revolutions begin with pervasive symptoms of social and political stress which lead to an initially moderate attempt at reform. But this moderation is superseded by a radical phrase of violent upheaval like the Terror of the French Revolution. Finally, there is a collapse into dictatorship. So, like the Biblical demoniac, the last state of the afflicted society is worse than the first.[23]

The American Revolution does not fit at all well with Brinton's fever chart, despite his best efforts at harmonization. If history is philosophy learned from examples, then the situation of the British Empire in 1763 is a confirmation of the old adage that pride indeed goes before a fall.[24] Triumphant in the Seven Years' War (1756-63), a great world war with the French for imperial supremacy, only sunshine and roses seemed ahead.[25] The war was won: the French had been driven from North America, and a worldwide empire had been created. The sober reality, however, was that the war had been very costly. Since, the reasoning ran, it had been fought largely in North America for the colonists, why not insist that they help pay for it?

Colonial society was far from democratic, but it was by contemporary standards remarkably free. The colonists enjoyed the cherished rights of

---

American Revolution Considered as a Social Movement (1925).

[21] Ralph Barton Perry has argued that in order to avoid revolution "the rate of change must be rapid enough to create a sense of movement within the life span of a generation." Ralph Barton Perry, *Puritanism and Democracy* (1944), 635.

[22] Crane Brinton, *The Anatomy of Revolution* (1965), 14–20; for the American Revolution, see 100, 128, 179, 185, 190, 235.

[23] Matthew 12:43–45.

[24] Dionysius of Halicarnassus (c. 60 BC–c. 7 BC), *Ars Rhetorica*, XI, 2.

[25] Called the French and Indian War by the colonists who named it for their enemies.

Englishmen.[26] They thought of themselves as the loyal subjects of a distant but benevolent king. But the truth was that this loyalty flourished in an environment of benign neglect. At times, the royal governors could be disagreeable. The Navigation Acts irritated primarily New England merchants, though they were often circumvented. Virginia tobacco planters had a depressing tendency to fall into debt to English middlemen, blaming not their all-too-common profligacy but a system they imagined was rigged against them. But none of this, or many other lesser irritants, was the stuff of revolution.

However, in 1763, flush with victory, the British began tightening the screws in a variety of ways. They prohibited colonial expansion beyond the Appalachians to prevent expensive Indian wars. They sent soldiers to North America to protect the colonists who were required to pay for their support. New custom duties were levied; then in 1765, the Stamp Act aroused powerful opposition by imposing a tax on all legal documents and newspapers.[27] These actions were taken at a time when the colonies were increasingly aware of their own strength and were completely free of any threat from the French Catholics of Canada. A series of crises, with only a few breathing spells, led ultimately to the revolution. The crises achieved in only a few years what over a hundred and fifty years of British policy had not done—impel the colonists to think of themselves more and more as a united people, not just inhabitants of particular colonies. After considerable agitation, including outright violence and intimidation, the tax was repealed.[28] However, the Declaratory Act of 1766 that repealed the Stamp Act also reaffirmed the right of Parliament to tax the colonies "in all Cases whatsoever."[29]

The immediate crisis passed, but things did not return to normal. Various minor irritations culminated in the Boston Tea Party of 1773 in which "patriots," thinly disguised as Indians, dumped 2000 chests of tea worth over 600,000 pounds into the Boston Harbor. The British response was the Coercive Acts of 1774, known to the colonists as the Intolerable Acts.[30] The British had hoped to subdue the radicals of New England without general resis-

---

[26] George Trevelyan observed that eighteen-century Englishmen enjoyed "Parliamentary control, and freedom of speech, press and person. . . . They looked with contempt on French, Italians and Germans as people enslaved to priests, Kings and nobles, unlike your freeborn Englishmen." See his *History of England* (1988; first ed., 1926), 22.

[27] Edmund S. Morgan and Helen M. Morgan, *The Stamp Act Crisis: Prologue to Revolution* (1953).

[28] The anti-British agitators were known as "Sons of Liberty." They were a very mixed bag, ranging from genuine patriots to thugs. The degree to which they were controlled by colonial leaders was sometimes uncertain. Middlekauff, *Glorious Cause*, 89–93.

[29] Middlekauff, *Glorious Cause*, 114.

[30] These acts closed the port of Boston (until the tea had been paid for), revoked the charter of Massachusetts, required the citizens of Boston to pay for the quartering of British soldiers, mandated trials in England for British officials and soldiers accused of crimes,

tance, but this was no longer possible. British policy led to the summoning of the First Continental Congress in September 1774.[31] Then shortly after the first armed clashes at Lexington and Concord in April 1775, the Second Continental Congress convened in May 1775.

During the crisis years from 1763 to 1776, there was an evolution of colonial policy. At first, the focus was on specific abuses with the goal of returning to Barzun's "good old days." Had the British heeded this sentiment, all might yet have been well—at least for a time. But they did not. Inevitably, the perspective broadened to encompass first the issue of taxation without representation which was resisted as an illegal taking of property. Then came the broader issue of the place of the colonies in the British Empire. Some envisioned a dominion status, such as the Galloway Plan of Union, which would have created an American colonial parliament with broader powers to regulate colonial affairs within the British Empire. It was narrowly defeated by the Continental Congress in October 1774—before the British had a chance to reject it.[32] Throughout the crisis years, the colonists became convinced that there was a conspiracy by corrupt British leaders to subdue them.[33] This profound distrust made any possible reconciliation more difficult.

Up to this point, the primary focus was almost entirely on relations with the British with little interest in either independence or domestic reform. The outbreak of fighting changed everything. Even so, it is an indication of the conservatism of the colonial leaders that they took a year after the war started to vote for independence. And it is only with independence that a host of other issues surfaced, including what kind of independent country the new country would be. Yet when Congress did declare independence, it also asserted its right to do so. Determining the origin and nature of this right is central to understanding the American Revolution.

Most of the colonists were Englishmen, transplanted in time and space, but English in heritage nonetheless. Many of the better educated among them were very much aware of the political evolution in England from the mid-seventeenth century to their own time. This was a history written largely by opposition centered in the emerging Whig Party to aggressive threats to civil liberty from an aggressive monarchy. The English Civil War of 1642–51 fits to

---

granted religious freedom to the Catholics of Quebec and transferred the land between the Ohio and Mississippi Rivers to the province of Quebec.

[31] These congresses reflect the new reality of colony-wide resistance. Both met at Philadelphia.

[32] Named for Joseph Galloway of Pennsylvania. The close vote shows that there was strong resistance to the idea of independence.

[33] See Gordon S. Wood, *The Creation of the American Republic, 1776–1789* (1969), 40–43. This obsession with conspiracy continued in the domestic political battles of the 1790s.

some degree into Crane Brinton's revolutionary fever chart—increasing radicalization of Puritan factions, though without the widespread Terror of the French Revolution, culminating in the authoritarian protectorate of Oliver Cromwell and the restoration of the Stuart monarchy of Charles II in 1660. Charles, however, pressed for greater powers against growing parliamentary opposition, so the opposition continued. The accession of the Catholic James II in 1685, and the prospect of an extended Catholic monarchy with the birth of his son, led to the Glorious Revolution of 1688 and the definitive triumph of the Whigs.[34] It is here that we should look—where the colonists looked— for the rationale of independence.

The Declaration of Independence was a foundational document for the American Revolution. The first two "self-evident truths" are that all men are created equal and "are endowed by their Creator with certain inalienable rights"—life, liberty, and the pursuit of happiness.[35] Furthermore, governments "deriving their just powers from the consent of the governed" are instituted among men to secure these rights. Virtually everything about the foundation of our government flows from these truths. Where did they come from?

The conventional view is to derive these principles largely from the thinkers of the eighteenth-century Enlightenment, more specifically from the English philosopher John Locke. Jefferson was strongly influenced by Locke when he wrote the Declaration of Independence. However, the concept of self-evident truths regarding human rights ultimately flows from the Biblical worldview. The most radical of all assertions justifying the American Revolution is the very one most deeply embedded in this heritage. The long-term view extends backward to the Genesis creation narrative with its foundational assertion that human beings were created in the image of God.[36] This is the ultimate source of human rights.[37]

The English Puritans reaffirmed this principle at a timely moment in the seventeenth century.[38] They emerged from the ferment of the Protestant

[34] Victors get to name things, and for the triumphant Whigs, it was indeed a Glorious Revolution.

[35] John Locke's triad was life, liberty, and property. "Pursuit of Happiness" was a rhetorical enhancement—to which the right of property was essential.

[36] Genesis 1:26.

[37] Carl L. Becker in his *The Declaration of Independence: A Study in the History of Political Ideas* (1922; repr., 1942) argues that the Declaration is based ultimately on the belief that God created a natural order of things, including human rights. The most fundamental influence on Jefferson and the Declaration, according to Becker, is the Enlightenment concept of "Nature and Nature's God" (37). This is not wrong but incomplete because it ignores the pervasive Puritan influence.

[38] Jacques Barzun observed that such seventeenth-century Puritan agitators as John Lilburne and "dozens of his fellow Puritan pamphleteers" declared and demanded "the

Reformation with its renewed emphasis on the priesthood of all believers and the equality of all Christians before God. In the context of English history, the Puritans were radical Protestants who wished to cleanse the Anglican Church of its papist impurities, a stance which put them at odds with both the monarchy and the Church of England.[39] Puritans believed that God, having created man in His image, endowed him with rights that cannot legitimately be denied by any human authority. This core belief survived all the vicissitudes of the English Civil War and the Protectorate of Oliver Cromwell. It survived the Restoration of the Stuart monarchy in 1660 and emerged during the crisis of 1685 and the Glorious Revolution of 1688. Thereafter, it was enshrined in the outlook of the emerging Whig Party. The New England Puritans were fully committed to the same belief, and this belief provided the rationale of the American Revolution. The revolutionaries were not claiming any new rights; they were simply asserting the rights that they already possessed.

In making this claim, they drew on the rich tradition of English political thought from the Puritan thinkers of the seventeenth century such as John Lilburne and John Milton as well as the teaching of New England Puritans. This Puritan tradition continued into the eighteenth century with the "so-called eighteenth-century Commonwealth men." These men never attained great fame, either in England or in America, and yet "in the fashioning of revolutionary ideology in America they had an influence that surpassed Locke's."[40]

However, it would be an oversimplification to attribute the success of the American Revolution solely to Puritan influence. Puritanism also had a powerful theocratic influence. Within Puritanism there was an inescapable tension between this influence and the primacy of the individual conscience and the distrust of governmental authority. What evolved in England and preeminently in America was a unique blend of the Puritan character with an optimistic political outlook which lent support to the democratic ideal. American colonial society was freer, less hierarchical than English society, so in this environment, the seeds of a greater democratic outlook germinated. Seventeenth-century Puritanism interacted with an emerging eighteenth-century democratic ethos to produce a uniquely American political synthesis

---

rights of man," yet because "these goals were justified out of Scripture, the substance of Puritan political thought has been eclipsed." These men, in fact, anticipated both Adam Smith and John Locke. See *Dawn to Decadence*, 263, 268–71 (quote 270).

[39] James I threatened to "harry" them "out of the land."

[40] Middlekauff, *Glorious Cause*, 132–35 (quote 132). Also see Bernard Bailyn, *The Ideological Origins of the American Revolution* (1967) for more on the significance of the Puritan influence, esp. vii–viii, 33–34 and Wood, *Creation*, 15, 19.

which was the indispensable political framework of the American Revolution.

This is the foundation which ensured the astonishing success of the American Revolution, particularly in contrast to the French Revolution. The American revolutionaries believed that all human beings lived in a kind of theocracy because all human beings possessed inalienable rights conferred by God, not by society. Governments can violate these rights—indeed much of human history is a melancholy record of such violations—but they cannot destroy them. This bedrock principle defines the primary responsibility of government which is to defend these rights; the legitimacy of any government is determined by its success in doing so.

This responsibility however, is easier to affirm than to implement, and the reason for this, according to the Biblical worldview, is that God created man in His image, but man chose evil; humanity is burdened with the deep wound of Original Sin.[41] This fundamental flaw has vast implications for all of life, including politics. The implications of this doctrine were not systematically challenged until the rise of the eighteenth-century Enlightenment philosophy with its virtual deification of Reason and its belief in the perfectibility of humanity.[42] But the enthusiastic adoption of this Enlightenment philosophy was in some respects deeply unreasonable. The flaw is not with reason itself but with an unreasonable belief in its total sufficiency in human affairs. It is, however, this philosophy, more than any other, which drives the utopian impulse, the ultimate source of modern totalitarianism, beginning with the French Revolution.

It was fortunate that while the American revolutionary Founders were influenced by the Enlightenment, the American Revolution was not simply an Enlightenment project.[43] The revolution unfolded in the context of that unique blend of Puritanism and democracy. The text of the Declaration of Independence embodies this blending of influences. Jefferson moves from the formulaic Enlightenment acknowledgement of "the laws of Nature and of Nature's God" to the Biblical affirmation that men possess "certain inalienable rights" which have been "endowed by their Creator."[44]

---

[41] It has always been easier to ridicule the concept than to ignore its consequences.

[42] It is certainly possible to acknowledge human imperfection without recourse to the Genesis narrative, but it is this narrative which presents the concept in its deepest embodiment in Western civilization.

[43] Carl L. Becker in *The Heavenly City of the Eighteenth-Century Philosophers* (1932; repr., 1958) interprets the Enlightenment in some ways as a radically secular version of Christianity with its linear view of history, the end point of which is the heavenly city of Christian eschatology on earth.

[44] See Michael Aton's review of Thomas G. West, *The Political Theory of the American Founding* (2018) in which he asserts that the core of the Founders' political theory is "a coherent

A perennial point of debate has always been the question of religion and the American founding.[45] Some of the Founders were Deists, not orthodox Christians. The United States was not founded as a Christian nation. However, religion, specifically Christianity, deeply informed its beginning and subsequent evolution. The American Revolution was primarily an effort to secure and safeguard those inalienable rights which the revolutionaries believed only God gave and only God could take away. The Founders were generally men of deep faith who were convinced that God was guiding their actions and would ultimately ensure their success. There has been little doubt on this score among historians. The debate has been on the issue of the degree to which they were Christian rather than Deist. But this debate is relevant only for the beliefs of the Founders. In the larger society, there was no uncertainty regarding the primacy of the Christian faith. The American Revolution itself unfolded with powerful support from the churches and pastors of the colonies. The American Revolution was regarded as a just war, even a holy war, to safeguard the God-given rights which were threatened by British tyranny.[46] Holy wars have a way of turning ugly, and the American Revolution certainly had its ugly aspects; yet it did not degenerate to the level of the European wars of religion which were a toxic brew of religious hatred and power politics.

Returning to the initial question: Was it a revolution? In 1775, neither the British nor the Americans had any difficulty in answering the question. But this relates only to its external aspect. After independence, unavoidable internal issues surfaced. A number of the Founders, perhaps most famously John Dickinson and Joseph Galloway, had been reluctant to declare independence, which raised a multitude of daunting issues summed up in Becker's

---

account of all human beings' equal natural rights." *New Criterion*, June 2018, 8–17 (quote, 13). Alexander Hamilton, in words that could have been echoed by many of contemporaries among the Founders, asserted that:

> The sacred rights of mankind are not to be rummaged for
> among old parchments or musty records. They are written,
> as with a sunbeam, in the whole volume of human nature
> by the hand of divinity itself, and can never be erased or
> obscured by mortal power.
> Harold C. Syrett, ed., *Papers of Alexander Hamilton*, I, 122.

[45] Jon Meacham discusses the long tradition of American public religion which flourished with relatively few constitutional objections. See *American Gospel: God, the Founding Fathers, and the Making of a Nation* (2006), 3-35.

[46] There was ambivalence among some Anglicans but hardly any elsewhere. For an exhaustive analysis, see James P. Byrd, *Sacred Scripture, Sacred War: The Bible and the American Revolution* (2013).

assertion about the issue of who would rule at home.[47] But it was not simply about who, but also about how.

However uncertain and conflicted many of the Founders were, Thomas Paine, for one, had no doubts.[48] A radical democrat and utopian, he hailed the revolution as "the birthday of a new world."[49] Opposed to this view was John Dickinson who cautioned that "a people does not reform with moderation."[50] The American Revolution was played out in the tension expressed in these quotations. It is clear that the American revolutionaries were initially concerned with the threat posed by aggressive British officials to colonial liberties. The whole crisis period (1763–76) was dominated by these issues. Once independence was established, however, internal political issues inevitably surfaced. How would the colonists become American citizens? What sort of government would be created? How would colonial society change as a result of the revolution?

Most historians agree that the American Revolution avoided the type of radicalism which later emerged during the French Revolution; nevertheless, some argue that it was radical. Historically this view was popular among the so-called Progressive historians who viewed the revolution through the lens of their own political ideology.[51] If it was radical, and this issue will be dealt with later, it was certainly not totalitarian. Paine's aspiration to "begin the world all over again" was, at bottom, a totalitarian project. Utopias are all well and good in the writings of Thomas Moore, Francis Bacon, and Samuel Butler; they do not wear well in real life. Utopian endeavors invariably produce totalitarian results. Trying to build a perfect society out of imperfect people is more daunting than the Labors of Hercules. Usually sooner rather than later, those in charge start reforming people by killing them. So the simple formula is: utopia+time (a variable)=dystopia.

The American revolutionaries never made the perfect the enemy of the good. They were not utopians. It is true, however, that there was an internal struggle to control the course of the revolution. All revolutions with any degree of popular participation release social forces which are difficult to control. Dickinson was right; the American Revolution was no exception. In fact, it was characterized by a good deal of intimidation and outright violence. The Sons of Liberty always had the frightening potential of veering

---

[47] Becker, *History of Political Parties in the Province of New York*, 22. Of course, for Becker the issue of who would rule at home was the cause of the war rather than a consequence.

[48] *Common Sense* (1776). Paine's radicalism triggered John Adams's visceral dislike; Adams grumbled that he was "a star of disaster." Quoted in Bailyn, *Origins*, 16.

[49] Thomas Paine, *Common Sense and Other Political Writings* (1953), 51.

[50] Quoted in Bailyn, *Ideological Origins*, 283.

[51] Prominent historians of this perspective are Charles Beard, Carl Becker, Louis Hartz, and J. Franklin Jameson.

out of control. Radical aspirations in any revolution are usually seen through rosy spectacles by Progressive historians. But the reality is often sobering. John Adams recalled meeting a common-man acquaintance during the revolution who expressed great enthusiasm for the cause because he thought that its success would mean the end of all courts of justice. Adams was properly horrified.[52]

The American revolutionaries rejected radicalism very much in the spirit of Robert Frost:

> I advocate a semi-revolution
> The trouble with a total revolution
> (ask any reputable Rosicrucian)
> Is that it brings the same class up on top.
> Executives of skillful execution
> Will therefore plan to go halfway and stop.
> Yes, revolutions are the only salves,
> But they're one thing that should be done by halves.[53]

The American revolutionary leaders were, by and large, in the Robert Frost school of semi-revolution.

The American Revolution was saved from self-destruction by an influential group of—the oxymoron is nearly unavoidable—revolutionary conservatives.[54] Perhaps the most prominent ones are John Dickinson, Robert Morris, James Wilson, Gouverneur Morris, and John Rutledge. Most of the prominent leaders of the revolution were conservative, including George Washington, John Adams, Alexander Hamilton, and, at this stage of things, even Thomas Jefferson and James Madison. The reasons for this "semi-revolution" go back to the primary influences—Puritanism and the democratic ethos. The Founders were deeply suspicious of unbridled democracy, so they did not attempt to achieve it. They were convinced that any form of representative government can succeed only with the support of virtuous citizens.[55] Quotations among the Founders on this point are abundant. John Adams

---

[52] John Adams, *Diary and Autobiography*, Adams Papers, Series 1, Diaries (1961), III, 326.

[53] Robert Frost, "A Semi-Revolution."

[54] See David Lefer, *The Founding Conservatives: How a Group of Unsung Heroes Saved the American Revolution* (2014).

[55] In his Farewell Address (1796, para. 27-28), George Washington asserted that:

Religion and morality are indispensable supports. In vain would that man claim the tributes of patriotism who should labor to subvert these great pillars of human happiness, these firmest props of the duties of men and Citizens.

It is, he concluded, "substantially true that virtue or morality is a necessary spring of popular government."

was the principal author of the Massachusetts Constitution of 1779, which states that:

> A frequent recurrence to the fundamental principles of the Constitution, and a constant adherence to those of piety, justice, moderation, temperance, industry, and frugality, are absolutely necessary to preserve the advantages of liberty, and to maintain a free government.[56]

The pervasive awareness of the importance of religion and the reality of human fallibility helped prevent the revolution from spinning off into utopianism.

There was another significant factor related to the issue of religion—the virtue of the Founders themselves. Despite their imperfections, they were men of virtue. The importance of virtue in leaders should be axiomatic, but, paradoxically, one sure sign of virtue is the awareness that one is not virtuous—at least not always:

> Unlike the French and Russian revolutionaries, the founders were always conscious of man's innate capacity for evil, and knew that they themselves were by no means exempt from the general taint.[57]

Perhaps the greatest safeguard against the abuse of power is the realization that the line between good and evil, as Aleksandr Solzhenitsyn reminds us, "runs right through every human heart."[58]

To return to the central question: Yes, it was a revolution. Progressive historians argue that it was also radical.[59] But part of the problem is a confusion of intent and consequences. Few historians have argued that the Founders set out with a blueprint for utopia—even Thomas Paine lacked a blueprint. But few have argued that the revolution left society unchanged. The best and most detailed case for the radicalism of the revolution has been made by Gordon Wood, but it is actually a case for the radical long-term results of the revolution.[60] Additional confirmation of this comes from Samuel Eliot Morison who made a similar distinction. "I have," he wrote:

---

[56] *Massachusetts Constitution* (1779).

[57] On the virtue of the Founders, see Myron Magnet, *The Founders at Home: The Building of America, 1735–1817* (2014). Michael Knox Beran, "The Private Faces of Public Virtue," review of *The Founders at Home, Claremont Review of Books*, Summer 2014, 65 (quote).

[58] Aleksandr Solzhenitsyn, *The Gulag Archipelago, 1918–1956* (1991). Not only through the hearts of his Soviet tormentors.

[59] The classic expression of this view is J. Franklin Jameson, *The American Revolution Considered as a Social Movement*. Samuel E. Morison dismissed Jameson's book as "a sort of Bible to our left-wing historians since World War II." See Morison, *Conservative Revolution*, 17.

[60] Gordon S. Wood, *The Radicalism of the American Revolution* (1992).

no intention to denigrate the radical achievements of the revolution—my thesis is that the conservative element was necessary to preserve these gains for posterity.[61]

The revolution did set in motion a long-term movement toward greater egalitarianism, wider opportunity, and increased social mobility. It introduced what might be called a kind of slow-motion radicalism which over time did transform colonial society into an independent democratic republic.

These conclusions are significant in light of our current ideological environment in a time when, one suspects, the Kingdom of Heaven itself would not satisfy leftist ideologues. The American Revolution succeeded beyond anyone's expectations because it avoided utopianism with its inevitable authoritarian implications.[62] The American Revolution was seen as remarkable in its own time, but it can now be seen as even more remarkable in contrast to the shipwrecks of later revolutions. The Founders bequeathed us a republic; every generation must reaffirm its determination to keep it.

---

[61] Morison, *Conservative Revolution*, 26.

[62] This authoritarianism is infiltrating our society like a slow virus. No victories in human affairs are ever permanent.

Chapter Two: If You Can Keep It: The Making of the Constitution, 1783–1789

On the last day of the grueling fifteen-week Constitutional Convention in Philadelphia, Benjamin Franklin, who despite his eighty-two years had played a significant role in its proceedings, was accosted by an anxious lady as he left Independence Hall. "Well, Doctor," she asked, "what have we got, a republic or a monarchy?" "A republic," Franklin replied, "if you can keep it."[63]

The years from 1776 to the end of the war in 1783 comprised a Dickensian best-of-times, worst-of-times era. The revolutionaries were engaged in a desperate struggle with the British superpower while also trying to create a new government. Yet they believed that they were equal to both tasks. They believed that free government could be sustained only by a virtuous people, and they were buoyed by their conviction that they were virtuous and, therefore, destined to succeed.[64] But they were not only virtuous, they also believed themselves to be united. The Whig worldview contrasted a virtuous, united people with a powerful, oppressive government. This was the bracing perspective which sustained their patriotic endeavor.

It is also true that this optimism is inconsistent with the prudent realism regarding human nature which was also characteristic of the revolutionaries. Perhaps this revolutionary euphoria served as a kind of Darwinian

---

[63] The notes of Dr. James McHenry, a delegate from Maryland, first published in the *American Historical Review* 11 (1906): 595-624 (quote, 618).

[64] Joel Barlow expressed this as succinctly as possible: "No virtue, no Commonwealth." July 4, 1787, oration quoted by Gordon S. Wood, *Creation*, 418. Quotations on this point could be multiplied virtually without end.

survival-mechanism which sustained the revolutionaries in their life-and-death struggle. As the end of the war approached in 1783, the euphoria had faded and a more somber assessment of human nature had reappeared. The Revolution succeeded without showing up on Crane Brinton's fever chart. However, forming a government proved to be an equally formidable task. The patched-together Continental Congress functioned as the frame of government until 1781. The Articles of Confederation had been proposed to the new states in 1777 but were not ratified for another four years, only two years before the war ended.

The reason for the delay was deeply symptomatic of the difficulties involved in forming a national government. The thirteen states were new, but the colonies from which they originated were very old by New World standards. People thought of themselves as Virginians, New Yorkers, or as members of whatever other colony they inhabited. The transition from colonies to states did not change the sense of belonging from the local to the national level. The Revolutionary War was fought and won by thirteen essentially independent states.

The ratification of the Articles of Confederation was delayed over a dispute between the states that had western land claims and those that did not. When Virginia and New York ceded their claims in 1781, the Articles of Confederation could finally be ratified. There was at last a national government. The Articles of Confederation reflected the determination to protect state power, which would also protect citizens against the danger of a government strong enough to threaten the liberties for which the war was being fought. But even though the government created by the Articles was not utopian, it certainly reflected naïve optimism.

The thirteen states retained their sovereignty, leading an exasperated British diplomat seeking to negotiate a commercial treaty to exclaim that he would need to negotiate thirteen treaties. The states could issue paper money and pass debt-relief laws nullifying contracts. It was the irresponsibility of the state legislatures which triggered much of the post-revolutionary disillusionment. James Madison was profoundly upset by this spectacle in which his own state of Virginia was an eager participant. There was no executive branch except a figurehead president. Congress could not impose taxes or regulate commerce. Nine of the thirteen states had to approve any legislation. Amending the Articles required unanimous approval.

These internal weaknesses loomed large in light of daunting external issues. The British were still in the Northwest forts in defiance of the Treaty of Paris. The Spanish threatened to choke off American trade on the Missis-

sippi River. The Native Americans, angered by repeated American incur-
sions, grew increasingly hostile. The new nation faced a sea of troubles.

The efficacy of the Articles of Confederation and the era during which
they were in force have been the subject of some debate. Most historians have
regarded the Articles as seriously defective and have seen that era as "the
critical period" for the new nation.[65] Still, both have had their defenders—
notably Charles Beard and Merrill Jensen. There is a political edge here.
The defenders of the Articles are generally Progressive historians who see
the Constitution as counter to the legacy of the Revolution. Jensen pushes
things very far by asserting that the supporters of the Constitution "frankly
disliked the political heritage of the Revolution."[66] He seems oblivious to the
absurdity of including George Washington, Benjamin Franklin, Alexander
Hamilton, John Adams, and James Madison in such company. Such men, it
may be said, were the legacy of the Revolution. The clearest evidence that
this was truly a critical period is their growing perception that the Articles
were not working and would have to be replaced in order to safeguard the
legacy of the Revolution. Two events in 1786, occurring almost simultaneously, seemed to justify this conviction. One highlighted the difficult issue
of interstate relations, and the second raised the alarm about the threat to
social stability.

In 1785, Virginia and Maryland negotiated the resolution of a dispute
regarding navigation on the Potomac River. The success of this meeting
encouraged James Madison to propose a general meeting of the states to
discuss the issue of congressional regulation of commerce. Invitations went
to all states to meet at Annapolis, Maryland, in September 1786. Only five
states sent delegates. The Annapolis Convention accomplished nothing.
The report of this truncated convention proposed a broader constitutional
convention to meet in Philadelphia in the spring of 1787. The Confederation
Congress reluctantly agreed to a meeting to consider piecemeal reforms, but
it had no intention of agreeing to its own death sentence.

Shays' Rebellion was more viscerally alarming. Daniel Shays, a Revolutionary War veteran, led a revolt of disaffected farmers in western Massachusetts protesting taxes, bankruptcies, and land seizures.[67] The rebellion
was put down by the state, fortunately with only mild reprisals. Still, the
rebellion sharpened the fear of Madison, Washington, and other leaders that

---

[65] See John Fiske, *The Critical Period in American History* (1916).

[66] Merrill Jensen, *The New Nation: A History of the United States During the Confederation, 1781–1789*
(1950), 426.

[67] On January 3, 1787, Jefferson wrote Madison that "a rebellion now and then is a good
thing." Madison declined to comment. Quoted in Jack N. Rakove, *Original Meanings:
Politics and Ideas in the Making of the Constitution* (1996), 34.

the new nation was on the brink of social chaos. The nightmare of democracy, the tyranny of the majority, seemed imminent.

In the light of these crises, many of the fifty-five men who assembled at Philadelphia that spring had no intention of merely revising the Articles of Confederation; their intent was to abandon them and try again. The model used to justify this bold step was the Massachusetts Constitution Convention of 1779–80, organized mainly by John Adams. The delegates to the convention were elected directly by the people, not by the state legislature. This special procedure had the intended effect of elevating the constitution to a level above that of ordinary law.[68] There was no legal justification for the announced intention of the Constitutional Convention. This was a sort of coup, revolutionary in both intent and result. The most compelling issue which initially confronted these men was the nature of state representation, specifically in the form of a division between large and small states. This led ultimately to the most significant issue of the Convention—the question of sovereignty, particularly in the context of federalism.

James Madison approached the Convention deeply disillusioned with the political situation, particularly as manifested by the state legislatures, and deeply anxious about a tyranny of the majority.[69] Therefore, he vigorously pushed for a powerful central government in which the state power was drastically reduced—a kind of mirror image of the government under the Articles of Confederation. He even advocated that the national government possess a veto power over state legislation. He pushed this position so intensely that nervous colleagues, aware of the power of the opposition, had to convince him to back off lest he blow up the very Convention he had worked so hard to assemble. Madison was also an advocate of what came to be known as the large-state plan (Virginia was one of the largest) in which representation would be proportional to population. The predictable small-state counter plan made representation equal among all states, regardless of size. This led to the Great Compromise which made the large-state plan apply to the House of Representatives and the small-state plan apply to the Senate. But despite this compromise, the even more fundamental issue—that of ultimate sovereignty—remained. It was never definitely resolved. The reason is simple but instructive: the risk was too great because of the danger that any precise statement would lead to an impasse. This is the reason for the continual reemergence of this issue with reverberations to the present.

---

[68] Gordon Wood observes that the constitutional convention was an "extraordinary invention, the most distinguished institutional contribution the American revolutionaries made to Western politics." See Wood, *Creation*, 342.

[69] Although Madison was not "the father of the Constitution," he was certainly the most pivotal figure in Philadelphia, and so he merits the closest scrutiny.

During the course of the Convention debates, two parties emerged—those who favored a repudiation of the Articles of Confederation and the creation of a new form of government and those who wished simply to retain the Articles. Since 1787, the first group is called Federalists and the second group is called Antifederalists. The men of the first group seized the name preemptively, leaving their opponents with a less-than-satisfactory alternative. The first group wished to lessen the power of the states in relation to the national government, while the second favored a more equal relationship.

The notable success of the Constitution during its over two-hundred-year history has retroactively worked against the reputation of the Antifederalists, though they continue to have defenders. Their fear of excessive governmental power, given our current metastatic administrative state, seems prophetic. Had they been more proactive in seeking to reform the Articles of Confederation, their positive contribution would have been much stronger. As it was, however, they supported a system which might have worked, but only if men were angels. Even so, as the Convention was winding down with the victory of the Federalists inevitable, the Antifederalists fought an important preemptive action in pushing for a bill of rights which would help guarantee freedom under the stronger national government.[70] Although the Federalists were initially opposed, claiming that it was not needed, they eventually realized how popular the idea was. Once the process of ratification began, the Federalists pledged to adopt a bill of rights by amendment once the new government had been established.

The Constitution would have to be approved by nine of the thirteen states. But if only several of the larger states rejected it, the whole project would have been in serious jeopardy. The debate was intense. Patrick Henry reflected the opinion of the Antifederalists generally when he asserted that the new Constitution "squints toward monarchy."[71] The debate triggered the drafting of *The Federalist* Papers, which were written chiefly by James Madison and Alexander Hamilton.[72] Despite their brilliance, most scholars have concluded that the majority of people opposed the Constitution. The seaboard areas of the states were more favorable to it than the rural areas

---

[70] Madison took upon himself the arduous and often thankless task of pushing the Bill of Rights through an exasperating Congress and the pettifogging caveats of Jefferson. See Burstein and Isenberg, *Madison and Jefferson*, 195–99.

[71] Speech of Patrick Henry to the Virginia Ratifying Convention, June 5, 1788.

[72] The deservedly best-known of the *Federalist Papers* is James Madison's *Federalist* number 10 in which he argues that large republics can flourish (in contrast to the then-current conventional wisdom) because the various factions and interest groups would serve as checks on each other, thereby preventing a majoritarian tyranny, his perennial nightmare. Here again is the tension between the Founders' commitment to a republic, which they believed required virtue, and their realistic assessment of the power of self-interest.

where voting was more difficult. The Federalists were better organized, more energetic, and more articulate. But even so, it was a very narrow victory.

So the nation had Benjamin Franklin's republic, which has enjoyed nearly unbroken praise throughout most of American history until the early-twentieth-century Progressive era. George Bancroft saw all of American history, in which the Constitution was embedded, as divinely guided.[73] His purpose was to "follow the steps by which a favoring Providence, calling institutions into being, has conducted the country to its present happiness and glory." The people of the United States, he asserted, "know their Constitution to be for them the ripened fruit of time."[74] He was by no means the only advocate of what might be called the providential view of American history. However, the limitations of this view are most poignantly seen in connection with the issue of slavery. It quickly became apparent at the Convention that this issue was not negotiable for the Southern delegates who insisted on counting every slave as three-fifths of a white man for purposes of direct taxation and representation in the House.[75] So people who could not vote served nonetheless to increase the representation of the slave states. Many at the Convention justified this action because of their belief that slavery was in full worldwide retreat; therefore, all concessions to Southerners would become moot. But Madison acknowledged the stark reality: "Great as the evil is, a dismemberment of the Union would be worse."[76] To this there was no answer. So Bancroft's providential view must be assessed in light of this tragic necessity.

The rise of the Progressive movement in the late nineteenth century led to a reevaluation of all of American history, including, inevitably, the Constitution itself. The movement was led to a significant degree by academics who regarded themselves as the rightful leaders of the country because of the keenness of their intellects and the purity of their intentions. They were the anointed or, actually, the self-anointed.[77] One of the many manifestations of the mentality of Progressives is an ill-concealed impatience with whatever is seen as an obstacle to their agenda—including the Constitution with

---

[73] See *A History of the United States from the Discovery of the American Continent* (1888), 4 vols., 1:3.

[74] George Bancroft, presidential address to the American Historical Association, April 27, 1886, published in *Papers of the American Historical Association* 2 no. 1 (1887), 3.

[75] Madison offered an unconvincing defense of this policy; see Burstein and Isenberg, *Madison and Jefferson*, 176–77.

[76] Jonathan Eliot, ed., *Debates in the Several State Conventions on the Adoption of the Federal Constitution*, 5 vols. (1827–30), *Debate in the Virginia Ratifying Convention*, 3: 452–53 (June 15, 1788).

[77] For a contemporary analysis, see Fred Siegal, *Revolt Against the Masses: How Liberalism Has Undermined the Middle Class* (2014).

its tiresome checks and balances, separation of powers, and guarantees of personal freedom.

Woodrow Wilson, the second Progressive president, repeatedly stressed the need for a "Darwinian Constitution," one that could be reinterpreted as Progressives think circumstances require. Here is a characteristic observation:

> The explicitly granted powers of the Constitution are what they always were, but the powers drawn from it by implication have grown and multiplied beyond all expectation, and each generation of statesmen looks to the Supreme Court to supply the interpretation which will serve the needs of the day.[78]

The Constitution becomes in the Progressive mind a kind of Rorschach blot of implicit meanings to be explicated as they wish and as circumstances require.

Another method of attack is to question the integrity of the Constitution because of the intent of its framers. In 1913, Charles A. Beard published a startling reevaluation of the Constitution. Breaking completely with previous historiography, he argued that the supporters of the Constitution had a "direct impelling motive" which "was the economic advantages which the beneficiaries expected would accrue to themselves, first, then from their action." Beard identified the culprits as those who were heavily invested in what he called "personalty," personal property which generally took the form of cash, public securities, manufacturing, and trade.[79] Those who opposed the Constitution were generally small farmers, large landed proprietors, and slaveholders. Supporters were also usually concentrated in cities along the coast.[80]

It is true that these significant economic differences generated some degree of tension—the reality of Madison's *Federalist*, Number 10, in action. The 1780s saw the beginnings of the market revolution which was to transform the trans-Atlantic economic system; any such dramatic change was bound to generate a strong level of resistance. In Beard's view, the supporters of the Constitution were counterrevolutionaries determined to create a strong government to facilitate their economic interests. They were also social conservatives who feared the dangers of unbridled democracy.[81]

---

[78] See his *Constitutional Government in the United States* (1908), 57 (Darwinian constitution), 158 (quote).

[79] See Charles A. Beard, *An Economic Interpretation of the Constitution* (1913), 18.

[80] An obvious exception to this position is none other than James Madison himself who, by Beard's standard, should have been firmly opposed to the Constitution

[81] Again, to some degree, Beard undercuts his own position. The most eloquent warnings about unbridled democracy he cites are from James Madison. See *Economic Interpretation*,

Early in his book, Beard informs us that, apart from the suppression of violence, the "primary object of government" is "the making of the rules which determine the property regulations of the members of society."[82] Beard has written an entire book criticizing the Founders for doing what he admits at the outset is the function of any government to do. But is the problem with who won? Suppose the owners of land (realty) had won. Would Beard then have written an expose of their activities? Was he an economic partisan, denouncing the evils of the commercial interests in favor of the agricultural interests? Was he a latter-day agrarian romantic in the Thomas Jefferson mold?

What is the current status of Beard's interpretation? It was generally accepted as intellectual orthodoxy during the Progressive era, extending into the New Deal era. Beginning in the 1950s, however, a reaction occurred, and so today the general consensus is to regard the book with, at the very least, a good deal of skepticism. Robert Middlekauff has put the case forcefully by saying that Beard's book is "perhaps the most influential interpretation of the drafting of the Constitution and the most harmful to understanding."[83]

This conclusion is based on rigorous analysis of the data presented in Beard's work. Perhaps the most detailed treatment is that of Forrest McDonald.[84] It is significant at the outset that McDonald acknowledges the undeniable fact that economic interests inevitably play a part of the formation of any government at any time. Rather, the issue is whether Beard is correct in the details of his analysis. The heart of McDonald's work is a highly focused evaluation of the data. McDonald's study is based on a broader database than that which was available in Beard's time. McDonald's conclusion is that there is simply no clear-cut economic division between the supporters of the Constitution and the opponents. In no state was the Constitution ratified without the support of farmers and "friends of paper money."[85] There was no simplistic division into personalty and realty. Perhaps the closest McDonald comes to a definitive conclusion is to state that most of the delegates voted in ways that reflected the interests of their states and local areas. But the important point is that interest is broader than economics. Georgia, for example, was motivated to support the Constitution because it needed a strong national government for protection from hostile Indians.

There is little support today among historians for an undiluted version of Beard's thesis. However, there is another aspect to this issue—its ideo-

---

24–25.
[82] *Economic Interpretation*, 13.
[83] Middlekauff, *Glorious Cause*, 654.
[84] Forrest McDonald, *We the People: The Economic Origins of the Constitution* (1958).
[85] McDonald, *We the People*, 162, 253, 416.

logical character. Beard was a prominent Progressive historian whose own life experience was rooted in left-wing causes.[86] As such, it is apparent that he had a quasi-Marxist sense that everything is fundamentally about economic interests—the interests of the capitalists, not the interests of the virtuous farmers. His book is important, and he is certainly correct in seeing economic motives at work. But his thesis is a crude oversimplification of a complex process; he is the man with a hammer who can see only nails.

Beard is an exemplar of the ideological historian whose work generates some responses which were early versions of politically correct orthodoxy.[87] In his introduction to the 1992 edition of *We the People*, Forrest McDonald recalls that in the 1930s and 1940s a dissent from Beardian orthodoxy was "virtually stifled."[88] When his own book was first published in 1958, it received generally favorable reviews; the *New York Times*, however, "disdained to review it."[89]

In 1934, over twenty years after *An Economic Interpretation of the Constitution* appeared, Beard delivered his presidential address to the American Historical Association with a doubtless intentionally provocative title, "Written History as an Act of Faith."[90] The address is very much a mixed bag. Beard is forthright in arguing that history is not science. He also argues against relativism, though he does not present any convincing arguments for his position. But where does faith come in?

First of all, he presents the classic possibilities for the movement of history: chaotic, cyclical, and linear. The historian, by faith, chooses the linear view—the standard Western perspective. The historian must see history as moving toward some goal "which can be only dimly divined." For Beard, there are basically only three possibilities: a capitalist dictatorship, a proletarian dictatorship, and a collectivist democracy. Beard picked the last based on "a study of long trends and on a faith in the indomitable spirit of mankind." Why only these three possibilities? Why are they all authoritarian? A collectivist democracy compared to what other kind of democ-

---

[86] See Herman Belz, "Selling the Framers Short," *Claremont Review of Books*, Fall 2013, online, for an analysis of Beard's Progressivism and an excellent historiographical survey. Belz observed that Beard had indoctrinated himself in "trade-union politics and Fabian socialist reformism."

[87] McDonald, *We the People*, xiii–xiv, xviii. He became a prominent noninterventionist in the 1930s during the crises leading to World War II. David Milne in *Worldmaking: The Art and Science of Diplomacy* (2015) observes that Beard had the "unfortunate fate to deploy relativism in opposing one of the few Manichaean conflicts in world history." Quoted by Richard Aldous in his review of Milne's book in the *Wall Street Journal*, September 26–27, 2015.

[88] McDonald, *We the People*, xiii.

[89] McDonald, *We the People*, xiii.

[90] *American Historical Review* 39 (1934): 219–29 (quotes, 228).

---

racy? The word "collectivist" gives the game away—a collectivist democracy sounds eerily like a people's republic. It seems deeply symptomatic that the leading Progressive historian of the early-twentieth century can see only authoritarianism of one form or another in the future of the human race.

It is interesting to note that while Beard's thesis in its undiluted form is no longer much in favor, some have argued that he was right in seeing the Constitution as, to some degree, an aristocratic document designed to curb the excesses of democracy and, as such, as counterrevolutionary.[91] But such accusations seem bizarre when pushed too far because they require us to believe that George Washington (a strong supporter of the Constitution and president of the Constitutional Convention) did not understand the legacy of the Revolution or, having understood it, was content to betray it.

But the obvious truth of the matter is quite simple. Yes, the Framers did distrust the dangers of unbridled democracy. James Madison at the Constitutional Convention warned of the dangers posed by men without property, observing that "either they will combine and so threaten the property of others" or they will become "the tools of opulence and ambition."[92] It is hard to find a more vivid statement of the problem they faced in 1787 or one that is more prophetic about the ongoing dangers any republic must confront.

The central dilemma faced by the Founders came from their idealistic belief in the necessity of virtue for the health of a republic and their realistic assessment of the primacy of self-interest.[93] The task they faced was to produce a constitution capable of functioning under these realities. An important aspect of this situation is simply that the Constitution was crafted to protect against undisciplined democracy in a way that made ongoing democratic reform possible. Veering too much in either direction would have courted disaster. So the Framers walked a tightrope which enabled the United States to thrive as the world's most enduring democracy.

In contrast to the idealism of the Declaration of Independence, there is the sober practicality of the Constitution which is not a blueprint for utopia but a set of rules for a real-world society. It is certainly possible to overstate this case. Certainly the Constitution, with its Bill of Rights and amendments, has been a vehicle of democratic reform, but it is largely immune from the spasms of overzealous reformers with utopian intentions. Herbert Butterfield has issued a valuable cautionary note, observing that

---

[91] Wood, *Creation*, 517–18, 524.

[92] Quoted in Max Farrand, *The Records of the Federal Convention of 1787* (1966), 4 vols., 2:203–4.

[93] See Forrest McDonald, *Novus Ordo Seclorum: The Intellectual Origins of the Constitution* (1985), 124, 162.

Men make gods now, not out of wood and stone, which though a waste of time is a fairly innocent proceeding, but out of their abstract nouns, which are the most treacherous and explosive things in the world.[94]

The perennial debate has always been focused on the methods of constitutional interpretation, involving the polarity of originalism and the so-called "living constitution" school.[95] On the one hand, originalism can easily become an exercise in an unproductive and stifling literalism predicated on the impossible task of long-distance mind reading. On the other hand, the "living constitution" viewpoint posits a dead Constitution which can be resuscitated to serve whatever current cause is clamoring for our attention. The task of constitutional interpretation must occur in the context of a wide-ranging immersion in the broad sweep of American history. There are no shortcuts. A middle-of-the-road approach seems best, one that avoids both "excessive reverence for words on a page" and a "complete disregard for their historical context in the name of evolving values."[96]

The Framers did create a *novus ordo seclorum*, a new order of the ages. Even the baffling ambiguities of the Constitution were to prove a source of strength because they reflect not only the political realities of the 1780s but also the inescapable complexities of self-government in the American context. And so it has endured. Given all this, we can quote the soaring words of Daniel Webster without apology or embarrassment.

Miracles do not cluster. Hold on to the Constitution of the United States of America and the Republic for which it stands—what has happened once in six thousand years may never happen again. Hold on to your Constitution, for if the American Constitution shall fail, there will surely be anarchy throughout the world.[97]

This discussion of the Constitution began with George Bancroft's providential view of U.S. history. After his magisterial analysis of the Constitution, Forrest McDonald permitted Otto von Bismarck, of all people, to have the last word. Bismarck is reported to have said that a Special Providence takes care of fools, drunks, and the United States of America, and, McDonald concludes, "Surely, the Founders believed the last of these."[98]

---

[94] Quoted in Bradford, *Original Intentions*, 18.

[95] The literature on this issue is voluminous. For a good introduction, see Elizabeth Corey, "Rationalism and Teaching the Constitution," *Academic Questions* 27 (2014): 300–8 and Michael Oakeshott, "Rationalism in Politics" in *Rationalism in Politics and Other Essays* (1991), 1–36.

[96] Corey, "Rationalism," 308.

[97] Speech at the celebration of the New York England Society, December 23, 1850.

[98] Quoted in McDonald, *Novus Ordo Seclorum*, 293.

Had the Founders been able to foresee the political battleground of the 1790s and beyond, they might have been even more grateful for the guidance of that Special Providence. Even so, perhaps the best last word is that of the British statesman William Gladstone who, on the occasion of the centennial anniversary of the Constitution, observed that he had "always regarded that Constitution as the most remarkable work known to men in modern times to have been produced by the human intellect at a single stroke (so to speak), in its application to practical affairs."[99]

---

[99] Letter to the committee in charge of the celebration of the centennial anniversary of the Constitution, July 20, 1887.

CHAPTER THREE: PARTY GAMES—THE 1790S

The Founders seemingly thought of everything. The genius of the Constitution confers on them the status of virtual omniscience. But while they dealt successfully with many issues, they ignored one salient issue—political parties. They had their reasons. Political parties, then called factions, were out of favor; they were associated with the politics of influence, patronage, and corruption characteristic of the Robert Walpole regime of eighteenth-century England. The idealistic ardor of the American Revolution had not yet disappeared, and, it was thought, Americans were capable of better things than such grubby, self-serving factions. The strong Puritan influence, deeply rooted in colonial history, should have counseled otherwise, but such cautionary voices were ignored, at least temporarily. In 1789, it seemed safe to do so. A powerful new Constitution had been written and ratified. The first administration with a galaxy of distinguished leaders headed by the universally acclaimed George Washington was poised to steer the new nation on a new course. But this auspicious year was the classic calm before the storm. The emergence of parties was to make the 1790s "one of the most passionate decades in American history."[100]

Alexander Hamilton was the first and the most consequential of all secretaries of the treasury. His far-reaching financial program was the initial catalyst for political opposition.[101] In a series of brilliant reports, Hamilton

---

[100] Gordon S. Wood, *Revolutionary Characters: What Made the Founders Different* (2006), 137. Part Two of Andrew Burstein and Nancy Isenberg's book *Madison and Jefferson* (2013) is appropriately entitled "The Pathological Decade and Beyond."

[101] Any standard monograph outlines this program; see Ron Chernow, *Alexander Hamilton* (2004).

proposed to create a national bank, fund the national debt by paying it off at face value to current holders, assume the unpaid state debts, and launch a vigorous effort to encourage manufacturing.[102] This program was designed in the short term to cement support for the fragile new republic by the "rich and well born." In the long term, Hamilton wished to effect a transformation of the fledging agrarian republic into a commercial and industrial power, an early version of a national market revolution. It was an ambitious program based on a broad interpretation of the Constitution's "necessary and proper" clause.[103] He succeeded in the creation of the bank with a twenty-year charter as well as funding the national debt and assuming the state debt.[104] He did not, however, succeed in his plan to encourage manufacturing. Jefferson and Madison could seldom raise their sights beyond the interests of the South in general and Virginia in particular.[105]

Powerful opposition quickly emerged, led initially by Hamilton's former ally James Madison, who was supported by the behind-the-scenes machinations of Thomas Jefferson, Washington's secretary of state[106]. Exploring the basis of their opposition leads directly into the appearance of the first political party system, lasting from about 1792 to 1816. The group supporting Hamilton's program simply adopted the Federalist label from those who had supported the Constitution. The Jeffersonian opposition party is known variously as Jeffersonians, Jeffersonian Republicans, Republicans, or even Democratic-Republicans. The simple term Republican seems the best option.[107]

Over the years, the Democratic Party, the successor of Jefferson's Republican Party, has embraced him as one of its chief icons. The Jefferson-Jackson Day dinners have long been a key fundraising event for the party. A major event in the Jeffersonian apotheosis was Franklin Roosevelt's dedication of

---

[102] This raised an ethical issue for Madison and Jefferson. Paying the debt at face value to current holders often rewarded speculators rather than many of the impoverished original holders who had sold the notes at a discount.

[103] Constitution, Article I, Section 8.

[104] The Bank of the United States aroused Jefferson's pathological hatred. In a letter to Madison on October 1, 1792, he asserted that anyone in Virginia who cooperated with the bank should be found guilty of treason and executed. "In other words," Chernow observes, "the principal author of the Declaration of Independence was recommending to the chief architect of the U.S. Constitution that any Virginia bank functionary who cooperated with Hamilton's bank should be found guilty of treason and executed." Chernow, *Hamilton*, 352.

[105] Chernow calls Hamilton "the prophet of the capitalist revolution in America" who was "a messenger from a future that we now inhabit." Chernow, *Hamilton*, 6.

[106] John Adams described Jefferson as a "shadow man whose greatest talent was hidden string-pulling." Quoted in Ellis, *Passionate Sage: The Character and Legacy of John Adams*, 115.

[107] The later Democratic Party is not Jefferson's party, but his flaws have had a persistent toxic effect on it.

the Jefferson Memorial in Washington, D.C., in 1943, on the bicentennial of his birth. This dedication was "against all the logic of the New Deal" which contained "nary a word about the beauties of small government."[108] The dedication elevated Jefferson in the minds of many to a status equal to that of George Washington and Abraham Lincoln. For the most part, mainstream historians have mitigated and rationalized his actions while extolling his words.[109] James Parton wrote in 1874 that "if Jefferson was wrong, America was wrong. If America is right, Jefferson was right."[110] But was he right?

In 1965, Richard Hofstadter wrote *The Paranoid Style in American Politics and Other Essays.* The term "right wing" puts in an appearance on the fourth line of the essay.[111] Although he does concede that paranoid thinking is "not always right wing," the main thrust of the essay is to show that it is the right-wingers who "feel dispossessed" and who also believe that the country is "infused with a network of communist agents."[112] Much of the subsequent historical literature is "infused" with the notion that the paranoid style is overwhelmingly a manifestation of those "dispossessed" right-wingers.[113] However, Prof. Hofstadter overlooked Thomas Jefferson, the man who can lay plausible claim to being the fountainhead of the paranoid style in American politics, even while being touted as an icon of Enlightenment rationality.

The main outlines of his political philosophy are scarcely the stuff of controversy. He was a small-government advocate who had implicit faith in the rationality of all people; therefore, he also believed that only limited government power was necessary.[114] He also was an unswerving agrarian, convinced that cities were evil, so the ideal citizen was the self-sufficient farmer. When men are detached from the natural agrarian environment, they become urban mobs who "add just so much to the support of pure government as sores do to the strength of the human body."[115] These views, however unexceptional they may appear to be, rest "on a seductive set of attractive illusions."[116] The evaluation of Jefferson as an American icon is largely based on his glittering generalities which are difficult to apply to the real world. And there is another aspect of his worldview which can be discerned only after a closer look at his approach to politics.

---

[108] Wood, *Revolutionary Characters*, 122.
[109] There are some welcome exceptions, most notably Joseph Ellis and Lance Banning.
[110] Quoted by Merrill Peterson, *The Jeffersonian Image in the American Mind* (1960), 234.
[111] Hofstadter, *Paranoid Style*, 3.
[112] Hofstadter, *Paranoid Style*, 23.
[113] Hofstadter, *Paranoid Style*, 25–26.
[114] See Ellis, *American Sphinx*, 10.
[115] Thomas Jefferson, *Notes on the State of Virginia* (1787), query xix.
[116] Ellis, *Sphinx*, x.

Anyone who studies the way Thomas Jefferson dealt with the issues of the 1790s is struck by his consistent paranoid style. Jefferson developed his own language with which to categorize his political opponents. These nefarious characters were not merely men with whom Jefferson disagreed. They were active agents of an elaborate conspiracy to destroy the fruits of the Revolution.[117] So his correspondence and private conversations are full of references to "monocrats," "aristocrats," and "monarchists," with other terms like "placemen" and "Anglomen." He never attempted to prove any of these allegations. Jefferson was not content to inhabit this Manichaean worldview alone. Those with whom he worked showed similar views. James Madison, among others, also employed such a vocabulary.[118]

The indiscriminate substitution of epithets for argument is intrinsically objectionable.[119] But what makes this whole approach virtually psychotic are the targets of this abuse.[120] Did Jefferson and Madison really believe that George Washington, John Adams, and Alexander Hamilton were conspirators planning to destroy the very revolution for which they had risked their lives?[121]

Jefferson uncritically accepted a complex of ideas known as British oppositionist thought, which originated among the Country Whigs of seventeenth-century England during their struggle with royal influence and the

---

[117] See, for example, John C. Miller, *The Federalist Era, 1789–1801* (1960), 1; Ellis, *Sphinx*, 12. Michael Lienesch, among many others, points out that Jefferson's correspondence is "bristling" with references to "aristocrats" and "monocrats." See Lienesch, "Thomas Jefferson and the American Democratic Experiment: The Origins of the Partisan Press, Popular Political Parties, and Public Opinion" in Peter S. Onuf, *Jeffersonian Legacies* (1993), 316–19. In a letter of December 31, 1795, to William B. Giles he asserted that the political conflict of the times is between "Republicans" and "Monocrats." Quoted in Nobel E. Cunningham, *The Jeffersonian Republicans: The Formation of a Party Organization, 1789–1801* (1957), 88.

[118] See his letter to Jefferson, April 18, 1796, in which he denounces "Monocrats" and "Monarchists" for casting a spell on the people. Quoted in Joseph J. Ellis, *American Creation: Triumphs and Tragedies at the Founding of the Republic* (2007), 199.

[119] At age seventy-five, Jefferson was still insisting that the party struggles of the 1790s were "contests of principle between the advocates of republican and those of kingly government." Quoted in Lance Banning, *The Jeffersonian Persuasion: Evolution of a Party Ideology* (1978), 13.

[120] Ellis characterizes this whole approach as a "preposterous distortion." See Ellis, *Creation*, 171.

[121] Washington was sometimes seen not as an active participant but as an unwitting dupe of the malignant Hamilton. Hamilton's notorious six-hour "monarchy speech" on June 18, 1787, at the Constitutional Convention lent credence to the belief that he was himself a monarchist. He called for a president and a senate to serve for life on good behavior. The British government, he said, was "the best in the world" (Wood, *Empire*, 92). However, he also recommended that the House members be elected every three years by universal manhood suffrage. This speech was "brilliant, courageous, and, in retrospect completely daft" (Chernow, *Hamilton*, 231). Hamilton went on to coauthor *The Federalist Papers* and work tirelessly for the ratification of the Constitution.

Court Whigs. These men interpreted the Glorious Revolution of 1688 as an effort to recover ancient liberties in reaction to the corruption and conspiracies of royal power. This English ideology contained a powerful agrarian bias which resonated with Virginia planters Jefferson and Madison.

There was also a curiously fanciful element—the Anglo-Saxon mythology. According to this view, the originally free idyllic society of the Anglo-Saxons was destroyed by the evil Normans; ever since, true reformers have been trying to undo the damage by restoring ancient liberties in the face of kings, corruption, and conspiracies.[122]

Elements of this ideology, particularly regarding corruption and conspiracy, were influential with the colonists before and during the American Revolution. But Jefferson adopted this seventeenth-century English ideology and applied it uncritically in post-revolutionary America against some of the most prominent revolutionaries. In doing so, he and Madison had a profoundly poisonous influence on the unfolding of the new American government in the 1790s, and they functioned as personifications of Hofstadter's paranoid style.

The starting point was the emerging opposition to Hamilton's financial program. Taken in its entirety, Hamilton's program had one great object: to create a financial system which would appeal to the self-interest of the wealthy to support the fragile, new government. Hamilton, Washington, and Adams, unlike Jefferson, were realistic about human nature. Patriotism was all well and good, but self-interest was vastly more reliable as a political motivator. This was a major policy issue, and it was a legitimate source of debate led by Madison who had undergone a rapid shift away from the nationalism he had supported in the 1780s.[123] Because of the compromises made at the Constitutional Convention, our system continues to have federal-state power issues.[124] The simplest explanation, therefore, is that Madison's type of nationalism could not accommodate the Hamiltonian centralizing program.[125]

---

[122] See Banning, *Jeffersonian Persuasion*, generally but especially 1–69. Banning, sympathetic as he is to Jefferson and Madison and the Republican Party generally, does not shrink from confronting the irrational aspects of this ideology and repudiating the characterization of Federalists as "conspiratorial counterrevolutionaries" (88). Ironies abound here. Jefferson, who was pathologically anti-British, swallowed whole the Country Whig ideology, including its Anglo-Saxon mythology.

[123] So there is a "James Madison problem." Jefferson was always a small-government ideologue, so his position is no mystery.

[124] Alexis de Tocqueville, the most famous of all nineteenth-century foreign observers, deals with this issue at length as a distinctive aspect of the American governmental system. See *Democracy in America* (1833, 1840).

[125] See Lance Banning, *The Sacred Fire of Liberty: James Madison & the Founding of the Federal Republic* (1995), 9, 42.

But there seems to be more involved here than philosophical abstractions. Jefferson was clearly the dominant partner in the relationship with Madison, so Jefferson's influence grew after Jefferson returned from France in the fall of 1789.[126] By this time, Madison was already cycling back into Virginia politics, and his political career hinged on his fidelity to the perceived interests of his own state. If Jefferson dominated Madison, so too did Virginia.[127] Hamilton's nationalist program was not well regarded in Virginia or in the southern states generally. It seems unlikely that political philosophy alone was a sufficient explanation for Madison's shift., The concept of states'-rights did represent a political philosophy, but it could also serve as a justification for strengthening one's political base.[128]

But there is an even more sinister issue—slavery—in play here. Jefferson and Madison, along with virtually all the prominent men of Virginia, were slaveholders. Lurking in the minds of many of these men was the fear that a government strong enough to enact Hamilton's program would also be strong enough to strike at slavery.[129] In 1790, at the very end of his life, Benjamin Franklin had, to the embarrassment of all of Virginia, raised the slavery issue once again on the national level after agreeing to serve as president of the Pennsylvania Abolition Society in 1787. The fear of abolition was expressed by the brutally visceral warning of Patrick Henry in 1788 while arguing against the Constitution: "They'll free your niggers."[130]

Jefferson and Madison were far more discreet than Henry, but they were also concerned about the implications a strong federal government might have for slavery. There is no real either/or choice to be made here. Hamilton's fiscal program did provoke opposition on its own merits, but the evidence is equally persuasive that Jefferson and Madison feared it because of its

---

[126] Ellis, *Sphinx*, xi–xii, 8. In a letter to Jefferson on October 15, 1794, Madison assures him that he is willing to "receive your commands with pleasure." Quoted in Wood, *Empire*, 148–49. Jefferson was at best only a lukewarm supporter of the Constitution and never abandoned his belief that America should be a loose confederation of sovereign states. See Wood, *Empire*, 10–11.

[127] E. James Ferguson, *The Power of the Purse: A History of American Public Finance* (1961), 298–99.

[128] See Ellis, *Creation*, 177. Ellis lays out the various explanations without drawing a specific conclusion (177–78). Joseph Charles asserts that the opposition of Jefferson and Madison was sectional from the beginning; they feared that Hamilton's program would benefit New England, not Virginia. Joseph Charles, *The Origins of the American Political Party System* (1954), 26.

[129] An excellent overview of the centrality of this issue is Ellis in *Founding*; see his treatment in a chapter appropriately entitled "The Silence," 82–119. It was largely a taboo subject; Madison's policy was one of "enlightened obfuscation" (114).

[130] Quoted in Jean Edward Smith, *John Marshall: Definer of a Nation* (1996), 119. Madison, arguing for the Constitution, tried to assure Henry that the new government would not have this power. See his speech to the Virginia ratifying convention on June 5, 1788, quoted in Magnet, *Founders*, 348–49.

---

implications for federal power over slavery.[131] This would seem to be a clear example of the Biblical proverb that the guilty flee "when no one pursues".[132] Certainly neither Washington, himself a slaveholder, nor Hamilton, an opponent of slavery, had the slightest interest in using the fiscal program as an antislavery Trojan horse.[133]

The importance of slavery and states'-rights for Jefferson and Madison can also be seen in the compromise of 1790 regarding the location of the national capital. They agreed to accept Hamilton's proposal to assume the revolutionary debts of the states, which Virginia strongly opposed, in exchange for the location of the capital on the Potomac where it would be "a physical projection of Virginia" and where there would be no difficulty for Southern congressmen bringing their slaves, unlike New York or Philadelphia.[134]

So it is evident that Jefferson and Madison were conspiracy-haunted, states'-rights protectors of slavery who loudly proclaimed their undying devotion to freedom and democracy.[135] It was very different with Hamilton:

> Many of the slaveholding populists were celebrated by posterity as tribunes of the common people. Meanwhile the self-made Hamilton, a fervent abolitionist and a staunch believer in meritocracy was villainized in American history textbooks as an apologist of privilege and wealth.[136]

Although it evolved over time, the Jefferson–Madison connection was crucial in the formation of political parties. Jefferson assumed his self-sanitizing mode. In 1789, he assured Francis Hopkinson that, "If I could not go to heaven but with a party, I would not go at all." [137] One might argue that this was before the parties had come into being, but then in 1796, he assured

---

[131] Ellis is very convincing on this issue. His arguments and supporting evidence seem very nearly conclusive. In addition to "The Silence," see also his *Creation*, 173–77. Slavery was always, he says, "the proverbial elephant in the room" (174).

[132] Proverbs 28:1 (RSV).

[133] Chernow, *Hamilton*, 629.

[134] Ellis, *Founding Brothers*, 79. See his chapter entitled "The Dinner" (at which the bargain was struck), 48–80.

[135] Samuel Johnson's question is still relevant: "How is it that we hear the loudest yelps for liberty among the drivers of negroes?" See "Taxation no Tyranny: An Answer to the Revolutionaries and Address to the American Congress," Samuel Johnson, *Works*, 3:85.

[136] Chernow, *Hamilton*, 629. Hamilton's reputation has fluctuated over the years while Jefferson and Madison have enjoyed general acclaim. Howard Zinn gives Jefferson a generous indulgence for slavery; he "tried his best" but political and economic forces "as well as his own weaknesses" were too much to overcome. And Hamilton? He was "one of the most forceful and astute leaders of the new aristocracy." Zinn, *A People's History*, 88 (Jefferson), 95 (Hamilton).

[137] Quoted in Wood, *Empire*, 160.

Edward Rutledge that he had "no interest in governing men."[138] Then as president and head of the party he had created, he told a correspondent that the "party division in this country is certainly not among its pleasant features."[139]

It is true that full-fledged political parties did not come into existence until the end of the 1790s, but they were evolving over the course of that decade. In May 1791, Jefferson and Madison left Philadelphia for a "botany trip" to the north to plan their strategy for opposing Hamilton's financial program.[140] This may be regarded as the unofficial beginning of the Republican Party. The initial domestic issues in 1789–91 were the final resolution of items left over from the Constitutional Convention, such as the Bill of Rights, Hamilton's program, and the location of the national capital. The period from 1791 to 1793 was a transitional period in party development; the period from 1793 to 1797 was the period of definite party development.[141] The defection of Jefferson, Madison, and their followers made the emergence of a Federalist Party increasingly obvious. Washington was reluctant to acknowledge this partisan reality, but the repeated clashes of Hamilton and Jefferson revealed the depth of their irreconcilable differences.

Jefferson's obsession with conspiracy was, perhaps, doubly ironic because from 1790 to the end of 1793 as secretary of state, he was a mole within Washington's administration. He clashed openly with Hamilton over his financial program without any success. Hamilton was brilliant, knowledgeable, and formidable in debate. Jefferson, though equally brilliant, knew little of finance and lacked Hamilton's strong personality. He compensated for this defect by orchestrating clandestine operations. Jefferson was appointed secretary of state primarily because of his service as minister to France from August 1784 to September 1789. However, when he joined Washington's administration, his record of public service was spotty. His term as governor of Virginia was a near-disaster because his fear of strong government prevented him from preparing to resist the British; the state suffered greatly during the Revolutionary War.[142]

Neither Jefferson nor Madison was able to match Hamilton's financial acumen; their objections were mostly political and rooted primarily in their states'-rights ideology. One of Jefferson's most dubious operations came

---

[138] The letter is dated February 27, 1796, quoted in Cunningham, *Jeffersonian Republicans*, 93–94.

[139] The letter, written in 1804, is quoted in John F. Hoadley, *Origins of American Political Parties* (1986), 19.

[140] Hoadley, *Origins*, 2. The conspiracy-phobic Jefferson engages in an undercover operation. See also Ellis, *Creation*, 170–71.

[141] For an overview, see Hoadley, *Origins*.

[142] See Michael Kranish, *Flight from Monticello: Thomas Jefferson's War* (2010). See also Ellis, *Sphinx*, 65–66.

about as a result of the botany trip. He planted Philip Freneau in the State Department as a "translator." But the public money he received would actually support him as editor of the newly established Republican newspaper, *The Gazette of the United States*.[143] This sordid maneuver was made even more distasteful by its aftermath. There were the inevitable denials and assertions of innocence. Jefferson actually expressed regret to Madison that Freneau's attacks had upset Washington.[144] He then lied directly at least twice to Washington, denying that he had any knowledge of Freneau's plan to criticize him.[145] He swore to Washington by "everything sacred and honorable" that he had not betrayed Washington's trust or engaged "in the bustle of politics or in turbulence and intrigue against the government."[146] When Hamilton, whose own intelligence system was functioning effectively, challenged this operation publicly, Freneau professed Jefferson's innocence, and Jefferson instructed Madison to defend him as well.[147]

Not only did Jefferson lie to Washington, he also began a whispering campaign, insinuating that a mentally incapacitated president was no longer up to the job.[148] By 1795, this whispering campaign became a fullbore Republican assault on Washington to destroy his reputation.[149] These attacks had to have been undertaken with the approval of both Jefferson and Madison. That the reputations of Jefferson and Madison themselves have survived largely intact is primarily the result of the indulgence of historians, who have been determined to see no evil in the face of such vicious behavior. It is hardly surprising that both Jefferson and Madison were permanently estranged from Washington. Jefferson was further exposed by the publication of his notorious letter to Philip Mazzei, an Italian friend, which was

---

[143] Ellis, *Creation*, 4, 7; Robert M. Rutland, *James Madison: The Founding Father* (1987), 115–16. See also Miller, *Federalist Era*, 90–97. Freneau was given exclusive access to foreign intelligence through Jefferson's State Department. See Ellis, *Creation*, 171–72. John Fenno's *Gazette of the United States* was a "semi-official" newspaper of the administration. See Chernow, *Hamilton*, 395–96.

[144] Thomas Jefferson to James Madison, June 9, 1792, quoted in Cunningham, *Jeffersonian Republicans*, 15–19, 28.

[145] See Thomas Jefferson to George Washington, September 2, 9, 1792, quoted in Cunningham, *Jeffersonian Republicans*, 15–19, 28.

[146] Jon Meacham, *Thomas Jefferson: The Art of Power* (2012), 297. Meacham admits that Jefferson had been "dishonest" in this affair (323).

[147] Ellis, *Creation*, 181–82; Miller, *Federalist Era*, 90–94.

[148] *James Madison Papers*, 2:805–7, cited in Ellis, *Creation*, 184. Ellis says that he was "spreading gossip that the once great man was past his prime." During the height of the debate over the Jay Treaty, Jefferson even quoted a line from Joseph Addison's *Cato* in a letter to Madison, March 27, 1796—"A curse on his virtues, they've undone his country." Quoted in Chernow, *Hamilton*, 499.

[149] Lance Banning, despite his Jeffersonian sympathies, writes of "venomous attacks" and "a shower of abuse." See Banning, *Jeffersonian Persuasion*, 242–44.

written in 1796 and published in American newspapers in May 1797. While the letter names no names, it is a blanket indictment of the Federalist Party as the "monarchical and aristocratic party" which had its head "shorn by the harlot England."[150]

In addition to conspiracy-mongering and backstabbing, Jefferson was also a great hater; his chief target was Hamilton, the man he never could stand up to face to face. In one of the ugliest letters he ever wrote, he accused Hamilton of cowardice. In 1793, Hamilton contracted yellow fever in Philadelphia. Hamilton was, Jefferson asserted, guilty of "excessive alarm," indeed even of "cowardice, hypochondria, and fakery" in the face of it.[151] To put this in perspective, Jefferson's chief military contribution during the Revolutionary War was being chased around his mismanaged state of Virginia by the British. Hamilton, among many other feats, led a bayonet charge at Yorktown.[152] A self-proclaimed champion of the people, Jefferson played the aristocrat card by denouncing Hamilton's career "from the moment at which history can stoop to notice him."[153] Hamilton was by no means a passive victim of Jefferson's malice; he often gave as good or better than he got.[154] One obvious difference, however, is that Hamilton attacked openly; Jefferson depended largely on proxies.

Jefferson had a lifelong obsession with Hamilton. During his tenure as secretary of the treasury, Hamilton was repeatedly investigated by Jeffersonians for fiscal wrongdoing; Hamilton was vindicated.[155] But the obsession continued. While president, Jefferson ordered Albert Gallatin to study government archives for evidence of wrongdoing and was disappointed by the lack of any incriminating evidence.[156] Jefferson pursued a dead man for the rest of his own life in "one of the most effective and resilient campaigns in the history of American politics."[157] This brief catalog of Jefferson's faults, with more to come, is no mere exercise in ad hominem sniping but rather

---

[150] Quoted in Miller, *Federalist Era*, 202–3. The letter was published in an Italian newspaper and then in the United States, first in Noah Webster's Federalist newspaper *Minerva*, May 14, 1787. See Ellis, *Sphinx*, 160–61.

[151] Jefferson to Madison, September 8, 1793, quoted in Rutland, *Madison*, 123. Even Madison saw this as "unkind." See also Chernow, *Hamilton*, 450.

[152] For Hamilton's military career, see Chernow, *Hamilton*, 164–65. He was a "certified hero" (165).

[153] Quoted in Knott, *Hamilton*, 20–21. Fellow Federalist John Adams, also jealous of Hamilton, took a similar line; he denounced him as "a bastard brat of a scotch peddler" in an 1806 letter to Francis Vanderkemp, quoted in Ellis, *Passionate Sage*, 63.

[154] See Chernow, *Hamilton*, 406–7. Chernow conceded that there was "something compulsive and uncontrollable" in Hamilton's public behavior (406).

[155] See Banning, *Jeffersonian Persuasion*, 173 and Ellis, *Sphinx*, 185.

[156] Chernow, *Hamilton*, 639, cites his son, James A. Hamilton. See *Reminiscences of James A. Hamilton* (1869), 23.

[157] Knott, *Hamilton*, 25.

speaks to a larger point. The Republican Party as a whole acquired much of the moral and ideological character of its founder. By contrast, no one person in the Federalist Party had an equal influence for good or for ill.[158]

If Hamilton's program was the catalyst for partisan differences on domestic issues, the French Revolution of 1789 was the catalyst for foreign-policy differences, although it affected domestic politics as well. The revolution began with a moderate phase in 1789 with the goal of establishing a liberal constitutional monarchy. It was hailed as a worthy successor of the American Revolution. However, by 1793 the Jacobins were in charge of a terroristic, totalitarian state at war with Europe. Many Americans turned away in disgust at the unfolding spectacle of mass executions but not Jefferson or Madison. Jefferson's attitude regarding the French Revolution is one of the most bizarre opinions adopted during his entire career. His stance was one of uncritical acceptance. In his eyes, the Jacobins could do no wrong.

The French Revolution in its bloodiest stage elicited one of Jefferson's most astonishing letters. Writing to William Short on January 31, 1793, at the height of the Terror, Jefferson asserted that he would see "half the earth desolated" in order to ensure the success of the French Revolution.[159] This exposed what Joseph Ellis has called "a chilling side of Jefferson's character."[160] Madison was equally bloodthirsty, though his language was more tempered.[161] Both men seemed oblivious to the sufferings of the Frenchmen who had aided the American revolutionaries.[162] For both men, ideology trumped simple humanity.[163]

Neither Jefferson nor Madison ever reconsidered his position. Furthermore, their hatred of England was as visceral and irrational as their infatuation with France down through the end of the Napoleonic era.[164] In 1794,

---

[158] During Washington's administrations, Hamilton comes closest because of his fiscal program, but he did not carry all Federalists with him. Adams had misgivings about him. See Ellis, *Passionate Sage*, 162–63.

[159] See Ford, *Writings*, VI, 153–57.

[160] Ellis, *Sphinx*, 127. In a letter to George Nicholas, March 15, 1793, Madison denounced the opponents of the French Revolution as "enemies of human nature." Quoted in Rutland, *Madison*, 121. The contrast with Adams is stark. Adams wrote that the philosophers Rousseau and Helvetius "preached to the French Nation *Liberty*, till they made them the most mechanical slaves; *equality*, till they destroyed Equity; *humanity*, till they became weasels and African panthers; and *fraternity*, till they cut one another's throats like Roman gladiators." Adams to Benjamin Waterhouse, May 21, 1821, Founders Online.

[161] See Ralph Ketcham, *James Madison, A Biography* (1940), 339–41.

[162] Lafayette was imprisoned for five years and his wife's family was exterminated. See Chernow, *Hamilton*, 433–34.

[163] On the occasion of the execution of Louis XVI, Philip Freneau's headline in the *National Gazette* was "Louis Capet Has Lost His Caput." Quoted in Wood, *Empire*, 177.

[164] Gordon Wood observes that Jefferson's affection for France and his hatred of England never dimmed and that he "generated his identity as an American from his hatred of

Jefferson expressed his desire to dine with a victorious French general in London after a French invasion.[165] He consistently preferred the Napoleonic dictatorship to the British monarchy, as did Madison.[166] This perspective further poisoned the political atmosphere of an already pathological decade.[167] It also provided the background for the first needless war in American history—the War of 1812.

In response to the war between England and France, Washington took the commonsense step of issuing the Proclamation of Neutrality in May 1793, which abrogated the Franco–American treaty of 1778; in deference to Jefferson's opposition, the word neutrality never appeared. The Proclamation recognized the new government of France and Edmond Genet as the French minister to the United States. Washington stated that the previous treaty would be honored but only to the extent that peace would not be endangered. The Jacobins had executed the king who had assisted the American revolutionaries. Nevertheless, the Republicans rose in opposition, arguing against both the substance of the Proclamation and its assumption of broad executive authority in foreign affairs.[168]

Near the end of Washington's first term, Jefferson resigned his position as secretary of state, abandoning his function as a mole within Washington's administration in exchange for assuming the role of a string-puller at Monticello. He had been defeated by the more aggressive Hamilton, who believed that his opportunities in Washington's administration were behind him; he followed Jefferson into retirement in January 1795.[169] Their departure did not significantly affect the ongoing political warfare. The struggle over foreign policy became even more intense during Washington's second term. Throughout this period, the Republicans pursued a bellicose policy toward England coupled with strong opposition to military preparedness. However, Washington was keenly aware of the weakness of the new republic which

---

England." Wood, *Empire*, 181. Jefferson would have cheerfully seen all kings, nobles, and priests packed off to the scaffold. Jefferson to William Short, January 3, 1793. Ford, *Writings*, 6:507–08.

[165] Jefferson to William Branch Giles, April 27, 1794, *Papers of Thomas Jefferson* (2000), 28:67.

[166] See Wood, *Empire*, 187

[167] Lance Banning concedes that the Republicans in general had been "blind for years" to the evils of French despotism and imperialism and that the issue embittered domestic politics to a degree not seen until the slavery controversy of the late 1850s. Banning, *Jeffersonian Persuasion*, 211.

[168] Washington was keenly aware that he was walking on untrodden ground in filling in the practical details of the Constitution in action. He consistently decided issues in favor of a strong executive.

[169] See Chernow, *Hamilton*, 479. Hamilton was in debt when he retired from public life and took up the practice of law to make ends meet—a conclusive refutation of the chronic Republican charge of venality and corruption.

had difficulty even in pacifying its western frontier. He sought to avoid war with either England or France.

The Whiskey Rebellion in western Pennsylvania, which had been simmering since 1791, finally erupted in 1794. The farmers bitterly resented the excise tax on whiskey which made it difficult to earn any profit from their corn crops. While their grievances were real, Washington did not believe that so direct a challenge to newly-established federal authority should go unanswered. Some of the rebels had employed the language of the French Revolution, so their defiance had Jacobin overtones.[170] An overwhelming show of force caused the rebellion to dissipate quickly. Washington balanced firmness with clemency, so the Federalist Party emerged from the affair with an enhanced reputation. Jefferson's comment on the whole affair was obtuse: "An insurrection was announced and proclaimed and armed against but was never found."[171]

By early 1794, the foreign affairs situation had become exceedingly dangerous. Relations with revolutionary France remained tense, and relations with England also deteriorated ominously. All this occurred against the backdrop of what Washington knew to be a pitifully weak new republic. Accordingly, Washington sent John Jay to England in May 1794 to pursue a treaty which, it was hoped, would avoid war by reducing Anglo–American tensions.[172] The treaty was signed by Jay in November 1794. By early 1795, the existence of the treaty became known, but its contents had not yet been disclosed, and it became the subject of feverish speculation. The Senate approved it by the required two-thirds majority, 20–10, in June 1795. Washington himself had some reservations but concluded that it was the best treaty possible under the circumstances. He signed it in mid-August 1795. By this time, its contents had been made public, and a tempestuous controversy had begun.[173] If any more proof were needed of the massive irresponsibility of the Republicans in general and Jefferson and Madison in particular were needed, the upheaval over the Jay Treaty provides definitive proof.[174]

---

[170] See Ellis, *Creation*, 195–96.

[171] Jefferson, *Papers*, 28:359. Here is an early example of the Fox Butterfield approach to reality. Butterfield, a reporter for the *New York Times*, earned unwelcome fame for his headline "Crime Keeps on Falling, but Prisons Keep on Filling." *New York Times*, September 28, 1997.

[172] Estes, *Jay Treaty*, 26, 34, 96.

[173] Gordon Wood has observed that Washington's determination to seek a treaty with England in the face of such intense and irrational resistance was one of his most courageous decisions. Wood, *Empire*, 196.

[174] Before the contents of the treaty had been revealed, Madison mournfully observed that the better the treaty would prove to be for Americans, the worst it would be for Republicans. See quote in Stanley M. Elkins and Eric L. McKitrick, *The Age of Federalism* (1993), 415–18.

Jefferson and Madison took the lead in viewing the treaty entirely through the ideological lens dictated by their hatred of England. The treaty was disappointing.[175] The biggest English concession was to evacuate the forts in the Northwest which they had already been obligated to do by the Treaty of Paris in 1783. There were only a few minimal concessions regarding the West Indian trade and no recognition of the American position on neutral rights. Commissions were established to deal with specific issues. Jay, nonetheless, did the best he could while playing a very weak hand. For Jefferson and Madison, however, the treaty represented the victory of "monarchists and "monocrats."[176] Washington had cast a spell on the people; the treaty established the triumph of "Aristocracy, Anglicanism, and mercantilism."[177] Therefore, it is no surprise that there were "raucous demonstrations reminiscent of revolutionary Paris."[178] All of this was designed to defeat a treaty intended to preserve the fledging republic from a war with the late-eighteenth-century superpower.

The Republicans had one last card to play. The commissioners established by the treaty had to be funded, and this gave the House Republicans an opportunity for more mischief. Edward Livingston called for Washington to turn over for inspection all the documents pertaining to the treaty. The clear implication was that the House as well as the Senate could pass on the merits of a treaty. Nevertheless, Livingston's petition passed in March 1796. Washington refused to comply. Madison was torn between his political opposition to the treaty and his uneasiness over the implications of Livingston's petition; his speeches of the time betrayed his inner conflict.[179] The tide of public opinion turned against the Republicans; eventually the House voted 51 to 48 to approve the funding of the commissioners. This whole controversy bears witness to the all-consuming nature of the Republican ideology. Perhaps an even uglier aspect was the willingness of Jefferson and Madison to encourage vile attacks on Washington from professional bottom-feeders such as James Callender and Benjamin Franklin Bache.[180]

The treaty was beneficial to the new republic. The Federalists triumphed politically in the short run. The treaty was a milestone in the development of political parties. The Federalists also used methods of political mobilization,

---

[175] For details, see Estes, *Jay Treaty*, 21–28.

[176] Madison to Jefferson, April 18, 1796, *James Madison Papers*, 2:933–35, quoted in Ellis, *Creation*, 201.

[177] See *Papers of Thomas Jefferson*, 39:95, quoted in Meacham, *Jefferson*, 294.

[178] Chernow, *Hamilton*, 487.

[179] Washington was able to show from a citation of the minutes of the Constitutional Convention that Madison himself had refused to grant the House any role in approving treaties. See Chernow, *Hamilton*, 499.

[180] See Estes, *Jay Treaty*, 99.

but they were never as effective at partisan warfare as the Republicans, so the tide was running against them.[181] All this was bad enough, but things were going to get worse because the Federalists were about to lose the greatest asset any American political party has ever enjoyed—George Washington. He was determined to return to his beloved Mount Vernon at the end of his second term. The Federalists never recovered from this loss.

John Adams was the obvious successor to Washington—a thankless task. The man who had spent eight unhappy years as vice president was now in line to spend four unhappy years as president. Federalist political power was in decline but was still sufficiently strong to turn back a challenge from Jefferson. Adams defeated Jefferson in the electoral vote 71–68. The Federalist Party was badly riven by factionalism. Because 59 electoral votes were cast for Thomas Pinckney, Jefferson, with the second highest total, became vice president.[182] The major troubles of the harried Adams did not result from having Jefferson as vice president but from his own prickly personality, from party factionalism, stemming primarily from Hamilton, and from a difficult diplomatic situation.[183]

The presidency of Adams was characterized by one vital achievement and one signal failure, both of which can be understood only in the context of the ongoing conflict with the Republicans. In 1796, the French revolutionary regime, though no longer Jacobin, was still authoritarian and aggressive and at war with most of Europe. However, its baleful influence was still powerful in the counsels of the Republican Party. Nothing the French did in these grim years gave any pause in the support of Jefferson, Madison, and many of their fellow Republicans. The issue, moreover, was not merely ideological but political. Citizen Adet, the French minister, appealed directly to American voters in November 1796 to elect Jefferson. Accompanying this appeal were several official French proclamations announcing the suspension of full diplomatic relations, a tougher policy on neutral shipping, and a comprehensive indictment of American policy toward France.[184]

In the face of this steady deterioration of U.S.-French relations, Adams pursued a classic carrot-and-stick policy. He continually held out the pros-

---

[181] David Hackett Fischer describes the vigorous but ultimately unsuccessful effort of the so-called "young Federalists" to capitalize on the democratic tide. See *The Revolution of American Conservatism: The Federalist Party in the Age of Jeffersonian Democracy* (1965).

[182] This anomalous outcome would be rendered impossible by the Twelfth Amendment to the Constitution in 1804, after another electoral debacle in 1800.

[183] The worst aspects of Hamilton's tempestuous personality surfaced only after his retirement, when he no longer benefitted from the direct tutelage of Washington, his mentor and father figure. He went from being the consummate insider to a resentful outsider. See Chernow, *Hamilton*, 514–16.

[184] Miller, *Federalist Era*, 199–200.

pect of a peaceful resolution of tensions while seeking a military build-up, including the creation of the Department of the Navy.[185] All of these efforts to strengthen the American military were consistently resisted by the Republicans. In fact, the behavior of some Republicans, unrebuked by Jefferson or Madison, is nearly beyond belief. Some freedom-loving Republicans, including a generous sprinkling of slaveholders, sang a ghastly song entitled "God Save the Guillotine," to the tune of "God Save the King" in addition to turning out for rallies wearing the French tricolor.[186] This occurred against the backdrop of growing naval tensions with the French. It injected more poison into American politics. Adams, in the teeth of this multifaceted crisis, kept a steady course of firm diplomacy and military preparation.[187] In July 1797, he sent three diplomats to France seeking to avoid war.[188] Jefferson and Madison opposed this peace effort.[189]

The result of this initiative was the explosive XYZ Affair.[190] The Americans had to deal with the oily French minister Talleyrand who suggested that bribes might lubricate the negotiations. The XYZ dispatches revealing the bribery attempt "electrified the country as no other event since the Revolutionary War."[191] Anti-French feeling was widespread, and the popularity of the Federalist Party soared as a result. The breakdown of negotiations led to what was called the Quasi-War with France. Adams refused to seek or declare war despite the urging of some of his own party. Even during this major crisis, the Republicans continued to vote against all funding for the military. Adams's policies succeeded, and a convention was signed in early 1801 ending the Quasi-War. It was too late to help him politically, but he had succeeded in avoiding an all-out war which the United States could have ill afforded.

The popularity of the Federalist Party, and of Adams himself, proved transient. A direct property tax imposed in 1798 alienated people across the country, leading directly to the 1799 uprising by John Fries in Pennsylvania.[192] The Federalist Party suffered a massive loss of support. While the

---

[185] "If you want peace, prepare for war"—Vegetius, *De Re Militari*, c. AD 500. See Wood, *Empire*, 241–45.

[186] Wood, *Empire*, 256.

[187] He also had to contend with a virulent anti-French faction, including Hamilton, who tended to see war as a first resort. Chernow, *Hamilton*, 566.

[188] Charles Cotesworth Pinckney, John Marshall, and Elbridge Gerry.

[189] Wood claims that the Republicans were afraid that successful peace efforts "might mean endorsing the Jay Treaty with Great Britain." Wood, *Empire*, 240. Peace with France might also mean peace with Great Britain.

[190] The letters are coded references to the three American diplomats.

[191] Miller, *Federalist Era*, 212.

[192] Fries was convicted twice of treason; Adams pardoned him in 1800.

direct tax could be justified as a way of meeting the cost of the Quasi-War, it is more difficult to defend the Alien and Sedition Acts of 1798.[193] The Alien acts restricting immigration were constitutional if unwise, but the Sedition Act was probably unconstitutional, even though, unlike its British counterpart, it did allow truth as a defense.[194] These acts represent a serious error by Federalists. Adams was not an enthusiastic supporter, but he did sign them into law. The saving grace was that the acts would expire early in 1801 at the end of his administration. But the grave mistake of the Alien and Sedition Acts was matched by an equally serious error by the Republicans.

In searching for a way of opposing the acts, Jefferson and Madison decided on what at first seemed to be a very strange tactic. They wrote resolutions for the Kentucky legislature (Jefferson) and the Virginia legislature (Madison) known as the Kentucky and Virginia Resolutions. But if the method was strange, the contents were ominous. Both resolutions asserted the right of state interposition to defend the citizens of a state against federal authority. Once again the compact theory of the federal union surfaces—the uneasy ghost of the Articles of Confederation. Jefferson's resolution, even after being toned down by Madison, espoused "secessionist views."[195] Matters became even more ominous in 1799 when the government of Virginia constructed an armory and armed its militia with the transparently absurd cover story that it feared a French invasion. This was too much even for Jefferson, who must privately have deplored the extent to which his followers actually moved to implement his theories.[196]

The salient question is why Jefferson and Madison chose this particular method. After all, the Sedition Act could easily have been challenged on First Amendment grounds. Historians have noted the applicability of this theory to states'-rights in defense of slavery. For example, Gordon Wood observes that they were not "primarily thinking about protecting slavery in 1798" but that the resolutions "certainly laid the basis for the nullification and states'-rights doctrines later used to defend slavery and Southern distinctiveness in the period leading up to the Civil War."[197] Once again Virginia and slavery had captured Jefferson and Madison. The toxic legacy of the Kentucky and

[193] The standard account is James Morton Smith, *Freedom's Fetters: The Alien and Sedition Acts and American Civil Liberties* (1956). Though deeply rooted in primary-source research, Smith's treatment is remorselessly critical of every aspect of Federalist policy. He gives no real account of the political context and no discussion of Republican pro-French excesses.

[194] The Federalists believed, quite rightly, that most immigrants would vote Republican.

[195] Wood, *Empire*, 271. Dumas Malone admits that Jefferson's zeal for states' rights "bordered on fanaticism." See Malone, *The Sage of Monticello* (1981), 356.

[196] Miller, *Federalist Era*, 241–42.

[197] Wood, *Empire*, 269.

Virginia Resolutions far exceeded any lingering fall-out from the Alien and Sedition Acts.

Despite all of Adams's presidential struggles, he had some significant successes, most notably in avoiding what would have been a disastrous war with France.[198] He would seek reelection, but the fortunes of the badly split Federalist Party were in an irreversible decline. He had mixed feelings about another four years in the White House. Would political vindication outweigh the prospect of more presidential misery? But, as it turned out, that was beside the point. The shadow man's time had come.

---

[198] His achievement is even more remarkable because of his hatred of the French Revolution and its poisonous ideology as a "form of religion." Ellis, *Passionate Sage*, 97.

Chapter Four: Utopia in Power, 1800–1815

Thomas Jefferson's slaves helped elect him president in 1800. He won the electoral vote 73 to 68, but because of the three-fifths compromise, the electoral strength of the slaveholding states was increased by at least twelve votes.[199] So for some embittered Federalists, Jefferson was denounced as the "Negro President."[200] Although this was the only presidential election in which the three-fifths factor was decisive, the political power of the slave-holding states enabled them to dominate the Republican Party and Andrew Jackson's successor Democratic Party down to the election of 1860.[201]

The election of 1800 provided some significant postelection drama. Aaron Burr, the Republican Party vice-presidential nominee, received the same number of electoral votes as Jefferson, and Burr, being Burr, decided to hold out for the presidency, thus throwing the election into the House of Repre-

---

[199]Chapter title: Borrowed from Mikhail Heller and Alexsandr Nekrich, *Utopia in Power: The History of the Soviet Union from 1917 to the Present* (1986).

See Paulsen, *Constitution*, 79.

[200] Garry Wills, *"Negro President": Jefferson and the Slave Power* (2003), 2 and 234, note 2. Although Wills informs his readers in his prologue that he "has admired Jefferson all my life and still do" (xii), his book is a convincing and systematic indictment of Jefferson and his Republican Party for their total enslavement to slave power. Jefferson's commitment to slavery was so strong that he turned down a $20,000 legacy (over $280,000 today) from his Revolutionary War friend, Polish patriot Thaddeus Kosciuszko, which was intended to enable him to free his slaves. When he died in 1826, his "most devoted servants were split apart." Henry Wiencek, "Master of Monticello," *Smithsonian*, October 2012, 40–49, 92–97 (95).

[201] Slaveholders dominated the presidency for thirty-two of the first thirty-six years, since twelve of the first fifteen presidents were either Southern slaveholders or Northern Democrats sympathetic to slavery. The election of Lincoln in 1860 signaled the end of this control; the response of the Democratic Party was secession.

sentatives, which caused a six-day deadlock. During this uneasy interval, Jefferson and the Republicans spoke of armed resistance.[202] Virginia and Pennsylvania began assembling their state militias. Jefferson was "getting desperate."[203]

At length, an unlikely hero emerged. Alexander Hamilton, believing that Burr was completely unacceptable, while Jefferson had at least "pretensions to character," spared "no energy" in working for Jefferson's victory.[204] Jefferson owed his success first to the "votes" of slaves, then to the actions of his archenemy.

Despite its unseemly aspects, it is possible that this was the most important presidential election because it resulted in the first peaceful transfer of power in a bitterly fought election. This accomplishment is all the more impressive, coming as it did after what still remains one of the most politically contentious decades in American history.

But was it really what Jefferson called it—the Revolution of 1800? Clearly it was not, according to Jacques Barzun's definition, but it certainly foreshadowed a distinct change in political philosophy and in governmental policies. The triumph of Jefferson and his Republican Party is usually seen as the triumph of democracy, particularly in contrast with the Federalist aristocrats.[205] However, the new nation was irrevocably set on a democratic course which would have unfolded largely as it did even if the Republican Party had shared the political perspective of the Federalist Party. One might even ask the unfashionable question as to which party showed the greatest fidelity to principle—the Republican Party, which prospered mightily with its democratic rhetoric, or the Federalist Party which, despite the efforts of the "Young Federalists," was consistently punished at the polls for its aristocratic prejudices, real or imputed?[206]

Jefferson started out on an ironic note with the famous announcement in his first inaugural that, "We are all Republicans, we are all Federalists." That is what he said. What he meant was, "We are all Republicans. You are all monocratic betrayers of the Revolution." Jefferson was never able to shed his paranoid obsessions and toxic ideology, so beneath his genial surface, the same old monsters lurked.[207] The Republican editor of the *Aurora* denounced

---

[202] Wood, *Empire*, 278–86; see also Wills, *"Negro President,"* 86–87.

[203] Wills, *"Negro President,"* 86.

[204] Wood, *Empire*, 284–85.

[205] While Wood's narrative in *Empire* is permeated with this class-obsessed perspective, Jefferson and Madison were agrarian aristocrats whose status was based on slave labor.

[206] See Fischer, *Revolution and American Conservatism*.

[207] Jefferson himself was the target of Federalist paranoia, particularly from Federalist Congregational clergy who denounced him as "some combination of pagan, infidel, atheist, and heretic." Ellis, *Sphinx*, 256. Jefferson was a fairly conventional Unitarian.

the Federalists as "secret enemies of the American Revolution—her internal, insidious, indefatigable foes."[208] Indeed, the Revolution had "for the first time arrived at completion" and "the reign of terror and corrupt government is at an end." Not the Jacobin reign of terror, of course, but the terror of the Adams administration. Leonard Levy observes that the key to the darker side of Jefferson was "his belief that America was in constant danger."[209]

The persistence of these pathologies was a bad omen for the success of his presidency. The evaluations of Jefferson as president are mixed. The general consensus is that his first term was a great success while his second term was marred by serious policy failures.[210] This view is true enough as far as it goes, but there is another aspect of this perspective. The great success of his first term was made possible by an unanticipated stroke of good fortune, while the failure of his second term was entirely his own responsibility. Jefferson was quick to implement his own political philosophy as president.[211] In terms of domestic policy, his essentially utopian view of the natural good-ness of humanity justified his own minimalist view of government. He was committed to shrinking government, retiring the national debt, reducing or eliminating taxes, and resisting what he thought was the excessive power of the judiciary.[212]

His foreign-policy prescriptions reflected the same utopian view of human nature. He distrusted the military and sought to reduce military spending on the army and navy to a bare minimum. He believed that nations should have only peaceful commercial relations with each other. He also believed that economic sanctions were more effective than military action.[213] This idealistic view of foreign-policy affairs was singularly unsuited for a

---

These beliefs were not noticeably different from those of John Adams and probably George Washington as well. The irony is that he was most savaged by his enemies for perhaps the most innocuous of his beliefs. For a good summary of his religious perspec-tive, see Wood, *Empire*, 576–81, 586–87, and John Ragosta, *Religious Freedom: Jefferson's Legacy, America's Creed* (2013), 7–39.

[208] *Aurora*, February 20, 1801, quoted in Banning *Jeffersonian Persuasion*, 270.

[209] Leonard Levy, *Jefferson and Civil Liberties: The Darker Side* (1963), 167. Levy engages in a systematic demolition of Jefferson's image as a staunch defender of civil liberties.

[210] Forrest McDonald writes of the "unparalleled success" of his first term and the "unmiti-gated failure" of his second. Forrest McDonald, *The Presidency of Thomas Jefferson* (1976), 30.

[211] A good overview is Ellis, *Sphinx*, 213–40.

[212] Wood observes that Jefferson believed that all people, except the British and Federalists, were willing to sacrifice "their selfish interests for the sake of the whole." This viewpoint was "one of the most idealistic in American if not world history." Wood, *Empire*, 301.

[213] See Banning, *Jeffersonian Persuasion*, 302. Banning observes that "experiments with economic coercion . . . had exposed an undeniable weakness in the principles on which the Republican Party had based its rule." Marshall

Smelser refers to "the derisory armed forces of the United States." See Smelser, *The Democratic Republic: 1801–1815* (1968), 160.

world in which Great Britain, the superpower of the age, was fighting for its life against Napoleon.

The story of the success of Jefferson's first term begins with the Louisiana Purchase, which, in turn, begins in St. Domingo, the western half of the island of Haiti. But there is a revealing backstory here which casts lurid light on Republican racial views. The Adams administration had supported the Haitian rebels led by Toussaint Louverture.[214] The administration provided naval support and encouraged Toussaint to declare independence from France. "The first revolutionary regime in the New World," Garry Wills writes, "was coming to the aid of the second one."[215] However, the election of Jefferson saw an abrupt change in policy. Jefferson showed "nothing but hostility" and refused diplomatic recognition.[216] Jefferson betrayed the Haitian revolution. Diplomatic recognition did not occur until 1862, during the Lincoln administration. Clearly the enslavement of Jefferson and his party to the slave power, with its visceral fear of slave rebellions, dictated this abandonment of the second revolution in the New World.[217]

In the larger scheme of things, the Haitian revolution is significant because of what happened next. In 1800, by means of the secret Treaty of San Ildefonso, France obtained title to the vast Louisiana Territory. When the appalling news of this transfer became known in the spring of 1802, Jefferson immediately grasped the potentially dire consequences. The transfer of Louisiana to an aggressive empire-building France in place of the tottering Spanish empire, particularly the acquisition of New Orleans, would be catastrophic. Jefferson concluded with a note of desperation that "we must marry ourselves to the British fleet and nation."[218]

But then came an astonishing change of fortune. Napoleon's efforts to subdue it proved so costly that he decided to sell the whole Louisiana territory, which Spain had retroceded to him, to the United States. It was a staggering piece of good fortune for the United States.

Napoleon's effort to subdue the rebellious slaves of Haiti had come to grief. Louisiana went on sale as "a providential gift from insurgent slaves and the malaria-carrying mosquitoes."[219] Jefferson was "not only lucky but also beholden to historical forces [i.e., the Haitian revolution] that he had actu-

---

[214] Wood, *Empire*, 537; Wills, "*Negro President*," 41.

[215] Wills, "*Negro President*," 41.

[216] Wills, "*Negro President*," 41, 43. Wills argues that most historians, solicitous of Jefferson's reputation, simply ignore the whole episode.

[217] Wills contrasts this with the support for Haiti advocated by Timothy Pickering and other Federalists. See Wills, "*Negro President*," 37–41, 44–45.

[218] Jefferson to Robert R. Livingston, April 18, 1802, Founders Online, https://founders. archives.gov/documents/Jefferson.

[219] Ellis, *Sphinx*, 246–47.

ally opposed." His dilemma was acute. The offer was too good to refuse, but his strict-constructionist view of the Constitution indicated that he should refuse it.[220] Nothing in the enumerated powers of the presidency indicates that the president has the power to acquire foreign territory in this fashion or to rule over the people of a territory as a virtual monarch. Fortunately, Jefferson had the good sense to override his constitutional misgivings and conclude what is still the greatest land acquisition in American history. Still, it must be noted that at this point the Republicans finally discovered the utility of the necessary-and-proper clause.

The Federalists, almost unanimously, opposed the Louisiana Purchase, for which they have been consistently criticized. This land acquisition would further diminish Federalist political fortunes. But the story does not quite stop here. The extra dimension to the story is that everyone knew that the new states to be carved out of that vast territory would be slave states. Timothy Pickering and other antislavery Federalists had more than narrow partisan reasons for their stance—quixotic though it proved to be.[221] One other point remains to be noted. The two Republican purists for whom not even Jefferson was strict enough, John Taylor and John Randolph, supported Jefferson vigorously on this issue.[222] Both men were intense proslavery zealots. So even in a good cause, the slavery issue persisted. But, lucky or not, the fact remains that had Jefferson been a one-term president, he would rightly be praised for a highly successful administration. He had implemented his political philosophy with no immediate apparent harm to the nation. He had concluded the epoch-making Louisiana Purchase. All seemed right with the world—and then came the second term.

The election of 1804 was a Republican cakewalk.[223] Jefferson won the electoral vote against the hapless Charles Cotesworth Pinckney 123–47. Jefferson's second term was a perfect storm of calamity, much, though not all, of his own making. But the disastrous second term began with a laudable success.[224] In 1804, goaded by the piratical tactics of the Barbary States against American shipping in the Mediterranean Sea, Jefferson dispatched a naval force to the area. In February 1804, Stephen Decatur entered the harbor at Tripoli and with a seventy-man force succeeded in burning the captured

---

[220] Wills, *"Negro President,"* 118, 124.

[221] Wills's discussion of this point is a significant revision of the standard view of the Federalists as embittered political dinosaurs. See *"Negro President,"* 115–16.

[222] Wills, *"Negro President,"* 116.

[223] Wood, *Empire,* 312; McDonald, *Presidency of Thomas Jefferson,* 86–87.

[224] Ellis, *Sphinx,* 241–43; Wood, *Empire,* 637–38. Schweikart and Allen call the action "America's first preemptive war." Schweikart and Allen, *Patriot's History,* 168. See also Brian Kilmeade and Don Yaeger, *Thomas Jefferson and the Tripoli Pirates: The Forgotten War That Changed American History* (2015).

USS *Philadelphia* before it could be deployed against American shipping. A follow-up force was dispatched in 1805, resulting in the end of depredations by the Barbary States. The problem, even in the midst of this success story, is that Jefferson failed to draw any salutary lessons from it regarding the use of military force. Both the army and the navy remained seriously underfunded.

All the deficiencies of Republican diplomacy were exposed in his second term. The Peace of Amiens, which provided a brief respite from the Napoleonic wars, ended in May 1803. The resumption of fighting resulted in renewed urgency on the issue of neutral rights. The details of American flounderings on this issue with a bewildering succession of futile trade regulations have been recounted many times.[225] Jefferson's pathological hatred of the British, shared by Madison, made any meaningful attempt at reconciliation impossible. His efforts to effect significant change in the behavior of a superpower fighting for survival by economic coercion were doomed to fail. The failure, already nearly a certainty, was also guaranteed by the Republican antimilitary ideology which saw armed force more as a threat to civil liberty than as a means of national defense. The whole Republican approach to the long-term global crisis was badly flawed, doomed to failure, and the direct cause of the needless War of 1812.

Jefferson's inflexible ideology led him to pass up an opportunity to reduce tensions with Great Britain. The Monroe–Pinckney commission produced a new treaty in August 1806, which was intended to replace the lapsed Jay Treaty and strengthen commercial relations between the two countries. The treaty was signed at the end of 1806. Jefferson received it in March 1807. He refused to send it to the Senate because it did not deal with impressment, even though the British pledged to be circumspect in resorting to it. Jefferson did not want any treaty with the British and was not willing to abandon the failed policy of economic coercion. This was "a great turning point in the Age of Jefferson" which passed up an opportunity to "substitute peace and prosperity for commercial restrictions and war." From this point on, Anglo-American relations steadily deteriorated.[226]

The culminating domestic disaster of this flawed diplomacy was the embargo. It is difficult to find anyone willing to mount a wholehearted defense of it. Wood, for example, asserts that Jefferson ended up "repressing his fellow citizens to a degree rarely duplicated in the entire history of the United States."[227] The triggering event was an egregious act of British

---

[225] See any standard account, such as Wood's chapter "Republican Diplomacy" in *Empire*, 620–58.

[226] It was negotiated by James Monroe and William Pinckney. Wood, *Empire*, 644–45; Donald R. Hickey, *The War of 1812: A Forgotten Conflict* (1989), 16 (quotes).

[227] Wood, *Empire*, 626.

aggression—the *Chesapeake–Leopard* incident in the summer of 1807. After the American captain of the *Chesapeake* refused a British demand to search his ship, the *Leopard* opened fire, forcing the *Chesapeake* to submit to being boarded, searched, and having several men impressed. Reaction was understandably intense. Jefferson considered drastic action, reflecting his ludicrously defective comprehension of American military resources. He initially contemplated a quick attack on Canada by militiamen authorized to fight only in their states, while gunboats defended the American coastline from the Royal Navy.[228] But Jefferson's fiscal policies meant that there was no money to finance even these limited actions. Fortunately, Jefferson's capable secretary of state Albert Gallatin provided the necessary reality check.[229]

At this point, Jefferson turned to the idea of an embargo, which went into effect in mid-December 1807, running its disastrous course until the end of his second term. It was, Wood notes, "with the exception of Prohibition, the greatest example in American history of ideology brought to bear on a matter of public policy."[230] The embargo represents the culmination of the fundamentally flawed effort at economic coercion which was clearly linked to the Republican aversion to the military.

The whole embargo effort brought to light another, somewhat paradoxical, aspect of the Jeffersonian worldview. Jefferson's public persona of genial sweetness and light only partially concealed the unrelenting Jefferson with the mailed fist. A number of commentators have noted the ferocity with which Jefferson sought to enforce the embargo which clearly ran deeply counter to the bedrock principle of Jefferson's political philosophy—that of limited government. In seeking to prevent war with Great Britain, Jefferson was, in effect, waging war on American citizens.[231] Jefferson was the only president to use the army for the routine enforcement of laws in peacetime. He expressed a willingness to execute those who defied the embargo. The man who had opposed even the use of militia to put down Shays' and Fries' rebellions turned the army on American citizens in 1807 when his policies were resisted.[232]

The embargo served other sinister aspects of the Jeffersonian ideology. Jefferson had always hated merchants, particularly Federalist merchants in New England. The embargo provided a perfect opportunity to punish the merchant class, his political opponents, and a recalcitrant region at once.

---

[228] Jefferson predicted that the conquest of Canada would be "a mere matter of marching." Quoted in Hickey, *War of 1812*, 73.

[229] Albert Gallatin to Jefferson, July 15, 1807, quoted in Wills, *"Negro President,"* 148.

[230] Wood, *Empire*, 649.

[231] McDonald, *Presidency of Thomas Jefferson*, 152.

[232] Levy, *Jefferson and Civil Liberties*, 107. He also used the navy in enforcement (113).

The strongest opposition came from "the monarchists of the north."[233] They got what they deserved. Would Jefferson have ever adopted any policy as harmful to Virginia planters as his embargo was to New England merchants? There was a regional aspect to the issue reflecting the sectional nature of the Republican Party.[234] Jefferson's party was a coalition of the solidly Republican slaveholding South and the emerging middling folk of the North. The paradox is that the party simultaneously was able to draw strength from the inherently democratizing forces at work in the country at large in ways that the Federalists could not while depending on the bastion of the solid, hierarchical, slaveholding South all the way to 1860.

The embargo was a grim display of all of Jefferson's ideological obsessions. The result was an unmitigated disaster; it failed to have any noticeable effect on British policy. Aimed at the British, the embargo punished Americans instead. Jefferson realized that things had gone badly wrong, so he served out the rest of his term in a state of helpless misery. At the end of his presidency, he confessed, "Never did a prisoner released from chains, feel such relief as I shall on shaking off the shackles of power."[235] But despite all his failures, his heir-apparent James Madison cruised to victory in the election of 1808, winning the electoral vote 122–53.[236] That outcome was a measure of the overall support enjoyed by the Republican Party and the ongoing decline of the Federalists, who had ceased to be a viable national political party, though they were still powerful in New England throughout the War of 1812.

The election of Madison ensured a continuation of Jefferson's already failed policies. Although the embargo was lifted, the same policy of economic coercion continued. The same domestic policies, including a continuation of military underfunding, were implemented. Madison's second term was as bad as his first. Even apart from the fruitless efforts at economic coercion, Madison faced many other difficulties. The emerging factionalism in the Republican Party, which had surfaced during Jefferson's presidency, increased. The less the Republicans had to fear a crumbling Federalist Party, the more they could indulge in the luxury of infighting. Madison would have faced daunting difficulties with the best of both policies and men, but he had neither. Poor choices, coupled with politically driven appointments, meant

---

[233] Jefferson to Thomas Mann Randolph, January 1, 1809, quoted in Jon Meacham, *Jefferson: The Art of Power*, 433.

[234] Wood, *Empire*, 531–33.

[235] Jefferson to P. S. Dupont de Nemors, March, 2, 1809, *Founders Online*, National Archives.

[236] The Federalists were divided between Charles Cotesworth Pinckney (47) and George Clinton (6). Madison was opposed by John Randolph and his faction which foreshadowed the divisions of the Republican Party during Madison's presidency. See Smelser, *Democrat Republic*, 181–82.

that he had inadequate personnel even at the cabinet level, with the notable exception of Albert Gallatin.[237]

Madison made no significant effort to prepare for war.[238] Nor was any effort made to achieve an accommodation with the Federalists. The result was that the War of 1812 was really a Republican war. He made no attempt to put government finances in shape to fund a war. There was no increase in taxes. The charter of the Bank of the United States was due to expire in 1811, and Madison made no effort to recharter it—at a time when the nation was on the brink of war. Most of the attention was devoted to the various failed efforts at economic coercion. The only really new aspect of these efforts was the opportunity they afforded Napoleon to engage in his own chicanery at the expense of both Great Britain and the United States.

In the midst of this dismal landscape, there are several incidents which reflect poorly on Madison. The first involves the notorious scoundrel James Wilkinson. Although Wilkinson is much less well known than Aaron Burr, he was by all accounts an equal, perhaps an even greater, villain. Yet despite his many villainies and manifest incompetence, he never paid anything like the proper penalty for his misdeeds.[239] His tenure as governor of the Louisiana Territory was a toxic brew of corruption and incompetence. A court-martial, however, was inconclusive, leaving the matter up to Madison, who chose not to pass judgment in deference to Wilkinson's influential Republican friends in Maryland. This decision was wrong in itself and damaged the morale of the army on the brink of the War of 1812.[240]

The other incident involved David M. Erskine, the British minister to the United States. In April 1809, he evidently exceeded his instructions by assuring Madison that the British would repeal the trade restrictions. Acting on this information, Madison announced a reopening of trade with Great Britain, only to learn in the summer that Erskine had been mistaken. But the story circulated that the repudiation of Erskine was the result of the anger that George III expressed over a comment that Madison, as secretary of state, had made in the aftermath of the *Chesapeake–Leopard* affair. Madison, calling for the punishment of Admiral George C. Berkley in connection with that incident, had observed that while he would not insist on further punishment, "he [was] not the less sensible of the justice and utility of such

---

[237] Madison went to war with "a group of incompetents rarely matched in U.S. history." Magnet, *Founders at Home*, 390.

[238] As good a source as any is Wood, *Empire*, 664–68; see also Smelser, *Democratic Republic*, 193–99.

[239] See Andro Linklater, *An Artist in Treason: The Extraordinary Double Life of General James Wilkinson* (2009).

[240] Robert Rutland, a sympathetic biographer, asserted that it was Madison's worst mistake. See Rutland, *James Madison*, 57–59.

---

an example, nor the less persuaded that it would best comport with what is due from His Britannic Majesty to his own honor." Angered by this not-so-subtle, unsolicited advice, George III, the story goes, insisted on repudiating any concession to the United States. But whatever the reason for the repudiation of Erskine's overture, the result was a renewed strain on Anglo–American relations.[241]

And then came Madison's declaration of war on June 18, 1812, at the very end of his first term. It was an unforced error; there was simply no compelling immediate cause for so drastic a step. It was just the culmination of over a decade of the failed policy of economic coercion. Also, the sad irony is that Madison's declaration of war came after Great Britain had suspended its Orders in Council but before that news reached America. A little patience would have saved much blood and treasure.[242] Neither he nor his Republican Party had any idea what to do except go to war. For all his Madisonian sympathy, Lance Banning put his finger directly on the problem by observing that Madison and his party held on to their "antiwar and antipreparation ideology so long and so stubbornly" that "the result was nearly a disaster for the United State."[243]

Madison took a badly divided country into war. The vote in the House was 79 to 49 and in the Senate 19 to 13, the closest vote for a declaration of war in American history. One of the many paradoxes of the War of 1812 is that the region and the political party most harmed by British policies were the strongest opponents of the war. Not a single Federalist voted for the war.[244] One measure of the strength of the Federalist opposition can be seen in the outcome of the election of 1812.[245] Even though the Federalist Party had been nearly moribund, Madison defeated DeWitt Clinton in the electoral vote only 128 to 89. The issue of the war and the energetic opposition of the Young Federalists revived Federalist strength. The Republicans went into the war believing that they confronted two enemies—the British and a

---

[241] Wood, *Empire*, 664–65; Smelser, *Democratic Republic*, 193–95. Most historians pass over the matter of Madison's comment. Kevin R. C. Gutzman comments that, if true, it was deeply ironic that Jeffersonian diplomacy, perhaps on the brink of success, would be derailed by a "characteristic Jeffersonian–Republican dig—the kind of gratuitously offensive thing that Madison and his friends had said and written about Federalists and foreign monarchs for nearly two decades." Kevin R. C. Gutzman, *James Madison and the Making of America* (2012), 307.

[242] It is possible to argue that the British suspension of the Orders in Council vindicated economic coercion. But no policy which takes over a decade to yield results can be considered a success. The British action came at a very low point in the war with Napoleon and could have been easily reversed once the crisis was over.

[243] Banning, *Jeffersonian Persuasion*, 293.

[244] Rutland, *James Madison*, 225.

[245] Hickey, *War of 1812*, 105.

"domestic faction" in league with them.[246] The declaration of war reignited the bitter partisan strife which had not really completely dissipated from the 1790s.[247] There was an ironic role reversal. The Federalists began talking the language of the Kentucky and Virginia Resolutions, while the Republicans were sounding like the Federalists of the Adams administration in support of federal authority.

Some Federalists, bitter in their opposition to the war, considered secession, though fortunately they were never able to carry the day.[248] They did have much by way of provocation.[249] The embargo had been a catastrophe which struck at the economic heart of New England. Federalists had before them the example of the Quasi-War in which Adams had defended the national honor with a calibrated use of force short of general war. Yet they saw the Republicans ignoring this achievement while blundering into war. It takes little imagination to predict how the Virginia planters would have reacted to any Federalist policies as damaging to their economic base as the embargo had been to the New England merchants.[250]

The Republicans under Madison plunged the nation into war under the worst possible circumstances. The country was badly divided politically, with grossly inadequate military preparation. The Bank of the United States was not rechartered in 1811 at the time when fiscal stability was most needed. There was a crisis of responsible, competent leadership both in the administration and in the military. Virtually no one, even Madison's most ardent defenders, disputes these facts. It is just that they refuse to connect the dots in their overall evaluation of him and his party. The War of 1812 was the first attempt at a politically correct war. Madison could not simply fight a war to win, but he had to fight it in an ideologically acceptable way.

[246] Richard Buel Jr., *America on the Brink: How the Political Struggle and the War of 1812 Almost Destroyed the Young Republic* (2005), 154.

[247] Smelser, *Democratic Republic*, 246.

[248] The role of the Federalists during the war has been the subject of much historiographical debate, which is clearly seen in two histories of the War of 1812. Donald Hickey's *War of 1812* takes a critical but judicious look at the party neither denying its faults nor exaggerating their impact. Richard Buel, however, consistently blames the Federalists for putting America in danger. Buel, however, does admit that economic coercion did not work, that the nation was not militarily prepared to fight, and that the Republicans denounced the Federalist Party as an enemy. See Buel, *American on the Brink*, 109, 150, 154.

[249] Gouverneur Morris denounced the war as an assault on New Englanders by claiming that resulted from "an administration of slave holders, who, envying the prosperity of the northern states, endeavoured to dry up its source by ruinous and commercial restrictions and have now, actuated by the same spirit, exposed them to the desolation of a war alike unnecessary and unjust." An Address to the People of the State of New York on the Present State of Affairs" (1812), from J. Jackson Barlow, ed., *To Secure the Blessings of Liberty: Selected Writings of Gouverneur Morris* (2012).

[250] One has only to look at their reaction to Hamilton's program which was in no way a direct assault on their economic interests.

Madison deliberately fought the war at less than full efficiency out of the grotesque obsession with saving our republican form of government.[251] He knowingly accepted administrative confusion and inefficiencies, military failure, and the opposition of both Federalists and even some members of his own party, believing that strong executive leadership would endanger the principles for which the war was being fought. Madison thought that it was better to allow the capital to be burned than to build up state power by the European model.[252] Being besotted by ideology is the only explanation for how a man of Madison's keen intellect could fail to see this as a ruinously false dichotomy. One also wonders if Madison had ever protested when Jefferson's embargo was used as a weapon against American citizens; it would almost seem as if Jefferson was more willing to use state power against domestic political opponents than against a foreign foe.

The war cost America 2260 killed in action and 4050 wounded. It is not known exactly how many died of disease, but the total number is estimated at 20,000 from all causes directly related to the war. The financial cost has been estimated at $105 million.[253] Was it worth it? Even if one assumes, against the available evidence, that the war was unavoidable, the follow-up question is: how many men died in order for Madison to fight a politically correct war and salve his Republican conscience? The Treaty of Ghent was signed on December 24, 1814, on the general principle of status quo ante bellum. The war ended as a costly stalemate.[254] Even so, there were some positive aspects. The nation had survived a war with the world's superpower. The war, furthermore, ended on a high military note—Andrew Jackson's stunning victory at New Orleans.[255]

So while Madison had squandered national resources in a needless stalemate of a war, he certainly seized firm control of the marketing angle. The man who subordinated military efficiency to ideology had no scruples about extolling the great achievement of the "second war for independence."[256] Added to this is the universal human instinct to claim victory in all wars if possible. Patriotic memory seeks to hallow even the most unjust wars with

---

[251] Wood, *Empire*, 698; see also Wood, *Revolutionary Characters: What Made the Founders Different* (2006), 170–71.

[252] Wood, *Empire*, 698.

[253] Hickey, *War of 1812*, 297, 303.

[254] Wood, *Empire*, 695. Ironically, the British never accepted the American position on neutral rights and impressment. The near–simultaneous ending of the Napoleonic war rendered the issues moot. See also Hickey, *War of 1812*, 289.

[255] It was fought on January 8, 1815—after the signing of the Treaty of Ghent.

[256] Wood, *Empire*, 699.

the patina of glory. Americans, citizens of a new republic, were perhaps even more vulnerable than other peoples to such blandishments.[257]

The Republican Party and Madison himself benefitted greatly from these factors. To this must also be added the final demise of the Federalist Party. The much-anticipated Hartford Convention, called by New England Federalists to address their grievances, met from December 15, 1814 to January 5, 1815—at the same time as the signing of the Treaty of Ghent. The moderates were firmly in control. The demands were not treasonous or even secessionist, but the timing was all wrong. Most Americans were ready to celebrate a great victory, so they had little patience with the New England Federalist naysayers, as the Republicans branded them. Federalists, particularly in New England, had rebounded during the war, but the conjunction of the Hartford Convention, the Treaty of Ghent, and the celebratory aftermath of the battle of New Orleans doomed the party to extinction.[258]

There is a final ironic twist to the story. To a considerable degree, the Federalists won the argument over economic policy. The Republican Party during the rest of Madison's second term turned to what some have called neofederalism, "The First Era of Big Central Government."[259] The plain truth was that the nation needed a new bank (Albert Gallatin had admitted this), basic transportation infrastructure (then called internal improvements), increased revenue, and a higher level of military capability. Even as the Federalists faded from the scene, their bitter opponents at length supported "a Hamiltonian wish list."[260] The nation had suffered greatly during the war because the Bank of the United States had not been rechartered in 1811. In addition to Gallatin, Madison himself had changed his mind on the issue, although he did not take a public stand because he "was afraid to admit that he had changed his mind."[261] In any case, a Second Bank of the United States was created with a twenty-year charter in 1816.

It is no exaggeration to say that the road system of the Roman Empire was superior to that of early-nineteenth-century America. The nation desperately needed to build roads and canals.[262] Madison conceded this point, but he insisted that a constitutional amendment was needed to enable federal money to be used to finance such projects. The obvious catch was that there

---

[257] Bradford Perkins commented that "seldom has a nation so successfully practiced self-induced amnesia." Quoted in Daniel Walker Howe, *What Hath God Wrought: The Transformation of America, 1815–1848* (2007), 71.

[258] Smelser, *Democratic Republic*, 298–09.

[259] The title of chapter six of Schweikart and Allen, *Patriot's History*, 179–218.

[260] Gutzman, *James Madison*, 330.

[261] Rutland, *James Madison*, 69–70.

[262] Wood, *Empire*, 485. In 1808, Gallatin had issued his Report on Roads and Canals in which he promised to secure an enabling constitutional amendment.

was no chance of such an amendment ever being passed in anything like a timely way. Matters came to a dramatic head on the last day of Madison's presidency when he "dropped his bombshell" by vetoing Henry Clay's Bonus Bill which would have used the bonus money from the new bank to finance internal improvements.[263] This action was clearly in line with Jefferson's longstanding belief in the necessity of a constitutional amendment. The nation had to make do with a primitive road system for many more years.[264]

Despite this setback, however, there were modest gains.[265] A protective tariff helped raise government revenue. A small standing army of 20,000 men increased military strength. In addition, Jefferson's ill-fated naval gunboat policy was "abandoned without a whimper of protest."[266] The result was that the Federalist philosophy lived on, admittedly in an attenuated form, in the Republican Party. Perhaps the crowning irony of this whole troubled era is that the Republicans finally adopted policies in peacetime which would have been immensely helpful before the war. The national euphoria which followed the war gave Madison, who served as the chief cheerleader, the political cover he needed. He cannot, however, escape the critical evaluation of historians. It is telling that some of his strongest apologists, nevertheless, have harsh things to say about critical aspects of his policies and leadership. [267] Madison and his party had led an unprepared and badly divided nation into an unnecessary war with incompetent leadership under the malign influence of a paranoid ideology. It is on these grounds that his leadership should be evaluated, not on whatever the mysterious combination of luck and Providence that enabled the new republic to survive into an Era of Good Feelings.[268]

---

[263] Rutland, *James Madison*, 205–06.

[264] Wood, *Empire*, 485. Many Republicans along with Jefferson continued to fear that a government strong enough to build roads and canals would also be strong enough to free the slaves, a fear which was inextricably woven into the fabric of the Republican Party and its Democratic successor. See John Henry Larson, "Jefferson's Union and the Problem of Internal Improvements" in Peter S. Onuf, ed., *Jeffersonian Legacies* (1993), 340–69.

[265] Banning, *Jeffersonian Persuasion*, 297.

[266] Rutland, *James Madison*, 196.

[267] Among the sympathetic historians with harshly critical treatments are Gordon S. Wood, Lance Banning, Kevin Gutzman, Robert R. Rutland, and Ralph Ketcham.

[268] Bismarck would not have been surprised.

CHAPTER FIVE: A LUCID INTERVAL, 1815—1828

Through a fortunate political application of Newton's law of gravity, the influence of Thomas Jefferson was seen in some sort of inverse proportion to the distance from his disciples. James Madison was never better than when Jefferson was an ocean away. James Monroe was also a clear beneficiary of this principle as the third and last of the Virginia Dynasty. The Jeffersonian ideology was strongest early in his career but weakened more over time than distance. Monroe did get off to a rocky start, faithfully reflecting even the irrational aspects of the Jeffersonian ideology. He bought unreflectively into the prevailing "Republican myth" that the Federalists sought to set up a monarchy.[269] He also reflected the Jeffersonian whitewashing of the French Revolution, noting that he had arrived after the "most spectacular scenes" had passed—surely one of the most euphemistic references to the Terror on

---

[269]Chapter title: Excerpt from "Mac Flecknoe; or, A satyr upon the True-Blew Poet c. 1676," by John Dryden (1631-1700), an attack on his rival, Thomas Shadwell.

> Shadwell alone, of all my sons, is he
>
> Who stands confirm'd in full stupidity.
>
> The rest to some faint meaning make pretence,
>
> But Shadwell never deviates into sense.
>
> Some beams of wit on other souls may fall,
>
> Strike through and make a lucid interval;
>
> But Shadwell's genuine night admits no ray,
>
> His rising fogs prevail upon the day.

Harry Ammon, *James Monroe: The Quest for National Identity* (1971), 371.

record.[270] In domestic politics, he was also a dependable Jeffersonian, refer-ring to John Adams as "our insane president."[271] In 1800, Monroe stood ready as governor of Virginia to call out the militia and take "drastic measures" in case the Federalists sought to negate the election of Jefferson, yet another example of the Jeffersonian paranoid style of politics.[272]

None of this is at all surprising in light of Monroe's early career. He grew up in the orbit of Republican politics. He became friends with both Jefferson and Madison in the 1780s. However, his diplomatic career almost ruined his prospects. Washington appointed him minister to France in 1794, but his pro-French position "nearly wrecked his career."[273] Monroe made a complete fool of himself in France. In private correspondence, he urged that the United States "seek redress" from Great Britain by "again appealing to arms," recom-mending that the United States invade Canada and seize the Bermudas.[274]

The nadir of Monroe's botched diplomatic career came during the negoti-ations leading to Jay's Treaty. He actually promised the French that he would permit them to see the text of the treaty; he requested a copy from John Jay, who naturally refused to send it. Monroe intended to use French opposition to the treaty to defeat it in the Senate. Its ratification, he wrote Madison, would "be one of the most afflicting events that ever befell our country."[275]

When Washington recalled Monroe in July 1796, he returned very much under a cloud. John Adams referred to him as "our disgraced minister" who was recalled for "misconduct."[276] Monroe reflected the bitter anti-Wash-ington animus of Jefferson by denouncing Washington's "ingratitude" and placing him among "a collection of superficial blunderers."[277] Perhaps the kindest thing to be said of Monroe at this dismal point in his career is that he had nowhere to go but up. And up he went. He returned to the familiar orbit of Virginia politics and was welcomed by Jefferson and Madison. He began a steady, if unspectacular, upward trajectory, first in Virginia, then in national politics.

---

[270] Ammon asserts that Monroe showed "an excellent understanding" of the French Revolution, including the "necessity of repressive measures." Ammon, *Monroe*, 131–32. In several articles in the *National Gazette*, Monroe equated the American and French Revolutions. Nobel E. Cunningham, *The Presidency of James Monroe* (1996), 4.

[271] Monroe to Madison, June 24, 1798, quoted in Ammon, *Monroe*, 168.

[272] Ammon, *Monroe*, 193.

[273] Cunningham, *Presidency*, 5.

[274] Letters to Edmund Randolph and Madison in November 1794, quoted in Ammon, *Monroe*, 128–29.

[275] Monroe to Madison, September 8, 1795, quoted in Ammon, *Monroe*, 145–46. Ammon can find no basis for defending Monroe's egregious behavior.

[276] Quoted in Ammon, *Monroe*, 168.

[277] Monroe to Madison, January 1, 1797, quoted in Ammon, *Monroe*, 157.

He had, for a time, an on-again, off-again relationship with Madison. His definitive entry into national politics came with his appointment as Madison's secretary of state in 1811. Even before this appointment, he began to show some signs of independence, differing with Jefferson on the United States policy toward Great Britain. During his tenure as U.S. minister to Great Britain (1803–07), he negotiated the Monroe–Pinckney Treaty (1806). However, Jefferson did not even bother to submit it to the Senate, so Monroe returned "in something like disgrace."[278] For his part, Monroe realized that the treaty was flawed but insisted that it was the best possible "when measured against the reality of British power."[279]

It seems that Monroe's tenure as minister to Great Britain provided a kind of reality therapy which changed him from a reflexive Jeffersonian into something of a realist. In retrospect, he came to see that Jefferson and Madison had "seemed to debase the nation by its dependence upon France."[280] It seems clear that by the time Monroe was appointed secretary of state, his recent experiences had prepared him well for the position, although he did share with Madison the erroneous belief that Great Britain would not be able to launch full-scale war against the United States.

Monroe's tenure as secretary of state was punctuated by several stints as acting secretary of war where he had to grapple with the real-life consequences of the Jeffersonian distrust of the military. He performed creditably in both positions, so was rightly seen as Madison's successor since the position of secretary of state was at that time viewed as the steppingstone to the presidency. It proved to be the case in the election of 1816. Monroe was elected by a party caucus over William Crawford by a vote of 65–54. Then, against the nominal opposition of Rufus King of the moribund Federalist Party, he cruised to a victory in the general election by an electoral margin of 183–34.

The election of Monroe occurred at a transitional time in the evolution of the American political party system. The first party system of Republicans and Federalists was breaking apart. The Federalist Party had been declining even before Jefferson's election in 1800. A brief revival during the War of 1812 quickly faded in the flush of victory and the stigma of the Hartford Convention. After 1815, the party ceased to exist as a viable national party.[281] The Republican Party had evolved beyond the bounds of Jeffersonian ortho-

---

[278] George Dangerfield, *The Era of Good Feelings* (1952), 96. See Chapter 4, p. 8.

[279] Quoted in Ammon, *Monroe*, 264.

[280] Ammon, *Monroe*, 491.

[281] Much of the Federalist economic program was ultimately adopted by the emerging Whig Party in the mid-1830s. Shaw Livermore Jr., *The Twilight of Federalism: The Disintegration of the Federalist Party, 1815–1830* (1962).

doxy, particularly during Madison's second term. The exigencies of the War of 1812 and the needs of a growing nation with increasingly variegated economic needs were straining the economic policies of an agrarian party to the breaking point.

The result was that Monroe inherited a party rent with profound divisions. The Old Republican fundamentalists of the John Randolph and John Taylor school continued to denounce what they saw as the manifold heresies of Madison and Monroe. For them, those insidious Federalists, defeated though they were as a party, were nevertheless succeeding by infiltrating the Republican Party with their pernicious ideas. With all these political complexities, the nation was undergoing an irresistible market revolution which carried it beyond the confines of Jeffersonian agrarianism. This was at the heart of Monroe's dilemma. He remained loyal to "those agrarian principles which he was so cautiously deserting."[282] But the point is that he did desert them; in doing so, he implemented the breakdown of the first party system.

Monroe began his presidency with a goodwill tour of New England in the summer of 1817, ostensibly to inspect frontier outposts and coastal fortifications but in reality to show himself in the Federalist stronghold.[283] The Federalist *Boston Columbian Centennial* of July 12, 1817, referred to "a demonstration of good feelings," a phrase which, transmuted into an "era of good feelings," was used to describe the political atmosphere during Monroe's presidency.[284] The reality was quite different. Although Monroe made cautious hints about bringing Federalists into his administration, the resistance of his fellow Republicans was too strong. The Federalists were "surprised and delighted" by Monroe's openness to their ideas, but there was no patronage payoff.[285] The phrase "era of good feelings" may be the last significant obeisance to the idea of a nonpartisan utopia. This was a transitional period of party development, but partisanship based on self-interest remained strong. Monroe was "bewildered" by "the chaos of contending factions" and endured what was actually an era of bad feelings.[286]

This transitional period was later to bewilder John Quincy Adams, who also witnessed the ongoing triumph of the democratic ethos. The Federalists would have had a difficult time in an age given over to the "curbing of privi-

---

[282] Dangerfield, *Era*, 101.
[283] Monroe departed from Jeffersonian orthodoxy in his conviction that creditable military force was essential, probably as a result of the military fiasco of the War of 1812,
[284] Dangerfield, *Era*, 95–96.
[285] Livermore, *Twilight*, 15.
[286] Ammon, *Monroe*, ix.

lege and the conquest of elites."[287] But it was not only the Federalists who felt the pressure of the evolving ethos. The Jeffersonians had developed "a theory of a natural aristocracy"—with themselves, naturally, at its center.[288] Once the democratic genie was out of the bottle, it was impossible to induce him to wriggle back in.[289] This transitional period was a prelude to the age of Andrew Jackson. An ever-stronger process of democratization is an unquestionably good thing so long as the people themselves attain the wisdom to use their freedom and influence wisely. But what if the democratization proceeds without a corresponding growth of wisdom?

Surveying the Monroe presidency as a whole, it is evident that he was sure-footed and confident in his conduct of foreign policy while less confident in his handling of domestic issues. The basic problem was attempting to steer a stable course between undiluted Federalism and traditional Jeffersonianism. But it is certainly to his credit that he did embark on this difficult venture.

On some issues, matters were fairly simple. Because the failure to recharter the national bank in 1811 had led to severe financial hardship during the War of 1812, both Madison and Monroe supported its recharter in 1816. The Old Republicans and the irreconcilable Jefferson continued their futile opposition. A similar trend was discernible in relation to the issue of the tariff. The nation was moving away from the agrarian simplicity extolled by Jefferson. The War of 1812 accelerated the growth of manufacturing. After the war, this newly established manufacturing sector was clearly threatened by renewed competition from the highly efficient British system. This led to the rise of the tariff issue. The pressures for tariff protection increased throughout Monroe's presidency. In 1816, Monroe supported a tariff which was enacted in April. It was "a temperate piece of legislation" and as such was not a powerfully divisive issue.[290] This one step forward did not resolve the issue as continued pressure for greater protection persisted throughout Monroe's administration. The result was another tariff in 1824. This time the vote was much closer, reflecting a growing sectional division as cotton, not manufacturing, was becoming king in the South; the planters were demanding cheap manufactured goods. Nevertheless, Monroe supported the tariff of 1824, signing the bill in May. This action was "an obituary in itself" of

---

[287] George Dangerfield, *The Awakening of American Nationalism, 1815–1828* (1965), 196.

[288] Livermore, *Twilight*, 7.

[289] This is really an outworking of the process analyzed by Gordon Wood in *The Radicalism of the American Revolution.* The radicalism was not immediately realized, but its implications were open ended.

[290] Dangerfield, *Awakening*, 14. The tariff of 1816 was supported by John Calhoun and other Southerners who hoped that the South would be able to develop its own manufacturing sector; this hope had faded by 1824.

the Virginia Dynasty.[291] Jefferson opposed the bill, though he did not directly blame Monroe for its passage.[292]

It was, however, the third major issue which proved by far the most contentious—the issue of the transportation infrastructure. The one act which had prevented Madison's "total immersion" in the Federalist program was his veto of the Bonus Bill to finance internal improvements.[293] And it was on this issue that Monroe's Jeffersonian scruples more or less held firm. He maintained the standard Republican position that internal improvements were necessary but could be undertaken only after the sanction of a constitutional amendment. But the reality was that internal improvements were necessary. Jefferson himself never learned. To him, the proposed Erie Canal, the single most important internal improvement in American history, was "madness."[294]

There was to be no definitive solution to this vexing issue during Monroe's presidency. In 1822, Monroe vetoed a bill authorizing repairs to the Cumberland Road, while admitting that Congress had the power to raise money and to appropriate it for the common defense and national benefit.[295] Despite these stops and starts, the nation muddled along with a series of ad hoc solutions. While Monroe argued against a system of internal improvements, Congress responded by issuing "a seemingly endless number of national projects by simple appropriations."[296] Monroe's willingness to move beyond the strictures of pure Jeffersonian orthodoxy served the nation well. Certainly, there were clouds on the horizon. Monroe was the leader of a rapidly evolving nation with greater economic complexity, in the context of resurgent sectionalism.

Slavery emerged as the most ominous sectional issue. The implications of the Jeffersonian coalition of the planters of the South and the Republicans of the North became more and more apparent over time. The complexity of the issue of internal improvements was made even more difficult by the ongoing need to protect slavery. Nathaniel Macon, in a letter in 1818, asserted that "if Congress can make canals, they can with more propriety emancipate."[297] The Tallmadge Amendment of February 1819 brought the whole slavery issue to the forefront in connection with territorial expansion. The amendment

---

[291] Dangerfield, *Era*, 310.

[292] Jefferson to Richard Rush, June 5, 1824, quoted in Dangerfield, *Era*, 310.

[293] Dangerfield, *Era*, 99.

[294] Quoted in Daniel Walker Howe, *What Hath God Wrought: The Transformation of America, 1815–1848* (2007), 117.

[295] Dangerfield, *Awakening*, 199.

[296] Stephen Skowronelk, *The Politics Presidents Make: Leadership from John Adams to George Bush* (1993), 100–7 (quote 105).

[297] Quoted in Howe, *Transformation*, 221.

would have barred the admission of Missouri to the Union as a slave state. It passed in the House but failed in the Senate. Fortunately, Maine was also applying for admittance. This happy coincidence enabled James Thomas to offer a compromise by which both states were to be admitted without reference to slavery, coupled with the future outlawing of slavery above the southern boundary of Missouri—the famous 36 30' line.

Monroe, himself a slaveholder, eagerly supported the compromise. But Jefferson famously described the episode as a "fire bell in the night" which "awakened me and filled me with terror."[298] Some northern Federalists opposed slavery and some northern Republicans had come to resent the political strength of Virginia, but there was not at this time enough passion for a general crisis. Monroe signed the Missouri Enabling Act on March 6, 1820. James Madison advised Monroe that "diffusion" was the ultimate solution to the slavery issue; therefore, slavery should be permitted to "go where it pleased."[299] The ordeal was not quite over because the Missouri constitution outlawed the immigration of free blacks into the state in defiance of the "privileges and immunities" clause of Article IV, Section 2 of the Constitution. After linguistic wrangling, Henry Clay crafted another compromise by means of a "toothless proviso." Missouri pledged not to do what the language of its constitution clearly enabled it to do.[300] The Missouri crisis made Southern Republicans even more intent on defending slavery against what they still thought of as Federalist plots.[301]

In contrast to perplexing domestic problems, Monroe enjoyed great diplomatic success. He benefitted, as any president would have, from the end of the long cycle of Napoleonic Wars. But he made the most of his opportunities, operating in close collaboration with his secretary of state, John Quincy Adams. Monroe's appointment of Adams as secretary of state was his most consequential Cabinet appointment. He selected a man with immense diplomatic experience with whom he could work effectively. There were two main emphases in the Monroe–Adams diplomacy—expansion at the expense of a tottering Spanish New World empire and the creation of a diplomatic sphere of influence in the face of potential European intrusion into the politics of Latin America. The result of their labors was to establish the United States as an expanding power with increasing significance in world politics. The Spanish New World empire was the "all-absorbing

---

[298] Jefferson to John Holmes, April 22, 1820, *Writings*, 1434.
[299] Madison to Monroe, February 10, 1820, quoted in Dangerfield, *Awakening*, 125.
[300] Dangerfield, *Awakening*, 132.
[301] Richard Hofstadter, *The Idea of a Party System: The Rise of Legitimate Opposition in the United States, 1780–1840* (1969), 201–3.

problem in foreign affairs."[302] Spanish weakness presented Monroe and Adams with opportunities they were ready to seize.

The inability of Spain to control the Florida Indians and establish a stable frontier gave Andrew Jackson the opportunity to take matters into his perennially aggressive hands. He invaded Florida, executed two British subjects for waging war against the United States, stormed Pensacola, and took control of West Florida. The political fallout was intense with complicated charges and countercharges of who knew what when and who, if anyone, had authorized Jackson's actions. Of all members of Monroe's Cabinet, Adams was Jackson's strongest supporter. Jackson's actions sent powerful signals to the hapless Spanish and undoubtedly rendered them more willing to sign the Adams–Onis Transcontinental Treaty of 1819. Spain ceded Florida to the United States. The treaty also established the western boundary of the Louisiana Purchase which ran from the mouth of the Sabine River on the Gulf of Mexico in the south, and then west and north along the Red and Arkansas Rivers and the forty-second parallel to the Pacific. The treaty was "one of the most outstanding achievements of early postwar nationalism."[303]

The second major achievement of the Monroe–Adams diplomacy was the Monroe Doctrine.[304] It too was a result of the break-up of the Spanish empire as various Spanish Latin American colonies revolted, declaring their independence. The European states of the reactionary post-Napoleonic Holy Alliance entertained the possibility of intervention on behalf of Spain. While this was never really a likely endeavor, either politically or logistically, it alarmed the British, who saw expanded commercial opportunity in newly opened Latin America. George Canning, the British foreign minister, proposed a joint Anglo–American declaration of opposition. But Monroe and Adams agreed that the time had come for an assertion of American diplomatic independence, so the doctrine, published in Monroe's Annual Message in December 1823, was a unilateral declaration that Latin America was off-limits to European powers. The United States had come a long way from Jefferson's fear of the possible need to "marry ourselves to the British fleet and British nation." The Monroe Doctrine is rightly seen as "the most lasting legacy of the presidency of James Monroe."[305]

As secretary of state, John Quincy Adams was Monroe's heir apparent, although he had rivals in Andrew Jackson, Henry Clay, William Crawford, and John C. Calhoun. The first American political party system was broken;

---

[302] Ammon, *Monroe*, 409.

[303] Dangerfield, *Awakening*, 72.

[304] It was not called the Monroe Doctrine until some years afterwards, but it could have been called with equal justice the Adams Doctrine

[305] Cunningham, *Presidency of James Monroe*, 163.

the second had not yet emerged. The result was intense political infighting which marred the latter stages of Monroe's second term. John Quincy Adams very much wanted to be president, but a combination of pride and Puritan conscience inhibited him from overt campaigning; every concession to political maneuvering offended his sense of propriety.[306] In 1824, Jackson won the popular vote with Adams a distant second, but the lack of a majority threw the election into the House.

A deadlock in the House was resolved by the infamous "corrupt bargain." Adams's opponents charged that Clay threw his support to Adams in exchange for being appointed secretary of state. Most historians believe that the agreement was "implicit but certainly not corrupt."[307] Adams and Clay agreed on much more than foreign policy. They shared a commitment to a nationalist program and sought to implement Clay's American System to provide "a positive thrust to the course of change."[308]

The difficulties of Adams's administration had two aspects: the nature of his program and the character of the American society in which it would have to be implemented. Adams wasted no time in alienating the public and galvanizing his political opponents. In his first annual message of November 25, 1825, he laid out an ambitious program modelled on the American System. He took Monroe's domestic program and then went far beyond it in calling for a nationalist agenda of expanded internal improvements, a protective tariff, and enhanced revenue from the sale of public lands. Adams incurred much ridicule by urging the adoption of the metric system, the establishment of a national university, and even a national observatory. All of this was urged in the context of an appeal for national unity which would be both "federal and national."[309] Adams acknowledged that the Constitution was a charter of limited powers while claiming in Hamiltonian terms that it permitted an ambitious national program. He concluded by urging Congress in the implementation of this program not to be "palsied by the will of our constituents."[310] This call for a "perilous experiment" was both "eloquent

---

[306] Samuel Flagg Bemis observed that no one was more fitted for the presidency "as a professional public servant and no man had less aptitude for political machinations." Samuel Flagg Bemis, *John Quincy Adams and the Union* (1956), 11.

[307] Bemis, *Adams*, 58. Adams and Clay were in almost complete agreement on foreign-policy issues, so the appointment made good sense for both men. However, the corrupt-bargain charge haunted Clay for the rest of his life. It proved to be "one of the most effective political weapons ever forged." Howe, *Transformation*, 247.

[308] Clay's American System supported the national bank, tariff protection, and internal improvements financed by the sale of public lands. Daniel Walker Howe, *The Political Culture of the American Whigs* (1979), 137.

[309] Bemis, *Adams*, 53.

[310] Dangerfield, *Awakening*, 232.

and fatal."[311] It would be difficult to imagine an address more calculated to arouse fierce opposition. The "palsied" phrase "convulsed the opposition."[312] The extent of Adams's program "dwarfed all previous interpretations of the reach of national power."[313] All of this was to be accomplished by abandoning party labels and governing by merit alone. Adams found himself caught in the contradictions "of a sweeping party program joined to a managerial defense of nonpartisanship."[314]

Whatever the merits of Adams's program might have been—and they were no doubt considerable—it was a program uniquely unsuitable for the political and social context in which it was presented. Even most of his own Cabinet viewed his first annual message "with dismay."[315] Jefferson, not surprisingly, saw it as a betrayal of 1776, "a single and splendid government of an aristocracy."[316] Henry Adams once described his grandfather as an "idealistic philosopher."[317] This would seem to indicate "that philosophers in government must either cease to be philosophers or cease to govern."[318] A contemporary toast to Adams sums up the case: "May he strike confusion to his foes as he has already done to his friends."[319]

However, the most important issue is not really the multiple travails of the Adams presidency but rather the nature of the opposition in the rapidly coalescing Democratic Party. There would surely have been trouble in any case because the elitism of the Adams approach would have aroused opposition. It was an age increasingly focused on the "curbing of privilege and the conquest of elites."[320] It was an age perhaps uniquely suited for the emergence of Andrew Jackson, who enjoyed in charisma what he lacked in programmatic detail. It was also an age of increased sectional tensions over slavery

Adams was the first president in a quarter of a century who was not a slaveholder, the first since his own father was president. Furthermore, George Washington became convinced that slavery was "morally

---

[311] Dangerfield, *Awakening*, 231.

[312] Robert W. Remini, *John Quincy Adams* (2002), 80. Remini, one of Jackson's most sympathetic biographers, credits Adams with a "bold, courageous, and statesmanlike program" (80).

[313] Skowronelk, *Politics Presidents Make*, 118.

[314] Skowronelk, *Politics Presidents Make*, 126.

[315] Dangerfield, *Era*, 348.

[316] Jefferson to W. B. Giles, December 26, 1825, quoted in Dangerfield, *Era*, 349–50. Dangerfield himself says that in the context of the time it was "Caesarism" (350).

[317] Henry Adams, *The Degradation of the Democratic Dogma* (1919), quoted in Dangerfield, *Era*, 350.

[318] Dangerfield, *Awakening*, 241.

[319] Skowronelk, *Politics Presidents Make*, 117–18.

[320] Dangerfield, *Awakening*, 196.

repugnant."[321] In his will, he freed all the slaves at the death of his wife Martha and urged that they be educated. He did this "in the face of Martha's and his family's bitter opposition."[322] In his memoirs, Adams recalled that he had hated slavery "from his earliest years."[323] He saw it as an insoluble problem since he was not an abolitionist and did not believe that colonization was a practical remedy. At the time of the Missouri controversy, Adams publicly supported the compromise, but he privately reflected that a breakup of the Union might be preferable to living under the dominion of the slave-holding South.[324] He came to express opposition to slavery openly during his post-presidential years as an antislavery congressman from Massachusetts, denouncing a South willing "to rivet into perpetuity the clanking chain of the slave."[325] Adams's presidency intersected with a steadily increasing Southern commitment to slavery. The cotton gin made the highly profitable short-staple cotton king over much of the South. As the South committed more and more to agriculture rather than manufacturing, the tariff became a sectionally divisive issue. Then came the terrifying revelation of Denmark Vesey's slave-revolt plot in Charleston, South Carolina.[326] In this troubled context, the South looked suspiciously at Adams.

All the difficulties of the Adams presidency were accentuated by the rise of Andrew Jackson and the Democratic Party. Although historians have written of the Age of Jackson, the behind-the-scenes architect of the Democratic Party was Martin Van Buren of New York, the "Little Magician" who, John Randolph observed, always "rowed to his object with muffled oars."[327] Van Buren was the principal opponent of Adams and the creator of the Jacksonian Democratic Party. From its inception, it was a proslavery party. Van Buren, harkening back to the political foundation of the Republicans, reforged the alliance of Southern slaveholders and the so-called "plain Republicans of the North."[328] The main point of this alliance was to exclude slavery from public debate and create a mass-movement, machine-politics political party based on an unparalleled use of patronage. For Van Buren,

---

[321] Gordon S. Wood, "Slaves in the Family," *New York Times Book Review*, December 14, 2003.

[322] Wood, "Slaves in the family."

[323] Adams, *Memoirs*, quoted in Kaplan, *Adams*, x.

[324] Adams, *Memoirs*, quoted in Dangerfield, *Awakening*, 125–26.

[325] Adams to Charles W. Upham, February 2, 1837, quoted in Bemis, *Adams*, 151.

[326] Slave revolt was the perennial nightmare of Southerners, the consequence both of rational fear and a guilty conscience. As a result, the antebellum South evolved into a police state, particularly in areas, such as South Carolina, where slaves outnumbered whites.

[327] Quoted in Dangerfield, *Era*, 360.

[328] Schweikart and Allen, *Patriot's History*, 197–98.

the best candidates, besides Jackson himself, would be "northern men of Southern principles."[329]

Van Buren was simultaneously creating this new Democratic Party and directing its fire remorselessly against Adams. He was "outraged" by Adams's plea for nationalism and tirelessly employed the states'-right issue as the rationale of resistance.[330] The result of his political ingenuity was the first modern political party which, however, did not represent "the triumph of the common man over aristocracy but the invention of machine politics."[331] But demagoguery, an inevitable manifestation of machine politics, is itself a form of exploitation, the principal means of exploitation in democratic systems.[332]

Adams was doomed to a troubled presidency. He had the wrong program at the wrong time, and he was confronting a new engine of political power which he was unable to resist. The rapidly coalescing Democratic Party waged a sustained campaign of sabotage against the Adams administration.[333] Van Buren's machinations were directed to the interests of his party. If the people benefitted, well and good, but their welfare was not really the prime objective. The trick was to make them think he was acting exclusively in their interest. But every issue for Van Buren was seen primarily through the lens of party interest.

While Southerners opposed internal improvements during Monroe's presidency, their opposition became even stronger during Adams's presidency because his support for a national scheme was even more threatening to those fearful of a government strong enough to strike at slavery. Even with the best of political leadership, the tariff would have been a complicated issue because of the need to balance out varying, sometimes competing, economic interests. The big division was the sectional split between the low-tariff South and protective-tariff North, but there were also many regional complexities. Adams generally favored a mildly protective tariff, though he said little about it publicly. It was, however, an integral part of the American System. The basic tariff problem, however, was simply Van Buren's obsession with using it to punish Adams and help Jackson in the run-up to the election of 1828. The result of his intrigue was the extraordinarily compli-

---

[329] Schweikart and Allen, *Patriot's History*, 200.

[330] Howe, *Transformation*, 489.

[331] Howe, *Transformation*, 241.

[332] There were some populist issues of vital importance to ordinary people where government relief would have been helpful. Debtor relief in the aftermath of the Panic of 1819, for example, was such an issue. Adams's reaction to this issue, was "inept." Hargreaves, *Presidency of John Quincy Adams*, 252.

[333] However, it will not do to exculpate Adams entirely. The mark of an effective leader is to convince and persuade. Adams could do neither effectively.

cated Tariff of 1828 which the ever-eloquent Randolph dubbed the "Tariff of Abominations." It was designed by Van Buren primarily "to manufacture a president."[334] As such, it was a "mere farrago of political tricks and undisguised appetites."[335] It passed Congress in May 1828; Adams reluctantly signed it. In this case, Van Buren nearly outsmarted himself. He had lit the fuse to a ticking time-bomb in South Carolina and bequeathed the resulting nullification crisis to Jackson.

Another issue that was caught up in the states'-rights question was the growing confrontation between Georgia and the Indians. While the attitude of Adams toward the Indians of Georgia and elsewhere could not meet contemporary standards, he was certainly much more enlightened than his Democratic opponents. He seems to have believed that the only fair solution would be gradual assimilation. The problem was that Georgia had ceded western land to the federal government in 1802 with the understanding that the Indian title to it would be extinguished.[336] But this had not been done. In 1825, a clearly fraudulent Treaty of Indian Springs was concluded; Adams signed it. He then had a change of heart, and a new treaty was signed which ceded some but not all Indian land. In December 1826, Georgia ignored this Treaty of Washington and began implementing the earlier Treaty of Indian Springs. Georgia was encouraged to do so by the Democratic Party generally, by other Southern states, and by Andrew Jackson. Adams's actions in the face of this determination were mixed. His nullification of the Treaty of Indian Springs was "unique in the history of the government's Indian relations."[337] In the end, however, all he could offer was a "holding action in defense of federal jurisdiction," which, unfortunately, was of little benefit to the Indians.[338] Still, it was an ineffective Adams who was on the right side of the issue in the face of his relentless Democratic opponents.

Land policy was another issue where there was a clear policy difference between Adams and the Democrats. In general, Adams wanted to use the revenue from the sale of public lands to pay off the national debt and to finance internal improvements, while Democrats pushed steadily for cheaper land. The Land Act of 1804 had reduced the price to $1.64 an acre for

---

[334] Howe, *Transformation*, 274.

[335] Dangerfield, *Era*, 401.

[336] For a succinct overview of the whole unhappy narrative, see Remini, *Adams*, 90–100.

[337] Howe, *Transformation*, 255.

[338] Hargreaves, *Presidency of John Quincy Adams*, 207. Remini's final judgment was that Adams lacked "the political dexterity, wisdom, or will to do what he knew was right." See Remini, *Adams*, 100. This harsh judgment comes from the sympathetic biographer of Jackson who was the implacable foe of Indians.

a minimum of 160 acres. In 1824, Thomas Hart Benton pushed to lower the price again, but Adams opposed his bill, so it was defeated.[339]

In 1820, the race issue surfaced in connection with Latin American affairs. Some of the newly formed republics called for a hemispheric Panama Congress. This would seem to be an innocuous enough proposal, so the Adams administration supported sending delegates. The Democrats reacted ferociously. The result was unseemly wrangling in Congress. The opposition was headed by John Calhoun and Martin Van Buren with John Randolph leading the way with inflammatory rhetoric. Finally, in mid-February 1826, Congress approved the sending of delegates, which "nearly blew the dome off the capitol building."[340] Adams believed that the United States' presence at the conference would be an opportunity to promote peace and good will—"the missionary theme."[341] But the Democrats were having none of it, and Adams knew the reason: "the darkest stain on the Senate's conscience was Haiti."[342] The idea of diplomatic contact with "mixed race" Latin American regimes was intolerable to Southern Democrats. By the time the U.S. delegates were finally sent, the conference was nearly over. Van Buren and Calhoun had played the race card to stymie the administration.

The termination of the Adams administration also ended the lucid interval of the period from 1815 to 1828, which was a time when both Monroe and Adams went beyond the constraints of an outmoded Jeffersonian ideological straitjacket. It was a period which saw the end of the first political party system and the birth throes of the second. It was an era which seemed to achieve some sort of balance between coherent public policy and an ongoing democratic evolution. Yet neither Monroe nor Adams achieved their goal of moving beyond partisanship, and it is difficult to see how they could have done so. Political parties, for all their faults, are the necessary vehicles of political change in democracies, while nonpartisanship is something of a utopian aspiration.

The Adams administration, for all of its manifold difficulties, came the closest to achieving this balance. Its downside, readily apparent at the time, was a certain distance from the aspirations of ordinary Americans; a paternalism which annoyed some and angered others had emerged. The rapidly changing social and economic landscape of a burgeoning America would

---

[339] The previous price in 1800 had been two dollars an acre for a 320-acre minimum. Richard B. Morris, ed., *Encyclopedia of American History* (1965), 461–62. The final outcome was the Homestead Act of 1862 which gave away 160 acres of public land to bona-fide settlers. Morris, ed., *Encyclopedia*, 463–64. See Remini, *Adams*, 86–87, for a brief overview. Adams was on the wrong side in terms of the evolution of land policy.

[340] Remini, *Adams*, 79.

[341] Hargreaves, *Presidency of John Adams*, 162.

[342] See chapter 3 for the approach of Jefferson to the Santo Domingo rebellion.

have posed a challenge for statesmen far more skillful than Adams. The effort of Adams to achieve an essentially nonpartisan nationalistic coalition failed. What would succeed? A newly constituted Democratic Party, led by a man nicknamed "King Andrew," would provide the answer. But first there was an election which provided very little suspense as to its outcome. It may well have been "the filthiest in American history."[343] There is no need to dignify the absurd charges and countercharges of both sides, yet reading about them surely explodes our belief that the contemporary political climate is uniquely poisonous. In the end, it was the outcome that mattered. Jackson won in a landslide. The result was only the culmination of a four-year campaign waged by Van Buren and the Democrats. Adams had no answer for their level of passion and organization.

The conventional historiographical narrative has been that the election of 1828 was a triumph of democracy against the forces of aristocracy and elitism—the recycled Jeffersonian paradigm. George Dangerfield argued that Adams and Clay "seemed to place the state at the service of one special interest."[344] But in reference to special interests, it seems significant that while Jackson won barely 50 percent of the vote in the free states, he won over 70 percent of the vote in the slave states. This is hardly surprising given that slavery was "the most significant issue" in the campaign.[345]

Jackson was "a giant figure," but what did he really stand for?[346] While it is true that Jackson was something of an outsider in 1828 and while it is also true that he lacked any specific program, he was certainly not without his own set of aspirations. He was committed to opening new lands in the west by removing the Indians. This was the fruit of the alliance of the "planters of the South and the plain Republicans of the North."[347] Van Buren clearly laid this program out in 1827, explicitly linking it with the defense of slavery. White supremacy, the expansion of slavery, and the expulsion of the Indians were the primary goals of the newly formed Democratic Party—a pernicious synergy of human-rights disasters. This was the alleged triumph of democracy.

---

[343] Remini, *Adams*, 116.
[344] Dangerfield, *Era*, 416.
[345] Bemis, *Adams*, 147–48.
[346] Dangerfield, *Awakening*, 297.
[347] Van Buren to Thomas Richie, January 13, 1827, quoted in Howe, *Transformation*, 279. The Republicans of the North are always "plain," doubtless to sustain the triumph-of-democracy narrative.

CHAPTER SIX: KING ANDREW AND THE PEOPLE, 1827–1837

It has been said that when God wishes to chastise us, He lets us see the consequences of our illusions. And so the elderly Jefferson was permitted to gaze on the disquieting figure of Andrew Jackson, and he did not like what he saw. Jackson was, Jefferson asserted, "a man of violent passions and unfit for the presidency"; he was "a dangerous man" who was "one of the most unfit men I know for such a place."[348] If Jefferson had ever dispassionately scrutinized his own ideology, the emergence of a Jackson would have been entirely predictable. Thomas Babington Macauley, surveying the political scene in the rapidly democratizing England of the 1830s, observed that "education was in a race to civilize democracy before it took over."[349] The emergence of King Andrew showed that, in the United States at least, education was losing the race.

The turbulent election of 1828 ended in a shattering victory for Jackson in what was widely interpreted by his supporters, and many subsequent historians, as a triumph of democracy.[350] Therefore, it seems fitting that at his post-inaugural celebration his followers:

---

[348] Quoted in Wood, *Revolutionary Characters*, 116. Jefferson made this assertion to Daniel Webster. Quoted in George T. Curtis, *Life of Daniel Webster* (1870), I, 222. Jefferson had more in common with Jackson than he was willing to acknowledge. Andrew Burstein comments that "the humane Jefferson, generally presumed Jackson's temperamental opposite, was merely quieter in his belligerence." Burstein, *The Passions of Andrew Jackson* (2004), 219.

[349] Quoted in Paul Johnson, *A History of the American People* (1997), 179.

[350] This is a major theme in Jacksonian historiography. An extended defense of this position is Sean Wilentz, *The Rise of American Democracy: Jefferson to Lincoln* (2006). Allen C. Guelzo's review is a convincing rebuttal. See Allen C. Guelzo, "Good Democrats and Bad Democrats," *Claremont Review of Books*, Summer 2006. He concludes that Wilentz's

acted out one of the most notorious scenes in American history, indiscriminately rushing through the front door [of the White House] and nearly crushing the president himself in their efforts to shake his hand. The celebrants' rowdiness ultimately compelled Jackson to seek shelter at his late lodgings. When the free-for-all died down, glass and windows had been shattered, some people had fainted, others left with bloody noses, and many had escaped through the windows because the doors were blocked.[351]

Democracy had arrived.

But what kind of democracy? John Quincy Adams summed up the Jackson years with the trenchant observation that the key to Jackson's success lay in the Jeffersonian alliance of "the Southern interest in slavery with the Northern riotous Democracy."[352] Jackson bitterly resented Adams's antislavery convictions, asserting in a letter in 1842 that he "ought to be confined to a hospital."[353] This champion of the common people believed that antislavery was a form of insanity.

The multifaceted Jacksonian movement, like any complex political phenomenon, is a kind of Rorschach blot subject to many possible interpretations.[354] The simplest and most flattering interpretation, and certainly the one still favored by Democratic Party historiography, is the Progressive viewpoint of Arthur M. Schlesinger, Jr., in *The Age of Jackson* (1945) with its Jackson as the rescuer of the common-man mythology.[355] Few contemporary historians take this simplistic position, and yet some are still inclined to shy away from the grimmer aspects of Jackson's presidency by using the averted-gaze approach. The Jackson administration began with an explosion of patronage excess and the darkly comic episode, although one with serious political implications, known as the "Eaton Affair," the "Eaton malaria," and various other names.

The sovereign principle for interpreting Jacksonian initiatives is to understand that the primary motivation was to benefit the Democratic Party. Jackson's revolutionary approach to patronage is the clearest example

---

book offers "a very usable past" for Democratic apologists, but it is "a mythic past, and in support of a mythic politics."

[351] Burstein, *Passions of Andrew Jackson*, 173.

[352] John Quincy Adams, *Diary, 1794–1845*, quoted in Richard B. Latner, *The Presidency of Andrew Jackson: White House Politics, 1829–1837* (1979), 207.

[353] Quoted in Robert V. Remini, *Andrew Jackson and the Course of American Freedom* (1981), 479. Remini neglects to mention that Adams opposed slavery and favored humane treatment of Indians. See Remini, *Course of American Freedom*, 109, 111–12.

[354] A good, very brief, overview is "When Historians Disagree: 'The Age of Jackson,'" in Alan Brinkley, *American History: A Survey, Volume I: To 1877* (1999), 296–97.

[355] Arthur M. Schlesinger Jr. is the quintessential Progressive court historian.

of this principle in action. Washington and John Adams together removed nine government officials from office; Jefferson removed thirty-nine; Madison, five; Monroe nine; John Quincy Adams, two. Jackson, removed 909.[356] The novelty of Jackson's patronage policy "lay not in appointments but in removals."[357]

The truth came straight from the Jacksonians themselves. During the campaign of 1828 Duff Green, one of the foremost Jacksonian journalists, announced that the goal of Jackson's patronage policy was to "reward his friends and punish his enemies." This was "not just a prediction; it was a threat."[358] Amos Kendall, one of Jackson's closest advisors, observed in a private letter that Jackson's supporters wanted "the privilege of availing themselves of the very abuses with which we charge our adversaries."[359]

The Jacksonians themselves in their public utterances speak grandly of democratic opportunity, the elimination of corruption, and the bracing effect of rotation in office. But such rhetoric has failed to convince most commentators. Even those who defend the policy, do so with serious reservations.[360] The closer one looks at Jackson's patronage policy, the more objectionable it appears. He had no inhibitions about granting positions to members of Congress.[361] Jackson appointed many newspaper editors to government positions; 71 percent of all government contracts went to Jacksonian editors.[362] Jackson's approach to patronage was a startling introduction to a common stratagem of his administration—touting as reforms policies designed almost entirely for the benefit of the Democratic Party. Jackson had the distinction of having introduced the full-blown spoils system which "diminished both the competence and the prestige of public service."[363]

---

[356] These statistics were gathered by James Parton and quoted by Jon Meacham, *American Lion: Andrew Jackson in the White House* (2008), 82. Donald Cole quotes Parton as saying that Jackson "was debauching the government." Parton's chapter dealing with patronage is appropriately entitled "Terror among the Office-holders." See his *Life of Andrew Jackson* (3 vols.; 1866). Donald B. Cole, *The Presidency of Andrew Jackson* (1993), 41.

[357] Howe, *Transformation*, 333.

[358] Quoted in Howe, *Transformation*, 331.

[359] Quoted from a letter to Francis P. Blair, February 14, 1829, in Howe, *Transformation*, 331.

[360] Van Deusen, for example, defends Jackson's policy, while admitting that the system became "a creeping blight" with the rise of "party hacks" and a "consequent degradation of government." Glyndon Van Deusen, *The Jacksonian Era, 1828–1848* (1959), 35–36. Remini admits that Jackson himself "stumbled again and again in his own appointments," making "inexcusable misjudgments." Remini, *Course of American Freedom*, 188, 290.

[361] Cole, *Presidency of Andrew Jackson*, 42–43. He appointed forty-one in his first years in office. Schlesinger spins Jackson's spoils system as a "sincere engine of reform" and an "essential step in the gradual formulation of a program for democratic America." See Schlesinger, *Age of Jackson*, 46–47.

[362] Cole, *Presidency of Andrew Jackson*, 43.

[363] Howe, *Transformation*, 334.

A second prominent early concern of Jackson's administration was the bizarre Eaton Affair. This unlikely crisis "took up more of the presidential time in his first year than any other issue."[364]Jackson wanted a close friend in his Cabinet, so he selected John H. Eaton as secretary of war. The affair centered on Peggy O'Neill Timberlake, with whom, rumor had it, Eaton had been having an affair prior to their marriage; her estranged husband had committed suicide. The outraged Cabinet wives shunned her. Jackson exploded with rage, demanded unqualified social acceptance, and announced that she "was as chaste as a virgin," which was "a defense even she herself would not have made."[365]

Jackson reacted with fury at the inability of his Cabinet members to override the powerful social conventions of their wives. Why such outrage? Jackson was a grieving widower whose wife Rachel had died suddenly just before his inauguration, probably of a heart attack. However, Jackson attributed her death to the anguish she had suffered from charges of adultery made by Adams' supporters during the vituperative election campaign of 1828. So for Jackson, Eaton's wife was yet another wronged woman to be chivalrously defended at all costs. This situation was complicated even more because there had been something dicey about Jackson's marriage. The evidence is clear that Jackson had really married a married woman and did so knowingly. The circumstances were not all that unusual for frontier Tennessee in 1794, but much had changed in time and custom by 1828.[366]

Despite its soap-opera quality, the affair had serious consequences. Jackson squandered a great deal of time and emotional energy on the issue. And the political fall-out was significant as well. Martin Van Buren, the wily secretary of state, had one great advantage over his Cabinet rivals; he was a widower who could shower the much-scorned Peggy Eaton with flattering and deferential attention. James Parton asserted that "the political history of the last thirty years dates from the moment when the soft hand of Mr. Van Buren touched Mrs. Eaton's knocker."[367]

The immediate consequence was that Van Buren rose immensely in Jackson's regard. He engineered a mass resignation of the Cabinet solely to obtain Eaton's removal to end the scandal without any attribution of guilt. In doing so, he parlayed the position of secretary of state into the vice pres-

---

[364] Howe, *Transformation*, 337.

[365] Meacham, *American* Lion, 115.

[366] Burstein observes that "in strictly legal terms Rachel did commit adultery and abandon her first husband." In 1828, Jackson was unwilling to acknowledge "the lower-class component of his frontier marriage." See Burstein, *Passions*, 248. His appendix (242–48) on the subject is thorough and judicious. Remini alludes only briefly to "the extraordinary circumstances of the Jackson marriage." Remini, *Course of American Freedom*, 118.

[367] Quoted in Howe, *Transformation*, 339.

idency and, in 1837, the presidency itself. The affair also had the effect of finalizing the growing estrangement of Jackson from Calhoun, who was not wholly innocent in the matter. Calhoun had disapproved of Eaton's presence in the Cabinet, and his wife Floride had taken the lead in ostracizing Peggy Eaton. Even so, the estrangement had deep roots and undoubtedly would have become irrevocable in any case.[368] The affair cast Jackson in an unfavorable light, although the damage was mitigated because the newspapers of the time did their best "to hush the story up."[369] Most people did not learn of the affair until the mass Cabinet resignations cast a lurid light on the whole business. Jackson's behavior had been bizarre, and in its aftermath, everything came down to one test: unquestioning loyalty. Anyone who crossed him "could expect to be condemned, vilified, and read out of the party."[370]

The most significant political events of Jackson's presidency were Indian removal, the Bank War, and the nullification controversy. Underlying all these events were the issues of slavery and states' rights. But the most important political development, which tied all these together, was the rise of the Democratic Party. In retrospect, it is easy to see that several factors combined to give impetus to the emergence of Andrew Jackson and the Democratic Party. The United States was an increasingly dynamic, rapidly changing society which was outgrowing its roots in Jeffersonian agrarianism. The result was that many Americans were experiencing heightened levels of stress. The Panic of 1819 resulted in growing demands for generous land policies, debtor-relief laws, lower tariffs, and the abolition of imprisonment for debt. For the first time, many Americans thought of politics "as having an intimate relation to their welfare."[371]

This more intense involvement occurred during a vast expansion of the electorate which came before the rise of the Democratic Party.[372] The party did not expand the electorate, but it certainly benefitted from the expansion.

---

[368] Michael F. Holt, *Political Parties and the American Political Tradition: From the Age of Jackson to the Age of Lincoln* (1992), 45. The deep roots of this estrangement originated in Secretary of War Calhoun's disapproval of Jackson's actions in Florida during Monroe's administration. He acted as a "wily despot" who "violated nearly every standard of justice" while executing two Englishmen on "flimsy legalistic grounds." See Burstein, *Passions of Andrew Jackson*, 131, and John W. Ward, *Andrew Jackson: Symbol for an Age* (1955), 39.

[369] Howe, *Transformation*, 340–41.

[370] Remini, *Course of American Freedom*, 321–22.

[371] Richard Hofstadter, *The Idea of a Party System: The Rise of Legitimate Opposition in the United States, 1780–1840.* (1969), 51.

[372] By 1828, nearly every state had universal manhood suffrage, and voter turnout rose from 27 percent in 1824 to 57 percent in 1828. Meacham, *American Lion*, 43. This expansion of the franchise meant that systematic mobilization of the electorate, buttressed by a party machinery, was increasingly important. Hofstadter, *Idea of a Party System*, 209–10. Howe, *Transformation*, 490. The emerging Whig Party also supported expanding voting rights (491).

Another factor was the awkward transitional period of party evolution. The disappearance of the Federalist Party, the fragmentation of the Republican Party, and the tentative, nonpartisan "amalgamation" policies of Monroe and Adams created a political void.[373] The void was filled by Andrew Jackson and Martin Van Buren. By 1824, Jackson had emerged as a dominant political figure based on his dramatic victory at New Orleans, his aggressive Florida campaign, and his charismatic, larger-than-life personality. Jackson had no well-thought-out political philosophy; his policies, rather, "derived from belief in the worth (and voting strength) of the common man."[374] He was a perfect fit for the United States of the early nineteenth century.[375]

His many defenders keep extolling his stature as a democratic hero.[376] For them this was the sovereign virtue which immunizes him against sustained criticism. There is no doubt that he was a gifted politician with a nearly unerring instinct for self-promotion and self-aggrandizement as well as the ability to gauge the winds of public opinion.

But behind the public persona of the democratic hero there lurked a powerfully domineering personality. He had "profoundly authoritarian instincts" and could be seen as a "Shakespearian tragic hero" whose fatal flaw was his inability "to countenance any form of dissent."[377] But Jackson rationalized this intolerance; he identified "totally with the people and believed that his will represented theirs," so his political opponents were engaged in "conspiracies to disrupt the processes of democracy."[378]

Jackson embodied authoritarian populism and he intended the Democratic Party to be its vehicle. This type of populism flowed naturally from Jefferson's lifelong fear of aristocratic conspiracy. The creation of the Democratic Party was the most significant longtime consequence of the Jacksonian era. The party was the work of many men, but the preeminent driving force was Martin Van Buren. It was Van Buren who identified Jackson as the indispensable vehicle of party success.[379] Van Buren is the architect of

---

[373] Robert V. Remini, *Martin Van Buren and the Making of the Democratic Party* (1959), 92.

[374] Van Deusen, *Jacksonian Era*, 36.

[375] John Ward, *Andrew Jackson: Symbol for an Age* (1955). does an excellent job of analyzing the various facets of Jackson's personality and their appeal to early-nineteenth-century America. Jackson's appeal was visceral, not intellectual. He was the polar opposite of John Quincy Adams. Jackson opposed the establishment of the Smithsonian Institution and "delayed the advance of scientific thought and experimental research." Howe, *Transformation*, 91.

[376] Schweikart and Allen observe that "the liberal spin on Jackson's presidency as champion of the common man is near universal." *Patriot's History*, 850, note 90.

[377] Howe, *Transformation*, 328; Burstein, *Passions*, 217–18.

[378] Remini, *Course of American Democracy*, 316–17.

[379] Perhaps the greatest measure of Van Buren's political acumen was his ability to always stay on the good side of the tempestuous Jackson by constantly remembering that

the fully developed American political party system. He did not have a major impact on Jackson's policies but certainly provided Jackson with the instrument to implement them. Van Buren is both the prototype of the professional politician and the creator of modern machine politics based on absolute party discipline held together by patronage.[380] The newly enfranchised electorate required incessant mobilization by a disciplined party machinery, direct appeals, and "an extensive chain of newspapers."[381]

But what was the ultimate goal of such intense effort? Was Van Buren the servant of a genuinely democratic polity or the author of a party-over-all philosophy? It is a truism to observe that reality is usually more complex than such sharp dichotomies. The best approach is to avoid sterile abstractions and proceed with an analysis of practical outcomes. The diligent student of the Jacksonian era is nearly overwhelmed by the rhetoric, often extravagant, of democratic renewal from the Jacksonians themselves and subsequent historians. But what did the party do in contrast to what it said? The basis of the party's strength lay in Van Buren's initial decision to sustain and strengthen that longtime Jeffersonian linkage of Southern planters with the so-called plain republicans of the north.[382] But sinister implications flowed inexorably from this decision. The linkage ensured that the Democratic Party would be the party of slavery until the end of slavery.[383] The Democratic Party never managed to force slavery on a largely unwilling America. By 1804, slavery had been abolished in all Northern states. But many Americans either supported slavery or were willing, for political and economic reasons, to tolerate it. Northern Democrats accepted policies calculated to sustain slavery in order to continue receiving the "life-giving manna of power and patronage."[384] In this tragic instance, the Democratic Party was certainly the party of the people.

But it did not stop with slavery. Expansion was linked to slavery. To be sure, many Americans who were not slaveholders moved west. Even so,

---

Jackson demanded "uncritical displays of devotion." Burstein, *Passions*, 197.

[380] Silas Wright, a Van Buren disciple, wrote in 1833 that "the first man we see step to the rear, we cut down . . . they must not falter or they perish." Quoted in Latner, *Presidency of Andrew Jackson*, 17.

[381] Holt, *Political Parties*, 40–41.

[382] Remini, *Van Buren*, 124–25.

[383] A historiographical analysis of historians, Democrats, and slavery would be a valuable study of evasion, apologetics, and rationalization. But the truth will out—and sometimes in surprising places. Jules Witcover's book *Party of the People: A History of the Democratic Party* (2003) has a flyleaf comment that the party was "nearly wrecked by the 'peculiar institution' of slavery," and the chapter on slavery is entitled "The Party Self-Destructs, 1853–1860."

[384] Alexander Saxton, *The Rise and Fall of the White Republic: Class, Politics, and Mass Culture in Nineteenth-Century America* (1990), 142.

slavery intensified an already strong expansionist impulse. The desire of the planters for fertile land was unquenchable. The Democratic Party represented the "high tide of manifest destiny."[385] The linkage between slavery, expansion, and white supremacy was unbreakable throughout the antebellum period. The "fundamental impulse behind Jacksonian democracy" was the "extension of white supremacy across the North American continent."[386]

The South generally resisted both internal improvements and tariff protection on economic grounds and because of the fear of government power which could be used against slavery. Fortunately, on both of these issues, the nation more or less muddled through. On the issue of internal improvements, Jackson continued to maintain the old Jeffersonian opposition on constitutional grounds. This meant that projects which could be interpreted as local would be opposed, so that no national plan, such as Adams had envisioned, would be implemented.[387] Jackson approached the issue almost entirely on political grounds. Internal improvements gave him the opportunity to "distribute favors where they would do the most political good."[388] Even so, a vast transportation revolution did occur during the Jackson presidency despite the general opposition of his Southern supporters.[389]

The tariff was a complex an issue; even the most diligent fine-tuning could not completely satisfy competing economic and sectional interests. The tariff of 1828 had been signed by Adams. It had been drafted by Silas Wright, one of Van Buren's "brightest lieutenants."[390] It particularly angered the South, but no other section of the country was happy with it either. The agrarian South opposed protective tariffs for both economic and political reasons; it objected to the high prices for manufactured goods any such tariff would entail. But it also feared that a government powerful enough to control the tariff could also strike at slavery.[391] So the tariff was "a major obstacle to Democratic Party unity."[392] But on this issue at least, Jackson was inclined to pragmatism, hoping that the tariff could adjust "competing local

---

[385] Saxton, *White Republic*, 192.

[386] Howe, *Transformation*, 357.

[387] The most famous case was his Maysville Road veto. This stretch of road was part of the National Road, but it had the disadvantage of being entirely within Kentucky, the home state of Henry Clay. Van Deusen, *Jacksonian Era*, 51–52.

[388] Howe, *Transformation*, 360.

[389] It was fueled mostly by state and local expenditures: $310 million (state); $125 million (localities); and $59 million (federal). Cole, *Presidency of Andrew Jackson*, 66.

[390] Remini, *Course of American Freedom*, 137. It seems to have been designed primarily to hurt Adams, but the tariff issue was too complex for even the political ingenuity of Van Buren.

[391] This fear was a political constant throughout the antebellum period from Jefferson to 1860.

[392] Latner, *Presidency of Andrew Jackson*, 68–69.

and national interests within a limited government framework."[393] Jackson wanted the tariff revenue to pay down the national debt, so he signed the Tariff of 1832.[394] There matters rested until the nullification controversy erupted.

But whatever pragmatism Jackson showed regarding internal improvements and the tariff was nowhere in evidence regarding Indian removal. Here the worst aspects of Jackson's personality combined with prevailing political and economic considerations to produce one of the greatest human-rights disasters in American history. Jackson brought to the presidency his longstanding view of Indians as uncivilized savages who constituted an intolerable obstacle to expansion and progress.[395] The Indian Removal Bill passed Congress in late May 1830. The analysis of the close vote is revealing. It passed the Senate by a party line vote 29–19 and in the House 102–97. The slave states supported it 61–15, while the free states opposed it 82–41. The three-fifths Southern vote premium made passage possible.[396]

Although Jackson's defenders conjure a realpolitik aura of inevitability, the truth is that the issue triggered the "strongest nation-wide democratic protest the country had yet witnessed."[397] A number of reformers, including Catharine Beecher and Theodore Frelinghuysen, "the Christian statesman," defended Indian rights; the Indians generally enjoyed the support of humanitarian reformers. They also had the law on their side. In two back-to-back cases the Supreme Court ruled that the Cherokee had a right to their land and that state law, specifically that of Georgia, had no jurisdiction in the matter.[398] Jackson may not have explicitly challenged the Court to enforce its decision, but that was clearly his position. Jackson never "allowed anything much less legal niceties to stand in his way if he was determined to do something."[399] So in defiance of the law, Jackson proceeded with removal by means of the Treaty of New Echota in December 1835. The result was the Trail of Tears which occurred in the fall and winter of 1838–39 during Van Buren's presidency. Casualty figures vary, but it seems that around four thousand Indians out of approximately twelve thousand died during the forced migration from the southeastern states, mainly Georgia, to the Indian

---

[393] Latner, *Presidency of Andrew Jackson*, 69.

[394] Cole, *Presidency of Andrew Jackson*, 106; Remini, *Course of American Freedom*, 360.

[395] Howe, *Transformation*, 343–45. The Cherokee showed the ability to assimilate.

[396] Howe, *Transformation*, 352.

[397] Howe, *Transformation*, 357.

[398] *Cherokee Nation v. George* (1831) and *Worcester v. Georgia* (1832). Alfred H. Kelly and Winfred A. Harbison, *The American Constitution: Its Origins and Development* (1970), 302–3.

[399] Meacham, *American Lion*, 204. Remini admits that Jackson "had encouraged Georgia in its intransigence." *Course of American Freedom*, 277.

Territory of Oklahoma. Other Indians besides the Cherokee also suffered high mortality rates during other forced migrations.[400]

Indian removal had broader implications. It says a great deal about Jackson himself, but it also shows "the myth of the Jackson Democrats as the party of small government."[401] Jackson exceeded Congressional authority and ignored the Supreme Court. Little wonder that his opponents began calling him "King Andrew."[402]

But why did he do all this? There are many reasons: contempt for the Indians, greed, political pressure, states'-rights ideology. But looming behind all these is the determination to protect and promote slavery. All the land snatched from the Indians represented the expansion of slavery; King Andrew owed fealty to King Cotton. He did this most effectively by stressing what slaveholders had in common with the rest of the country—westward expansion, racial paternalism, and the acquisition of private property. In the broadest sense, this tragic episode is a dramatic opening to the emerging linkage of slavery, imperialism, and expansion which was to convulse the nation until the Civil War.[403] The Democratic Party gave no quarter to those who questioned this human-rights nightmare. Martin Van Buren during the Trail of Tears praised the policy, saying:

> The wise, humane, and undeviating policy of the government in this most difficult of all our relations foreign or domestic has at length been justified to the world in near approach to a happy and certain consummation.[404]

It takes a "Little Magician" to transform an atrocity into benevolence.[405]

Another issue central to the economic life of the nation was the Second Bank of the United States. Jackson designated the most powerful financial institution in the country not under his control the "Monster." There is more involved here than mere name-calling. Monsters cannot be managed; they can only be destroyed. It is, however, certainly true that there were serious problems with an uncritical pro-bank position. The bank, in the person of

---

[400] Howe, *Transformation*, 416.

[401] Schweikart and Allen, *Patriot's History*, 207.

[402] The National Republicans, evolving into the Whig Party in the mid-1830s, opposed his actions as the Whigs of England had opposed royal power in the seventeenth century. See https://www.history.com/topics/19th-century/whig-party.

[403] Rogin, *Subjection of the American Indian*, xxvii.

[404] Howe, *Transformation*, 416–17; From his second annual message, December 2, 1838, quoted in Rogin, *Subjection of the American Indian*, 247.

[405] The assessments of some historians seem influenced by political considerations. Schlesinger in his *Age of Jackson* ignores the Trail of Tears almost completely. Van Deusen gives us a Teflon Jackson with the blame conveniently shifted to "unscrupulous government agents." *Jacksonian Era*, 49.

its imperious president Nicholas Biddle, did possess an unhealthy concentration of power. The ideal solution would have been a reasonable compromise: keep the bank and establish additional safeguards against abuse. But neither man was willing to do this. So the Bank War began. The most immediate political impact of the Bank War was the development of the second American political party system, which had been in gestation for some time. Jackson's imperious behavior provoked the formation of the Whig Party in opposition to "King Andrew."[406]

The twenty-year charter of the Second Bank of the United States was due to expire in 1836, near the end of Jackson's second term. Henry Clay and Biddle decided to make it a campaign issue in 1832 by pushing for an early recharter. The bill to recharter the bank passed the House in July 1832 by a vote of 107–85. A significant number of Democrats supported recharter. Jackson, however, saw this as "a declaration of war."[407] He issued a ringing veto message on July 10. It was perhaps "the most important veto message in history."[408] Biddle and Clay, both astute politicians, had blundered badly in extending what Jackson saw instantly as a personal challenge. But then they compounded their initial error by badly misjudging the impact of the veto message. It was a political attack; its language was "resounding and demagogic," but politically effective.[409] They actually distributed the veto message as a campaign document, which it proved to be—but for Jackson, not against him. During the 1832 campaign, the Democrats had no party platform: "Jackson was its platform and the Bank veto was the chief plank."[410] The election of 1832 resulted in an easy Jackson victory over Clay by an impressive 219–49 electoral-vote margin. He won 88 percent of the popular vote in the deep South. The party adopted a national-convention methodology with its required two-thirds vote for nomination which gave the South "a veto over Democratic candidates for the next hundred years."[411] The Democrats dominated the South, "where the two-party system had never really flourished."[412] The Democratic–Whig Party nomenclature was generally adopted during and after the 1832 campaign.[413]

---

[406] The standard Democratic mythology is to depict the Whigs as elitists after the fashion of the Federalists and to market themselves as the defenders of the people. A favorable account of the Whig Party is Daniel Walker Howe, *The Political Culture of the American Whigs* (1979).

[407] Howe, *Transformation*, 379.

[408] Howe, *Transformation*, 380. It was important because of its immediate impact on the banking system and its significance in establishing the foundation of an imperial presidency.

[409] Schlesinger, *Age of Jackson*, 90.

[410] Van Deusen, *Jacksonian Era*, 17.

[411] Howe, *Transformation*, 384–85.

[412] Remini, *Course of American Freedom*, 390.

[413] Cole, *Presidency of Andrew Jackson*, 137–38.

Jackson's reelection doomed the bank. Biddle began to restrict credit in a misguided effort to demonstrate how important the bank was. However, what he succeeded in demonstrating was that he really did have too much power. Jackson pressed the attack on the bank in what was a pattern of escalating lawlessness. He removed government deposits and began placing the money in his notorious "pet" banks, all headed by loyal Democrats. Jackson had to dismiss two secretaries of the treasury, Louis McLane and William J. Duane, before the compliant Roger B. Taney took office in September 1833. His actions were "a stunning display of power by the chief executive" who was willing "to flout the Constitution to get his way."[414] The Monster was slain as the bank charter expired in February 1836. The nation saw a spectacular rise in inflation, driven largely by western public-land sales. Jackson's last major economic legislation was the Specie Circular in July 1837 mandating that only hard money would be accepted for the purchase of public land. This was followed by a crash and the Depression of 1837. What was Jackson's responsibility for this sequence of economic disasters?[415]

The Bank War was rich in irony. The man who hated banks created many more of them throughout the country. The man who believed in democracy acted like an absolute monarch. For all of Jackson's invocation of "the people," there is no real evidence that they benefitted from any of his actions.[416] The predictable efforts to make the Bank War a great democratic crusade are unconvincing. A familiar pattern is revealed in connection with Jackson and the Democratic Party generally—much inflated democratic rhetoric to justify power grabs which benefit insiders rather than ordinary Americans.

One of Jackson's strongest critics sees the nullification controversy as "his finest hour" in which he "combined firmness with conciliation."[417] The crisis unfolded amid a deepening estrangement of Jackson and Calhoun, but more was involved than personal animosity. Calhoun had come to believe that ultimate sovereignty lay with the people of a state, not with the national government.[418] This would have remained a mere constitutional abstraction except for the growing resentment of South Carolina over the tariff. Behind

---

[414] Schweikart and Allen, *Patriot's History*, 216. His action stood. Clay engineered a feel-good but meaningless motion of censure in the Senate in March 1834, which was expunged in January 1837.

[415] Richard Hofstadter, a Jackson advocate, holds him responsible, while Schweikart and Allen, among his severest critics, attribute the problems mostly to international factors. Hofstadter, *Idea of a Party System*, 62; Schweikart and Allen, *Patriot's History*, 216–17.

[416] Howe, *Transformation*, 394.

[417] Howe, *Transformation*, 405.

[418] See his *South Carolina Expositor and Protest* (1828), written to protest the "Tariff of Abominations."

the tariff issue lay that of slavery. The tragedy of Calhoun was that he used his immense talents for the purpose of "immobilizing the federal government in the service of a slave economy."[419]

The immediate context was the Tariff of 1832. This compromise tariff, pushed through by Adams, more or less satisfied most people but not those of South Carolina. The economy of the state was depressed. George McDuffie's forty-bale theory held that the tariff drained away 40 percent of the planters' profits.[420] The South Carolina legislature passed its nullification ordinance November 19, 1832. As he always did, Jackson saw this as a personal challenge. He issued his Proclamation to the People of South Carolina on December 10, upholding federal sovereignty and warning in stark terms of the consequences of treason.[421] The crisis was resolved quickly in early 1833. No other Southern states joined South Carolina. Jackson asked Congress for authority to enforce the revenue laws, and the Force Bill passed Congress by wide margins on January 16, 1833. At the same time, Calhoun worked with Clay to produce a compromise tariff. The Force Bill and the tariff both passed Congress on March 1, 1833. South Carolina nullified both its own nullification ordinance and the Force Bill on March 11, 1833. But even in his moment of greatest triumph, Jackson simply could not stay on the high road. He pocket-vetoed Clay's Distribution Bill, which he had earlier favored, rather than "acknowledge that Clay deserved credit for a comprehensive resolution of the nullification crisis."[422]

All Jackson really needed to know was that the nullifiers were defying him. Beyond that, it is hard to gauge his level of understanding. He seemed inclined to believe that the nullifiers were capable of intriguing with Clay "to blow up a storm on the subject of the slave question."[423] But this unlikely prospect reflects Jackson's reluctance to acknowledge the importance of slavery to the nullifiers because he needed to frame the issue in terms which did not include striking at slavery. But the issue could not really be states'-rights either. After all, Jackson "had encouraged Georgia in its intransigence" over the issue of Indian removal, so it was not unreasonable for the nullifiers to think that they could "get away with their defiance as Georgia had

---

[419] Howe, *Transformation*, 399.

[420] Howe, *Transformation*, 396.

[421] Jackson upheld national sovereignty with such eloquence that Lincoln used his remarks as a model for his similar defense in his First Inaugural. Cole, *Presidency of Andrew Jackson*, 160–61.

[422] Howe, *Transformation*, 409. Clay thought of the bill as part of the compromise package because distributing the revenue of public-land sales to the states would help reconcile Northerners to future tariff reductions.

[423] Latner, *Presidency of Andrew Jackson*, 163.

done."[424] The simple truth seems to be that Jackson responded to what he conceived as a personal challenge and used impressive nationalistic rhetoric to justify his response. Fortunately, in this instance at least, his response dovetailed with the best interests of the nation as a whole.

But if some issues had been resolved, the issue of slavery remained unresolved; it was the dominant issue of Jackson's presidency. The relationship of politics and slavery during Jackson's presidency "awaits scholarly treatment."[425] Perhaps the sharp contrast between Jackson the man of the people and Jackson the inveterate defender of slavery is too painful for some historians to contemplate, but the issue will not go away. It seems clear that Jackson's presidency is a watershed; it represents a transition for Jackson and the Democrats from the earlier guilt-ridden, uneasy defenders like Jefferson and Madison to a more aggressive and unapologetic proslavery stance.

Jackson was himself a slaveholder and evidently a harsh one. He has the dubious distinction of being the only president to have personally driven a slave "coffle," a convoy of chained slaves.[426] He once approved of a punishment of three hundred lashes for a runaway slave.[427] As president, Jackson pursued an aggressive proslavery policy. World opinion was turning decisively against slavery, yet Jackson made no effort to suppress the notorious African slave trade.[428] Antislavery sentiment by the 1830s was coalescing more and more into organized groups. Jackson responded with fierce anger and resistance. He publicly called abolitionists "monsters," supported federal censorship of the mail, and gave local postmasters the right to publish the names of anyone receiving antislavery material.[429] This represented "the largest peacetime violation of civil liberty in U.S. history."[430] The "gag rule" controversy erupted at the end of Jackson's presidency. Southern politicians were angry and embarrassed at a profusion of antislavery petitions from Northern abolitionists. Both the House and the Senate adopted the practice of receiving the petitions, then immediately tabling them without discussion. This prac-

---

[424] Remini, *Course of American Freedom*, 277, 388.

[425] Latner, *Presidency of Andrew Jackson*, 254.

[426] Review of Fergus M. Borderwich, *The American Slave Coast* by Ned and Constance Sublette, *Wall Street Journal*, January 23, 2016.

[427] Runaway slave ad by Jackson in the *Tennessee Gazette*, October 3, 1804, p. 3. Jackson offered to pay anyone capturing the runaway ten dollars for every one hundred lashes given him to a total of three hundred.

[428] Howe, *Transformation*, 361.

[429] Howe, *Transformation*, 428–29. He had proposed a law outlawing antislavery mailings, but Southerners, fearing federal power, suggested giving discretion to local postmasters—the result was essentially the same. Van Deusen, *Jacksonian Era*, 108.

[430] Howe, *Transformation*, 430.

tice protected Southerners from the horrors of antislavery petitions while avoiding potential constitutional problems related to outright censorship.[431]

With both Jackson and the Democratic Party expressing public abhorrence of antislavery activists, it is significant that the decade of the 1830s was one of the most violent in American history.[432] Many Americans of the time worried about the strain of violence in American life, and in 1838, Abraham Lincoln, then a young Whig from Illinois, distinguished contemporary violence from protests during the Revolutionary era and was "an evangelist for obedience to the law."[433]

There were many causes of riots and urban violence generally. American society was subject to various tensions, uncertainties, and fears which sometimes found violent expression—there were anti-Catholic riots, workingmen's union riots, and anti-immigration riots among others. But in all this, there were also anti-abolition riots which expressed the deep anger many, even in the North, felt at the rise of organized antislavery movements. There was a direct link between rioting and organized antislavery.[434] One of the paradoxes of the riots is that they were often led by "gentlemen of property and standing" for whom antislavery had become a monster which threatened their control of society.[435]

But if Jackson and the Democrats were not solely responsible for all the violence, neither can they be completely exonerated. Jackson's detestation of abolitionists was well known. His willingness to circumvent the law was common knowledge. He was a kind of "anarchic hero" who believed he could act outside the law because of the rectitude of his own character.[436] It is not surprising that this attitude found expression as an outgrowth of the popular Jacksonian democracy which emphasized the rights of the common man to act in his own defense.[437] This was actually "a variant of majoritarian ideology."[438] Violence was "integrated into the political and social processes of Jacksonian society."[439] By the end of the 1830s, the intense phase of the

---

[431] Van Deusen, *Jacksonian Era*, 107–8; Howe, *Transformation*, 512–13. Ultimately 79 percent of northern Democrats voted in favor of it. Cole, *Presidency of Andrew Jackson*, 277–78.

[432] Cole, *Presidency of Andrew Jackson*, 320.

[433] Howe, *Transformation*, 438.

[434] See David Grimsted, "Rioting in its Jacksonian Setting," *American Historical Review* 77 (1972): 375.

[435] Leonard L. Richards, *Gentlemen of Property and Standing: Antiabolition Mobs in Jacksonian America* (1970), 170.

[436] Grimsted, "Rioting," 307.

[437] Michael Feldberg, *The Turbulent Era: Riot and Disorder in Jacksonian America* (1980), 90.

[438] Feldberg, *Turbulent Era*, 97.

[439] Feldberg, *Turbulent Era*, 126.

violence had subsided, but the underlying hostility of Jackson and the Democrats to antislavery remained a deep political reality.[440]

The linkage between Jackson, the Democrats, and slavery was firmly fixed.[441] But while Jackson and the Democrats were linked to slavery, they were also linked to territorial expansion and imperialism. Democratic dominance "rested on an alliance with slavery and aggressive advocacy of territorial expansion."[442] Jackson worked constantly to create the "New South expansive in its desire for land, cotton, and slavery."[443] This linkage, furthermore, perpetuated the growing conflict over slavery.

The paradox of Jackson's presidency is that it failed because it succeeded. The dictionary definition of a demagogue is one who leads the people, but arguably a demagogue is also one who is compelled by the people to give them what they want. This is the irony of seeing Jackson as the embodiment of the age. Jackson both led and was led. He and many people wanted the same things.[444] What they wanted most was land, expansion, and slavery—by whatever means. Even the imperious Jackson was a mere servant of the people.

A standard defense of Jackson and the Democratic Party is that it was either slavery or disunion, so they loved the Union more than they disliked slavery.[445] This rationalization ignores the simple fact that Jackson and a great many others around him were zealous defenders of slavery and all that it represented. In addition, this begs the question of what democratic leadership should be—which is not just getting elected by appealing to the lowest common denominator of a democratic wish list. In the last analysis, there should be a type of democratic leadership which is neither the tone-deaf paternalism of John Quincy Adams nor the abject pandering of Andrew Jackson and his Democratic Party. Jackson's presidency, for all of its lofty democratic common-man rhetoric, laid the foundation for imperialism, secession, and war.

---

[440] Richards speculates that the growth and activity of the antislavery societies lessened after 1837, while people had grown more or less resigned to their presence. Richards, *Gentlemen of Property*, 156–59.

[441] Cole observes that "one of the legacies" of the party "was its accommodation to slavery." Cole, *Presidency of Andrew Jackson*, 275. Some historians engaged in extended rationalizations. Robert Remini denies that the Democrats "as Jacksonians" were committed to preserving slavery even though they "abhorred abolitionists" and thought that the nullifiers were "aided and abetted by abolitionists" who were conspiring to put "blue light Federalists back in power." *Course of American Freedom*, 343.

[442] Saxton, *White Republic*, 105.

[443] Mark R. Cheathem, *Andrew Jackson, Southerner* (2013), 204, quoted by Melissa J. Gismondi in her review in the *Register of the Kentucky Historical Society* 112 (2014): 667.

[444] See Ward, *Andrew Jackson: Symbol for an Age*.

[445] Cole, *Presidency of Andrew Jackson*, 225–26.

Chapter Seven: Adrift: From Jackson to Polk, 1837–1844

The Federalists would have been delighted to run George Washington for president to all eternity, and the Democrats of 1836 thought the same about Andrew Jackson. Since this was not possible, it was only fitting that they should run Martin Van Buren, the architect of the Democratic Party, who was in an excellent position to benefit from Jackson's popularity.

The newly organizing Whigs were not in a position to run an effective campaign. They were reduced to the desperate expedient of running three candidates, hoping to throw the election into the House of Representatives.[446] The result was a clear but unexpectedly close victory. Van Buren got only 50.9 percent of the popular vote, yet he prevailed in the electoral vote 170 to a combined Whig total of 124.[447] John Quincy Adams viewed this result with deep apprehension; he foresaw "a succession of Presidents" who would:

> snarl with impotent fury against a money broker's shop, to rivet into perpetuity the clanking chain of the slave, and to waste in boundless bribery to the west the invaluable inheritance of the Public Lands.[448]

He was not far off the mark, particularly regarding "the clanking chain of the slave."

---

[446] The three candidates were William Henry Harrison, Hugh Lawson White, and Daniel Webster. Norma Lois Peterson, *The Presidencies of William Henry Harrison and John Tyler* (1989), 17.

[447] Howe, *Transformation*, 487; Peterson, *Presidencies*, 21. The election result was no great victory for the common man. The Democratic Party leadership was often "as wealthy as the supposedly aristocratic Whigs." Howe, *Transformation*, 489; Holt, *Political Parties*, 55.

[448] Letter to Charles Upham, February 2, 1837, quoted in Howe, *Transformation*, 488.

Martin Van Buren provides another example of the truth of that old admonition: be careful what you wish for. As the quintessential politician of the Jacksonian era, his whole career was pointed toward the presidency which, once obtained, promptly turned to ashes in his mouth. All seemed well at first with Van Buren looking forward to a serene administration amounting basically to Andrew Jackson's third term.[449] While his inaugural message was "clothed in humility," it was proslavery. His administration was "imperiled by the tsunami that struck at almost the exact moment he took office."[450] The "Little Magician" quickly became "Martin Van Ruin."[451]

The Depression of 1837 was caused by a combination of factors, both foreign and domestic, among them Jackson's Bank War and other fiscal policies.[452] In one of history's ironies, although Van Buren had stayed aloof from Jackson's economic program, it was he who had to pick up the pieces. Problems were also caused by the inflationary impact of Mexican silver coupled with a restriction of credit by the Bank of England. There was no Bank of the United States to give any meaningful control over the national economy. One of the many ironies of Jackson's Bank War was that it resulted in over twice as many banks in 1836 as there had been in 1830. Many of these banks followed bad business practices, contributing to the debacle. These state banks also issued paper money despite Jackson's preference for hard money.[453]

Another contributing factor was the impact of Jackson's Specie Circular.[454] Intended to discourage rampant land speculation, it had the unintended consequence of draining specie from the banking system, particularly in the East. Nevertheless, Van Buren decided to retain it in the face of strong criticism because he was reluctant to break with Jackson. Nevertheless, it was repealed by a Congressional joint resolution in 1838. In the inevitable blame game, Democrats blamed the banks, while Whigs blamed Jackson and the Specie Circular.[455]

---

[449] Howe, *Transformation*, 483.

[450] Van Deusen, *Jacksonian Era*, 115. He pledged to oppose abolition in the District of Columbia and to avoid interference with slavery in the South; abolitionists were "outraged." Edward L. Widmer, *Martin Van Buren* (2005), 107.

[451] Howe, *Transformation*, 505.

[452] Howe, *Transformation*, 503.

[453] Major Wilson, *The Presidency of Martin Van Buren* (1984), 44–45. See also Van Deusen, *Jacksonian Era*, 116–17.

[454] Van Deusen, *Jacksonian Era*, 120; Wilson, *Presidency of Martin Van Buren*, 48, 51–52. Howe believes that it was the major factor in the Depression of 1837. Howe, *Transformation*, 503–4.

[455] Most commentators believe that the Whigs had the better of the argument. Howe, *Transformation*, 503.

Perhaps the crowning irony of the whole situation is seen in Van Buren's response to the crisis.[456] His policies as outlined in his message to a special session of Congress in September 1837 were designed "to solve the embarrassment of the national government" rather than to cope with the economic problems of the country which "made clear his narrow view of governmental responsibility." He added insult to injury by saying later that:

> Those who look to the actions of this Government for specific aid to the citizen to relieve embarrassments arising from losses by revulsions [sic] in commerce and credit lose sight of the ends for which it was created and the powers with which it is clothed.[457]

The people must suffer the consequences of misguided governmental policies. In the light of this perspective, it was appropriate that the "central domestic issue" of Van Buren's administration was the creation of an Independent Treasury to divorce governmental finance from the national economic system.[458]

The Whigs and some conservative Democrats resisted the Independent Treasury Act; its legislative history was torturous. It was defeated in June 1838 but passed in June 1839. Then it was again repealed in 1841 in the aftermath of the election of 1840. Finally, it was again passed in August 1844. It then remained in effect until the Federal Reserve Act of 1913.[459] The Democrats prevailed, but it was a hollow victory since it did nothing to benefit the economy.[460] Van Buren's only remedy for the economic crisis was "to seek protection for the money of the federal government."[461] Meanwhile, the Whig Party, which had benefitted greatly from these economic travails, was unsuccessful in its persistent attempt to charter another national bank. So the Democrats, the putative party of the people, did virtually nothing to relieve the sufferings of the people, blaming the banks for the disaster—the very banks which their own policies had called into being.[462]

In its economic policies, the Democratic Party had linked itself to the past., It resurrected the centrality of agriculture with "the neo-physiocratic concepts of John Taylor."[463] Van Buren had "dismantled Hamilton's finan-

---

[456] Van Deusen, *Jacksonian Era*, 121.

[457] From his third annual message, December 4, 1839, quoted in Howe, *Transformation*, 505.

[458] Wilson, *Presidency of Martin Van Buren*, 61.

[459] One overview is Richard B. Morris, ed., *Encyclopedia of American History* (1965), 182, 184, 196.

[460] The hard times lasted until 1843, a prolonged period of economic depression exceeded only by the Great Depression of 1929. Howe, *Transformation*, 505.

[461] Paul H. Bergeron, *The Presidency of James K. Polk* (1987), 1.

[462] Wilson, *Presidency of Martin Van Buren*, 71. See also Schweikart and Allen, *Patriot's History*, 222.

[463] Van Deusen, *Jacksonian Era*, 122.

cial apparatus" and so "had reached the limits of Jeffersonian doctrine."[464] The Democrats were reduced to blaming the depression on the national sin of departing from true Jacksonian virtue.[465] But grappling with the ghost of Alexander Hamilton was no way to prepare the country for the growing complexities of the nineteenth-century economy. It is impossible to know with any certainty how successful Whig economic policies might have been. However, it does seem clear that the Democrats held forth the impossibly restrictive idea "of a republic that was essentially immune from disruptive change in the economic and social sphere" —while presiding over the Depression of 1837, a juxtaposition hardly likely to foster confidence in their stewardship of the economy.[466]

Although the economic situation was the dominant issue of the Van Buren administration, there were other issues also worthy of attention. Andrew Jackson's human-rights disaster known as Indian Removal was actually implemented by Van Buren, complete with a self-serving rationalization. He sealed Jackson's white supremacist policy by implementing it.[467] Van Buren also pursued a war against the Seminoles which was fought at the insistence of slaveholders who resented the Indian refuge for runaway slaves. The war cost over 500 million dollars in present-day value. His Indian policy was so egregious that his favorite niece hoped that he would lose the election of 1840.[468]

In terms of slavery, Van Buren proved true to the overall perspective outlined in his inaugural address. The Democratic Party was the party of slavery and white supremacy. It abandoned even the pretense of adhering to the doctrine of natural rights "enshrined in the Declaration of Independence" while glorifying "the mudsill theory of society."[469] The party was not content merely to defend slavery in the South, it also sought to defend it by playing on the racial prejudices of Northerners and stirring up fears of free blacks competing for their jobs. In doing so, the party "proved adept at manipulating these feelings" in Northern workers.[470] The predictable anomaly was that some of the supposedly elitist Federalists and Whigs supported

---

[464] Widmer, *Martin Van Buren*, 102.

[465] Wilson, *Presidency of Martin Van Buren*, 88.

[466] Wilson, *Presidency of Martin Van Buren*, 88, 91.

[467] Howe, *Transformation*, 516–17.

[468] Widmer, *Martin Van Buren*, 118.

[469] Van Deusen, *Jacksonian Era*, 168.

[470] Howe, *Transformation*, 545. This lent credence to the slave-power conspiracy theory which stressed the degree to which the South dominated national politics right down to the Civil War. Northern Democrats, not without reason, were "accused of being allies of the Slave Power." Indeed, the strategy was to keep Northern Democrats at the very least "largely subservient" on the issue of slavery. See Leonard Richards, *The Slave Power: The Free North and Southern Domination* (2000), 4, 112.

black suffrage while the supposedly democratic Democrats opposed it.[471] It is certainly symptomatic that Van Buren himself had been a slaveholder in New York before state emancipation had occurred in 1827.[472] Van Buren was committed to maintaining the proslavery policies which were already in place. The Gag Rule remained in effect from 1836 to 1844 with Clay, Adams, and other Whigs vigorously opposing it.[473]

In the high-profile *Amistad* case in 1839, Van Buren would have sent the mutinous blacks back into slavery. Adams rose to denounce the administration in a speech described as "one president putting another president on trial."[474] By a 6 to 1 vote, the Supreme Court declared the slaves to be free.

Van Buren "spent four years dodging the most important issue of the day, slavery."[475] But he was dodging the issue from the proslavery default position of the Democratic Party. It is true enough that Van Buren was no John Calhoun; he was not going into the trenches for a full-throated defense of slavery as always and everywhere a positive good. But he was most certainly willing to subordinate virtually everything, including the freedom of a multitude of human beings, to the interests of the Democratic Party.

But it is perhaps the crowning irony of Van Buren's entire career that events were about to overtake him and first weaken, then ultimately destroy, the proslavery equilibrium he had painfully put in place. The issues of Texas and expansion undermined Van Buren's relative moderation; his inherent caution proved to be his undoing. The ground was shifting under his feet. Without intending to, "the great politician of the age had checkmated himself."[476] Van Buren was keenly aware of the profoundly divisive nature of the issue of Texas, as explained below. Even Jackson had recognized this and, uncharacteristically, moderated his demands on Mexico in order to help Van Buren in 1836.[477] There were some cautious discussions regarding the annexation of Texas during Van Buren's administration. But John Quincy Adams made these discussions public, and Van Buren quickly backed down. Texas annexation "was one concession the South did not get from Jack-

---

[471] The Whigs divided over the issue of slavery and certainly from time to time compromised on it. Howe, *Transformation*, 511, 586. But they never regarded slavery as a positive good and they never accepted the extreme racial views of Democrats. The Northern Whigs formed the core constituency of the emerging Republican Party.

[472] Howe, *Transformation*, 508. His son married the daughter of a wealthy South Carolina planter. Widmer, *Martin Van Buren*, 112.

[473] Howe, *Transformation*, 513, 515.

[474] Howe, *Transformation*, 522–23.

[475] Schweikart and Allen, *Patriot's History*, 233.

[476] Widmer, *Presidency of Martin Van Buren*, 123.

[477] Howe, *Transformation*, 670. He had recognized the independence of Texas on his last day in office.

son's otherwise compliant successor."[478] But the issue of Texas annexation "replaced states'-rights as the political mantra of Southerners who embraced the new doctrine of the 'positive good' of slavery."[479] For Van Buren, the party was everything, but it was the party itself which was to turn against him. It was one of his own protégés, John L. O'Sullivan, who coined the "electric phrase" of expansionist ideology, "Manifest Destiny."[480]

However, the problem was not immediately obvious, simply because the dominant issue of the election of 1840 was the shattered economy. The stereotypical view of the election of 1840 was that it was mere "mindless hoopla" in which the Whigs were content to embrace the electoral tactics of the Democrats.[481] But the election was important for several reasons. It was the first manifestation of "a truly nationwide party system" with the emergence of the Whigs as a national party.[482] The Whigs, sensing victory, were much better prepared in 1840 than they had been in 1836. The selection of William Henry Harrison at the Whig convention was a mild surprise.[483] He was a war hero who, as a relative outsider, lacked the liabilities of Henry Clay. The Democrats sneered that he was a doddering old man content to sit in front of his log cabin with a mug of hard cider.[484] This was a tone-deaf mistake. He was the "scion of an old aristocratic Virginia family," the son of Benjamin Harrison who had signed the Declaration of Independence.[485] But the Democrats helped transformed him into a Jacksonian man of the people.

The election of 1840 did offer a significant contrast of party positions, particularly regarding economic policy. The Democrats issued the first official party platform.[486] It had nine clauses, six of which were proslavery. Basically, they supported hard money and laissez-faire while saying nothing about the economic depression. The Whigs supported the American System with an emphasis on soft money, internal improvements, a protective tariff, and, in general, the activist role of the government in the management of

---

[478] Howe, *Transformation*, 671.

[479] Howe, *Transformation*, 677

[480] Widmer, *Martin Van Buren*, 148. It came from his "Argument for the Annexation of Oregon and California," in the *New York Morning News*, December 27, 1845.

[481] Howe, *Transformation*, 576. The Whigs did adopt the tactics of mass appeal. A rueful Democrat commented in 1840 that, "We have taught them how to conquer us." Quoted from the *Democratic Review* in Wilson, *Presidency of Martin Van Buren*, 486.

[482] Schweikart and Allen, *Patriot's History*, 234.

[483] The party selected John Tyler, a states'-rights strict constructionist from Virginia, to balance the ticket and appeal to Southern Whigs.

[484] Howe, *Transformation*, 574.

[485] Wilson, *Presidency of Martin Van Buren*, 196.

[486] Howe, *Transformation*, 573–74.

the economy.[487] Beneath the contrast in policy specifics, however, there was also a significant difference in social philosophies. There was a connection between Whigs and the evangelical movement flowing out of the Second Great Awakening. Evangelicals wished to "enlist the power of the state on behalf of reform."[488] The Whigs, always more sympathetic to a variety of reform movements, were in line with a kind of "political postmillennialism," an anticipation of the later Social Gospel movement.[489] The practical consequence was that the Whigs wanted to "transform the United States into an economically developed nation" while the Democrats were content to keep the country as it was.[490]

These basic philosophic differences were submerged in the campaign of 1840. The outcome was hardly surprising. The Whigs prevailed handily in the electoral vote 234 to 60 and also controlled both the House and the Senate.[491] Even so, the vote in some states was very close, so that Van Buren saw his defeat as only a temporary setback. But the Whigs in fact had suffered a most dramatic defeat. The death of Harrison a mere thirty-one days into his presidency cost them their only viable chance to implement their economic program. John Tyler quickly revealed that he had no Whig sympathies; his administration was a four-year Whig nightmare.

After Harrison's death, Tyler quickly claimed the full rights of the presidency in the face of constitutional ambiguity.[492] There were dissenters who believed with John Quincy Adams that Tyler was a "vice president acting as president." Tyler was a Virginia slaveholder who was really a strict-constructionist, states'-rights Democrat who became a Whig only because he opposed Jackson on the Force Bill and the removal of the bank deposits.[493] These positions had grave implications for the Whig domestic program. In addition, he was also an ardent expansionist and an intense defender of slavery. He was "horrified" at antislavery petitions and employed harsh, almost violent, rhetoric in denouncing them.[494]

Tyler's impact on the Whig domestic program was mixed but mostly negative. He accepted the repeal of the Independent Treasury, then turned

---

[487] Howe, *Transformation*, 574. In 1840, a young Whig named Abraham Lincoln called for a new national bank, making it "a central theme in his campaign speeches." Wilson, *Presidency of Martin Van Buren*, 199.

[488] Howe, *Transformation*, 580; see also Howe, *The Political Culture of the American Whigs* (1979), 150–80.

[489] Howe, *Transformation*, 580.

[490] Howe, *Transformation*, 582; Van Deusen, *Jacksonian Era*, 150.

[491] Wilson, *Presidency of Martin Van Buren*, 207; Peterson, *Presidencies*, 29.

[492] See U.S. Constitution, Article II, Section 1, Paragraph 6; Peterson, *Presidencies*, 48.

[493] Howe, *Transformation*, 591; Van Deusen, *Jacksonian Era*, 154.

[494] Richards, *Slave Power*, 129.

around and vetoed the centerpiece of the Whig program, Clay's bank bill, in August 1841. The Whigs lacked the votes to override his veto. The other domestic issues were dealt with in a way that satisfied neither side. There was a linkage between the tariff issue and land policy. Whigs wanted a high tariff and a land act which provided for the distribution of the proceeds to the states.[495] However, the Democrats wanted the money to go to the federal government in order to keep the tariff as low as possible. The result was a compromise settlement.[496] The Tariff of 1842 returned rates to the level of the Tariff of 1832, while the Land Act of 1841 had its distribution provisions repealed in August 1842. All of this drove the Whigs into expelling Tyler from the Whig Party. He responded by purging Whig appointees and replacing them with states'-rights Democrats.[497]

The struggle over domestic economic policy was deeply frustrating for the Whigs, but it was overshadowed by the growing conflict over Texas, expansion, and slavery. This increasingly powerful linkage was to shape the national political debate until the outbreak of the Civil War. The linkage of slavery with Texas was a matter of geography; Texas settlers had ignored the Mexican prohibition of importing slaves. The slave population of Texas had grown faster than the white population. Tyler had decided to make Texas annexation the issue with which he hoped to win reelection, so slavery became the dominant issue of his administration.[498]

But annexation had only "some small sentiment for it in the north," while abolitionists "were up in arms against it."[499] Tyler continued to frame the issue in the context of slavery, conjuring British "plots to 'abolitionize' Texas."[500] On April 12, 1844, John C. Calhoun, Tyler's new secretary of state, signed a treaty of annexation with Texas.[501] Tyler attempted to keep it a secret until after the Senate had approved it. However, Benjamin Tappan, "a maverick antislavery Democrat," leaked the treaty to the press. The Senate vote confirmed Tyler's worst fears. It was defeated 35–16. Slave-state Democrats approved it 10–1. Northern Democrats voted 7–5 against it. Northern Whigs opposed it 13–0 while even Southern Whigs opposed it 14–1.[502]

---

[495] This distribution was intended to encourage internal improvements at the state level to avoid constitutional objections.

[496] Morris, ed., *Encyclopedia*, 463, 519; Howe, *Transformation*, 592–93; Peterson, *Presidencies*, 104–8.

[497] Howe, *Transformation*, 593–94.

[498] Howe, *Transformation*, 677; Van Deusen, *Jacksonian Era*, 177.

[499] Van Deusen, *Jacksonian Era*, 179.

[500] Howe, *Transformation*, 678.

[501] He had replaced Daniel Webster, who had been the last Whig in Tyler's cabinet. Van Deusen, *Jacksonian Era*, 180.

[502] Howe, *Transformation*, 680.

Tyler had only himself to blame. When he proposed the treaty in October 1841, he had "inflamed sentiments" on both sides of the issue.[503] He had pushed the issue, despite its divisiveness, which enabled "rabid proslavery annexationists" to dominate the debate.[504] Despite Tyler's attempt to sweeten the deal by reaching out for Oregon and California, he was unable to compensate for the polarization of the slavery issue. There was a proslavery cabal around Tyler which wanted to acquire Texas "by whatever means necessary."[505] Despite all his scheming, he was left without a viable political future.[506] He was a man between parties, denounced by the Whigs and regarded by Democrats as only a useful but temporary ally. The very intensity of the treaty debate in the Senate frightened key members of both parties into thinking that the Texas issue was just too hot to handle.

Henry Clay and Martin Van Buren, the frontrunners in the presidential campaign of 1844, wanted to ignore the Texas question. The significant difference is that the Whigs rallied behind Clay, but the Democrats did not rally around Van Buren. He believed that:

> Those who have wrought great changes in the world never succeeded by gaining over chiefs; but always by exciting the multitude. The first is the source of intrigue and produces only secondary results, the second is the result of genius and transforms the universe.[507]

But "exciting the multitude" is a two-edged sword. Van Buren had excited the multitude all his political life, but when he tried to put the quietus on the slavery issue, the excited multitude of Southern Democrats and their Northern Democratic sympathizers were having none of it. In 1844, the man who had been the effective creator of the Democratic Party must have shared the feelings of Dr. Frankenstein when this same party, with the full support of Andrew Jackson, rejected him in favor of James K. Polk, an avowed expansionist.[508] The excited multitude had spoken. "Van, Van," was indeed, as the 1840 Whig campaign ditty had it, "a used-up man," used up by his own party.

---

[503] Peterson, *Presidencies*, 176.

[504] Peterson, *Presidencies*, 177.

[505] Peterson, *Presidencies*, 187.

[506] He ran on a third-party ticket without a running mate, supported mostly by federal officeholders seeking to hang on to their jobs. Howe, *Transformation*, 681.

[507] Quoted in Widmer, *Martin Van Buren*, 70. Cited only as "private notebook entry."

[508] Widmer seeks to put the best possible spin on Van Buren's opposition to the annexation of Texas; this was "Van Buren at his best." Widmer, *Martin Van Buren*, 150. This absolution would be much more convincing if Van Buren had not spent his entire career exploiting the issue of slavery for the benefit of himself and the Democratic Party.

Chapter Eight: War, Arsenic, and Compromise, 1844–1850

Nevertheless, going into the Democratic convention of 1844, Martin Van Buren did not feel like a used-up man. Things seemed under control. He was the longtime leader of the party. He had the support of Andrew Jackson, and memories of his difficult presidency, blasted by the Panic of 1837, had faded. The most immediate concern was Texas, but this thorny issue also appeared manageable. Both Jackson and Van Buren, while showing initial interest, had backed off pushing for annexation. Another reassuring factor was that Henry Clay, the probable Whig nominee, was opposed to any immediate annexation of Texas. For him annexation was "a diversion, and a war for Texas [would be] senseless."[509] Van Buren had visited Clay at Ashland, his Kentucky estate, in 1842. Did they discuss Texas at that time? No one knows for sure, but they were certainly in agreement on the issue. As the party conventions approached in 1844 and the annexation treaty reached the Senate on April 27, 1844, both Clay and Van Buren dispatched public letters opposing the measure.[510]

But it is at this point that the political ground began an ominous shift beneath Van Buren's feet. Andrew Jackson, despite his earlier caution on Texas, was "an avid expansionist" who, following the publication of Van

---

[509]Chapter title

Ralph Waldo Emerson predicted that the United States would conquer Mexico, but, he warned, "it will be as the man who swallowed the arsenic, which brings him down in turn. Mexico will poison us." Edward Waldo Emerson and Waldo Emerson Forbes, eds., *Journals of Ralph Waldo Emerson* (10 vols.; 1909–14), 7: 206.

Amy S. Greenberg, *A Wicked War: Polk, Clay, Lincoln and the 1846 Invasion of Mexico* (2012), 47.
[510]Van Deusen, *Jacksonian Era*, 182.

Buren's letter, "spent the few days mourning." Then he came out vigorously for fellow Tennessean James K. Polk."[511] It is at this point that Van Buren became "a used-up man." The proceedings at the convention were anticlimactic. The Polk forces pushed through adoption of the two-thirds rule which prevented a quick Van Buren victory. On the seventh ballot, Polk was nominated. He sought to mend fences by pledging to serve only one term, by denying that he had been working against Van Buren, and by insisting that he had not been consulted about the two-thirds rule. It was "a masterful political apologia."[512]

But if the ground had shifted under Van Buren, it had also shifted under Henry Clay. He easily gained the Whig nomination, but he was running against an ardent pro-Texas expansionist in an expansionist era. Expansionism was the key topic of the ensuing campaign. This was no problem for Polk, but it was a big one for Clay who was driven to "wiring in and out" on the Texas issue.[513] Clay, generally a brilliant political strategist, succeeded only in falling between two stools and convincing many voters that he was untrustworthy. Clay could not match the popular Democratic expansionist position which unambiguously called for the annexation of Texas, California, and Oregon "at the earliest practicable period."[514]

Against this expansionist program, the Whigs could offer only a focus on "economic development, and social reform."[515] The Whig Party was the reform party. For Democrats, reform programs generally were tainted with the specter of abolitionism. Any government strong enough to reform anything was strong enough to threaten slavery. So the Whig support for "all kinds of improvements to promote economic growth and upward mobility" was anathema to the stagnant Democratic focus on slave-driven agriculture.[516] But the Democrats had the winning issue in expansion. They also had the immense advantage of newspaper support. Most of the newspapers of the time "owed their existence to the Democratic Party" and they "loyally supported" the slaveholders' agenda.[517]

---

[511] John D. Eisenhower, "The Election of James K. Polk," *Tennessee Historical Quarterly* 53 (1994): 76–77. Polk's nickname was "Young Hickory."

[512] Eisenhower, "Election of Polk," 81.

[513] Peterson, *Harrison and Tyler*, 243.

[514] Howe, *Transformation*, 683.

[515] Howe, *Transformation*, 686.

[516] James M. McPherson, *Battle Cry of Freedom: The Civil War Era* (1988), 28.

[517] Schweikart and Allen, *Patriot's History*, 237. Michael Holt refers to the Democrats' "extensive chain of newspapers" which "brought the Jacksonian gospel to the people." Holt, *Political Parties and the American Political Tradition: From the Age of Jackson to the Age of Lincoln* (1992), 41.

After a vitriolic campaign, reminiscent of the election of 1828, the result was an election which proved to be "one of the closest and most momentous in American history."[518] The campaign was complicated by a number of factors, most importantly, perhaps, the antislavery Liberty Party candidacy of James G. Birney. In retrospect, this was Clay's best shot at the presidency, but he fell short in the electoral vote 170 to 105 and in the popular vote by a razor-thin margin of 1,337,243 to 1,299,062. The election of Polk in 1844 is an excellent example of the threshold effect, revealing a seismic shift in the Democratic Party which had been developing more or less imperceptibly for some time. It was not merely that Polk was not Van Buren but also that the Democratic Party of Polk was not the Democratic Party of Van Buren. The election of 1844 is the first election from which it is possible to draw an ominous line leading to 1860.

Van Buren had been able to maintain the morally compromising but nonetheless effective North–South coalition. But now the magic was gone, so the balance was shifting inexorably to the South. The Democratic Party "its humanitarian pretensions left hopelessly behind, was dedicated to expansion and was driven into proslavery policies by the increasing dominance of southern interests in its counsels." Polk became the head of "the new Democracy."[519] The intense focus of the Democratic Party on expansion was not only about the expansion of slavery, important as that was. It also had to do with the overall political balance of power by bringing in new slave states to maintain the power of the South, particularly in the Senate. Polk himself supported the possibility that Texas could be made into five slave states.[520]

But this raises a very important issue. Slavery could not be threatened in the slave states because of ironclad constitutional guarantees. Abolitionist rhetoric could not change this basic reality. Abraham Lincoln vainly offered such reassurances in 1860–61, but this was never enough. The goal of the Democratic Party from the time of Polk onward was not the defense of slavery but rather the expansion of slavery and the acquisition of the political power necessary to support it.[521] Despite the fraying of the old Van Buren coalition, Southern Democrats continued to benefit from significant support from Northern Democrats.[522]

---

[518] Howe, *Transformation*, 682.

[519] Van Deusen, *Jacksonian Era*, 186.

[520] William Dusinberre, *Slavemaster President: The Double Career of James K. Polk* (2003), 145–46.

[521] The South ceased to be an open society. The Democratic Party "substantially curtailed" freedom of speech. The mildest reservations about slavery were met with "withering objections," while Southern Whigs were attacked as "traitors to the vital interests of the South." Dusinberre, *Slavemaster President*, 159.

[522] Leonard L. Richards, *The Slave Power: The Free North and Southern Domination, 1780–1860* (2000), 165–77.

Territorial expansion, under the sunny rubric of Manifest Destiny, presented a sharp contrast between rhetoric and reality which challenged the optimism of Jefferson's "empire of liberty."[523] The somber reality was that Manifest Destiny was "based on the assumption of white supremacy" in which nonwhite land claims were not taken seriously.[524] During the debate over Texas, John Quincy Adams had come to realize that "slavery as well as freedom might be extended over the continent."[525]

There was also a sharp contrast between the political parties.[526] The Whigs supported American development "more in terms of qualitative economic improvement than quantitative expansion of territory." They supported "economic and cultural imperialism through expanding trade and Christian missions." Many Democrats, however, tended to be "indifferent or contemptuous" of such reforms as temperance and women's rights.[527]

Manifest Destiny can best be understood as a manifest design of the Democratic Party. Expansion was "neither accidental nor innocent."[528] The whole process can be understood in a very broad economic and political context. The intense Democratic focus on expansion, in addition to concerns over slavery and the political balance of power for the South, was also rooted in a pervasive neo-Jeffersonian worldview characterized by "a vision of a rural arcadia" and a deep fear of modernization.[529] Although Manifest Destiny is often interpreted in the context of nationalism, in the hands of Polk and the Democrats, the focus was on states' rights and slavery. It was the Whigs who were the nationalists. The domestic program of the Democrats—opposition to internal improvements and a national bank, for example—all related to their states'-rights perspective.

The neo-Jeffersonian aspect of this approach is heightened by the continuation of the old dream of economic coercion through control of vital raw materials. The result was "a unique brand of mercantilism" which sought to control other nations by "holding a virtual monopoly over vital resources such as cotton and foodstuffs."[530] To complete the picture of a reappearance

---

[523] Howe, *Transformation*, 703.

[524] Howe, *Transformation*, 703.

[525] Frederick Merk, *Slavery and the Annexation of Texas* (1972), 23.

[526] Howe, *Transformation*, 706.

[527] Thomas R. Hietala, *Manifest Design: Anxious Aggrandizement in Late Jacksonian America* (1985), 112.

[528] Hietala, *Manifest Design*, 94.

[529] Hietala, *Manifest Design*, 97. The chapter arguing this viewpoint is entitled "Jefferson Redivivus: The Perils of Modernization."

[530] Hietala, *Manifest Design*, 56.

of Jeffersonianism was that old foreign-policy standby—hatred of the Brit-ish.[531]

It is more accurate to speak of Jacksonian expansion than of Jackso-nian democracy.[532] The Democratic Party was the vehicle for the protection and extension of slavery as well as the advocate of a retrograde economic policy of agrarianism in clear contrast to the Whig commitment to progress, economic diversity, and caution regarding the extension of slavery.

But before the inauguration of Polk, there was still John Tyler. Although his own bid for the presidency in 1844 had been a fiasco, he was "grimly exultant" at Polk's election, determined to move ahead to admit Texas, not by treaty but by a joint Congressional resolution.[533] He argued that Polk's election was a mandate on Texas annexation which made "further objec-tions futile."[534] The obvious advantage of a joint-resolution approach is that it avoided the two-thirds majority required to ratify a treaty. So Tyler claimed authority by virtue of Article IV, Section 3 of the Constitution which provides that "New States may be admitted by the Congress into this Union." Tyler claimed that this provision "fully empowered" him to move ahead, but the problem was that Texas was a sovereign nation, not a new territory seeking statehood.[535]

The process of getting the joint resolution passed moved forward ominously in the context of virulent agitation and paranoiac anti-British obsessions. Tyler has been accused of lying about British intentions both directly and through his friend and agent Duff Green, who conjured "a monarchist alliance" between antislavery leaders and the British who were seeking to "abolitionize" Texas.[536] The paranoia continued even after Edward Everett, the U.S. ambassador to Great Britain, denounced the "baselessness of Duff Green's tale."[537]

Despite all of Tyler's machinations, the joint-resolution strategy trig-gered strong opposition from Whigs and some Northern Democrats. It is significant that Albert Gallatin, the "bearer of the Jeffersonian tradition in

---

[531] Hietala, *Manifest Design*, 7. The abolition of slavery in the British Empire in 1833 was an additional reason to hate Great Britain.

[532] Hietala, *Manifest Design*, 7.

[533] Van Deusen, *Jacksonian Era*, 190.

[534] Greenberg, *A Wicked War*, 61.

[535] Peterson, *Harrison and Tyler*, 229..

[536] Merk, *Slavery and the Annexation of Texas*, xii–xiii, 32. The British preferred an indepen-dent Texas and exerted some influence to that end. But the idea that they would take a direct role in the matter or that Texas would welcome British interference is absurd. Nevertheless, the level of Anglophobia reached "almost hysterical proportions" while Jackson described alleged British activities in "near-apocalyptic terms." Sam W. Haynes, *James K. Polk and the Expansionist Impulse* (1997), 104, 106.

[537] Merk, *Slavery and the Annexation of Texas*, 32.

American politics," opposed the "new doctrine of a legislative annexation of Texas."[538] After an intricate process of negotiation, the joint resolution passed Congress during the lame-duck session in December 1844. The resolution passed the Democratically controlled House 120–98 and squeaked through the Senate 27–25.[539] Tyler signed the measure at the very end of his presidency on March 1, 1845.[540] All Democratic senators supported it while only three out of fifteen Southern Whigs voted for it. Antislavery leaders in the North saw it as "a national catastrophe."[541] John Quincy Adams asserted that the action reduced the Constitution "to a menstrous [sic] rag."[542] He saw it as the triumph of the Slave Power, "the heaviest calamity that ever befell my country." It was "the apoplexy of the Constitution."[543] The joint resolution "reassured slaveowners about the security of their form of investment and its potential for further expansion."[544] Tyler regarded the annexation of Texas as "the crowning achievement of his administration." This position makes perfect sense from the perspective of his passionately proslavery convictions.[545] Apparently proslavery success trumped the requirement of simple honesty.[546]

In response to the annexation of Texas, Mexico "immediately broke off" diplomatic relations.[547] So Polk, who had strongly approved of Tyler's actions, entered his presidency with a dangerous but welcome situation on his hands, which was rendered even more explosive because of the unresolved boundary issue. The United States and Texas both claimed the Rio Grande boundary, rather than the assertion by Mexico that it should be the Nueces River. The case for the Rio Grande boundary was "flimsy at best."[548]

---

[538] Schweikart and Allen, *Patriot's History*, 240.

[539] It was generally "acclaimed by Democrats and lamented by Whigs." Merk, *Slavery and the Annexation of Texas*, 159.

[540] The passage was made possible by Southern Democrats, "most northern Democrats," and a "handful of Southern Whigs." Howe, *Transformation*, 700.

[541] For Merk, the roots of the Civil War "lay deep in the soil of Texas." Merk, *Slavery and the Annexation of Texas*, 181.

[542] Howe, *Transformation*, 699, quoted from his memoirs.

[543] Peterson, *Harrison and Tyler*, 257, quoted from his memoirs.

[544] Howe, *Transformation*, 700. Howe notes that the price of prime field hands rose 21 percent within a year of the acceptance of annexation by Texas, and it continued to increase throughout the 1850s with the integration of a "flourishing international pricing network for southern staple crops and the commodified human beings who produced them." Howe, *Transformation*, 700.

[545] Antislavery petitions "horrified" him, and he looked at abolitionists "with horror." Richards, *Slave Power*, 129, and Peterson, *Harrison and Tyler*, 206.

[546] Merk is caustic regarding Tyler's dishonest circulation of "manufactured propaganda" while downplaying the issue of slavery. Merk, *Slavery and the Annexation of Texas*, 50.

[547] Schweikart and Allen, *Patriot's History*, 240.

[548] Haynes, *James K. Polk*, 118.

But Polk intended to claim the Rio Grande boundary "however laughable those claims might be."[549]

But for Polk, even Texas with the Rio Grande boundary was not enough. He wanted the vast California and New Mexico territories as well. In the interests of the Slave Power, the Democratic Party continually strengthened its position as the party of a ruthless imperialism. He relished the highly volatile situation he inherited from Tyler because he was committed not only to slavery but to the expansion of slavery. He was himself a zealous slaveholder who did not wish to be seen as such. While president, he bought and sold slaves with no regard for the slave families involved, while maintaining the fiction that he held only "a few family retainers."[550] He had been "acculturated by a lifelong reliance on slave labor." In 1830, he voted against a Tennessee proposal to outlaw whipping slaves and professed himself to be "delighted" at the passage of the Gag Rule.[551]

Polk was very much an entrepreneurial slavemaster who ran his Mississippi plantation like a business. He bought and sold slaves simply to "make his cotton plantation more profitable."[552] His primary motive was to "expand his cherished plantation enterprise" and so "commercial success, not a paternalistic sense of duty to 'family negroes' was the driving force behind Polk's forays into the market for enslaved labor power."[553] Polk was an ambitious slaveholder, committed to profit, and deeply resentful of those opposed to the slave system. He made diligent efforts to conceal the degree to which he engaged in slave-trading. He was largely successful even with historians until a path-breaking master's thesis brought the matter to light.[554] Not for nothing did Polk earn the nickname "Polk the Mendacious."[555] It has also been noted that he never seemed plagued with self-doubt; he had "a moral certitude and self-righteousness that he carried to the White House."[556]

The most positive evaluations of Polk's presidency generally come from historians who downplay or even ignore the issue of slavery or who argue that Polk just did not know what he was doing. For example, at the beginning of his book, Paul Bergeron promises that he will give a highly favorable view of Polk as president, while admitting that some historians "have

---

[549] Greenberg, *Wicked War*, 67.

[550] Howe, *Transformation*, 702.

[551] John Seigenthaler, *James Polk* (2004), 86–87.

[552] Dusinberre, *Slavemaster President*, 13.

[553] Dusinberre, *Slavemaster President*, 22.

[554] Dusinberre, *Slavemaster President*, 22. The thesis was written by Richard Marsh at North Texas University in 1977.

[555] Haynes, *James K. Polk*, 77. The nickname was originally conferred on him by Alexander Stephens. Merk, *Slavery and the Annexation of Texas*, 106.

[556] Seigenthaler, *Polk*, 1.

handled him severely."[557] He does this by the simple expedient of ignoring the slavery issue almost completely. A variant line of defense is that Polk simply did not anticipate that the issues of slavery and expansion would prove to be so difficult. Charles Sellers depicts a Polk who was "strangely blind to the great convulsion over slavery that was shaping before his eyes." Sellers also saw in Polk a "disingenuous, a slippery quality that served him in good stead."[558] Polk denied any link between slavery and the Mexican War in his diary entry for January 5, 1847, and in other places as well. It seems likely that he wrote this and other passages with Clio, the Muse of History, looking over his shoulder.[559] Certainly the Wilmot Proviso, introduced on August 6, 1846, made it plain for all to see that Polk "had opened Pandora's box of the territorial slave issue."[560] It also seems significant that Polk and the Democratic Party consistently attempted to link abolition with the Whigs, "taunting" them with their "supposed alliance with abolitionism."[561] Is it at all plausible that slavery was a powerful issue for the Democrats at all times and everywhere except in Texas and the West generally? Polk was either unbelievably obtuse or was, once again, acting out his role of "Polk the Mendacious."

In March 1845, he was confronting a major crisis which he relished as a great opportunity, one which he had zealously helped to create.[562] Any schoolboy confronted by a playground bully has two choices and one hope: fight, flight, or adult intervention. In 1846, Mexico had two choices and no hope of intervention.[563] Polk wanted a war, and flight was impossible. Mexico had broken diplomatic relations with the United States in response to the joint-annexation resolution. Texas joined the United States in February 1846, resulting in an uneasy standoff. However, Polk did not want a standoff; he wanted a war.

---

[557] Paul H. Bergeron, *The Presidency of James K. Polk* (1986), xiii. His preface does not contain the words "slavery" or "expansion" and the index of the book has no entry for "slavery."

[558] Glyndon Van Deusen's review of Charles G. Sellers, *James K. Polk, Continentalist, 1843–1846* (1967) in *American Historical Review* 72 (1967): 1095. Haynes also notes that the Polk administration was "strangely oblivious to the sectional rancor that had been a byproduct of its conquest of the west." Haynes, *James K. Polk*, 196.

[559] Dusinberre, *Slavemaster President* , 79. Dusinberre characterizes these entries as "disingenuous" (142). Yet Whigs consistently predicted trouble; some Northern Democrats were cautious as well.

[560] Dusinberre, *Slavemaster President*, 80. The Proviso would not permit slavery in any territory acquired from Mexico. See below, p. 116.

[561] Dusinberre, *Slavemaster President*, 127.

[562] Young Hickory was reassured by Old Hickory's belief that "the God of the universe . . . intended this great valley [Texas] to belong to our nation." Quoted in Seigenthaler, *James Polk*, 72.

[563] Van Deusen, *Jacksonian Era*, 214.

First he laid down a diplomatic smokescreen by dispatching John Slidell to Mexico in November 1845 to demand that Mexico sell New Mexico and California and accept the Rio Grande boundary with Texas. The Slidell mission lasted until end of March 1846, but it was an obvious failure by January 1846. The mission was "clearly coercive in manner."[564] It provided "only a show of negotiating" and, worse yet, was intended to "incense the Mexicans."[565] Polk himself was already incensed, telling his Cabinet in early February 1846 that the failure of the mission would mean war.

Time passed, and Mexico, despite breaking diplomatic relations and rejecting Slidell's ultimatum, showed a disconcerting reluctance to declare war. Polk, desperately trying to "manufacture a war," dispatched Zachary Taylor's forces into the disputed territory up to the Rio Grande boundary on January 13, 1846.[566] Rains delayed his advance until early March. Finally, Polk received the gratifying news that the Mexicans had attacked. Polk, who had been prepared to declare war without an attack, now had his *casus belli.* Garrett Davis, a Kentucky Whig, summed it up best: "It is our own President who began this war."[567]

The outcome of the Mexican War was a foregone conclusion, but its course and consequences were not. The war began with an outburst of patriotic zeal and high hopes, reflecting as it did the high tide of Manifest Destiny perceived in its most idealistic aspect. The Congressional vote for war was 40 to 2 in the Senate and 174 to 14 in the House. However, the magnitude of these approval rates is misleading. Once the brief initial euphoria subsided, opposition to the war quickly became a formidable political force. Whigs were deeply skeptical of the war from the beginning. They distrusted Polk, questioned his war aims, and were deeply uneasy about the consequences of the war in relation to the slavery issue. Even so, they were not able in any substantive way to alter its course or consequences. This was true, in part, because of divisions within the party.[568] During the war, there were differences between Southern Whigs who were somewhat more inclined to support the war, albeit sometimes reluctantly, and Northern Whigs, some of whom earned the appellation "Conscience Whigs" because of their growing opposition to slavery.[569]

---

[564] John H. Schroeder, *Mr. Polk's War: American Opposition and Dissent, 1846–1848* (1973), 12.

[565] Greenberg, *A Wicked War*, 78.

[566] So observed Anson Jones, president of Texas. Quoted in Howe, *Transformation*, 733. This was deliberately provocative. John Calhoun, Andrew Jackson, and John Quincy Adams had all accepted the Nueces River boundary. Schroeder, *Mr. Polk's War*, 11.

[567] Quoted in Howe, *Transformation*, 742.

[568] Schroeder, *Mr. Polk's War*, 145.

[569] This group was an important factor in the rise of the Republican Party. Free blacks in the North voted "as a solid Whig bloc" while "Democratic egalitarianism was for whites

Polk and the Democrats resorted to intense efforts to compel acquiescence. Polk's administration "did everything they could to stifle discussion, questions, and dissent."[570] Six months after the war began, in his first annual message, Polk branded all opponents of the war traitors; he "complained frequently" about "the Federalists"—Whigs who opposed the war.[571] The tactic alarmed many Whigs who remembered the War of 1812 as the death knell of the Federalist Party. One Whig congressman announced that he favored "war, pestilence, and famine" as a survival strategy.[572] But in addition to the Whigs' own indecision and the accusations of disloyalty, Polk had another way of dragging the Whigs along. His legislative strategy was simple but effective—bundling. He deliberately forced Whigs who opposed the war to also oppose supplies for the troops, thus exposing them "to the politically fatal charge of disloyalty" with the additional peril of seeming to endanger the troops in the field.[573]

In the short term, Polk got his way and his war, but it became impossible to stifle mounting criticism from prominent opponents and the nation at large. The most powerful political alliance in opposition was the partnership of ex-president John Quincy Adams and future president Abraham Lincoln, whose "Spot Resolutions" of December 22, 1847, demanded to know exactly where the war began.[574] This was a "devastating rebuke to Polk."[575] For his part, Adams denounced it as "a most unrighteous war."[576] The war was also opposed by virtually all the leading antislavery activists, literary figures, and reformers in the North who feared that the nation "had forsaken its true mission" by seeking material gain and slavery expansion.[577]

The war Polk could not wait to start was becoming increasingly difficult to manage. Then came an unexpected thunderbolt in the form of the Wilmot Proviso. David Wilmot was a Democratic congressman from Pennsylvania; his Proviso affirmed that slavery would not be permitted in any new territory acquired from Mexico. In August 1846, Polk had requested a two-million-dollar appropriation to acquire land from Mexico. In characteristic Polk fashion, he wanted it kept secret with a short time limit on approval because

---

only." McPherson, *Battle Cry of Freedom*, 30.

[570] Howe, *Transformation*, 741.

[571] Greenberg, *A Wicked War*, 195. Schroeder, *Mr. Polk's War*, 72.

[572] McPherson, *Battle Cry of Freedom*, 47.

[573] Schroeder, *Mr. Polk's War*, 14–17.

[574] There is a fitting symmetry here. Adams was a Whig before there was a Whig Party and Lincoln remained a Whig after the party disappeared.

[575] Greenberg, *A Wicked War*, 248–49. Lincoln paid a political price for this in Illinois but did not back down.

[576] Van Deusen, *Jacksonian Era*, 224.

[577] Schroeder, *Mr. Polk's War*, 119.

of impending Congressional adjournment. But the whole scheme blew up in his face. The Whigs insisted that publicity "would be the price of their support."[578] The Wilmot Proviso was the second and most important of a two-punch combination. It was in some ways "the culmination of a series of intraparty rivalries that took a sectional form within the Democratic organizations."[579] Wilmot was not an antislavery activist. His Proviso was intended to keep blacks out of the West and protect it as a whites-only area. This was also the thrust of the emerging Free-Soil Party. Polk eventually got his appropriation, and the Proviso "was a catalyst and its importance as such cannot be overstressed."[580] Politics never really returned to normal. Polk had set in motion the inescapable and increasingly divisive issue of slavery in the territories. The work of Emerson's arsenic had begun.

In the meantime, there was a war to wage, and Polk, ever the micromanager, sought to keep his fingers on all the buttons. The U.S. Army officer corps was overwhelmingly Whig, and the two leading generals of the Mexican War, Zachary Taylor and Winfield Scott, were not only Whigs but potential political rivals. They were "the bane of his presidency," and he hated them "more than Mexicans."[581] His relations with Scott were particularly difficult, and the fault was not entirely Polk's—there were reasons why his nickname was "Old Fuss and Feathers." But while Polk, who had no military experience whatsoever, professed to have little regard for Scott's generalship, Scott was praised by the Duke of Wellington as "the greatest living soldier."[582]

Polk's relations with Taylor were not good either, but his relations with Scott had a soap-opera quality, culminating in Polk's dismissal of him and subjecting him to a Court of Inquiry in early 1848 over Scott's dismissal of Gideon Pillow, a Polk favorite. The court "whitewashed" Pillow's behavior but did not rule on the merits of the case against Scott.[583] The proceeding had served its real purpose by keeping Scott out of politics and aborting any chance he had of being the Whig presidential candidate in 1848. Robert E. Lee observed that "to suspend a successful general in command of an army in

---

[578] David M. Potter and Don E. Fehrenbacher, *The Impending Crisis: America before the Civil War, 1848–1861* (1978), 19.

[579] Potter, *Impending Crisis,* 27. The Van Buren wing of the party resented the growing Southern dominance of the party.

[580] John Mayfield, *Rehearsal for Republicanism: Free Soil and the Politics of Antislavery* (1980), 54. Polk denounced the Proviso as "a mischievous and foolish amendment." Potter, *Impending Crisis,* 64. But it is possible to argue that by the standard of the Northwest Ordinance, Thomas Jefferson was the "real author of the Wilmot Proviso." Potter, *Impending Crisis,* 54. But Jefferson's "Empire of Liberty" was "becoming "an empire for slavery" as a result of the work of his political descendants. McPherson, *Battle Cry of Freedom,* 51.

[581] Potter, *Impending Crisis,* 3.

[582] Bauer, *Mexican War,* 322.

[583] Howe, *Transformation,* 791–92.

the heart of an enemy's country [and] to try the judge [Scott] in place of the accused [Pillow] is to upset all discipline."[584] Polk provided Lincoln with a timely example of how not to deal with wartime generals.[585]

There was no way the Mexicans could win the war, but they were determined not to lose it. In late fall 1846, Polk ordered Scott to attack Vera Cruz. By the spring of 1847, the war seemed won, but once again the Mexicans fought stubbornly on. The war was won but not yet over. In the meantime, antiwar protests increased, the debate over slavery in the West simmered, and an unwelcome movement to annex all of Mexico gained strength. Polk dispatched Nicholas P. Trist to Mexico to negotiate an end to the war.[586] He was to demand recognition of the Rio Grande boundary and vast land acquisitions in California, Nevada, Utah, most of New Mexico and Arizona, and part of Wyoming and Colorado—"next to the Louisiana Purchase the largest single addition to the national domain."[587] Despite the seriousness of the issues involved, Trist's mission had a kind of comic-opera quality. He and Scott quarreled, then reconciled. Negotiations with the Mexicans were conducted at times in a surrealistic atmosphere. Scott took Mexico City in mid-September 1847; the Mexicans became more amenable. Then came the final monkey wrench. Polk decided to demand more for less and also decided to recall Trist in early October 1847.

Trist was close to persuading the Mexicans to agree to Polk's original demands. Scott's troops in central Mexico were being harassed by guerrillas and disease, and Trist feared the emergence of a Mexican war party which would continue the fighting. So he did "something unheard of in American diplomacy; he refused to come home." He wrote a sixty-five-page letter explaining his actions. Polk was "dumbstruck" and wanted him "physically thrown out of army headquarters."[588] Despite Polk's disapproval, the Treaty of Guadalupe Hidalgo was signed in late December 1847. Its terms fulfilled Polk's original instructions.[589] Trist's action "was insubordinate but courageous."[590] It ended the war on favorable terms, extricated Scott's army from its ongoing peril, and aborted an increasingly powerful movement

---

[584] Quoted in Howe, *Transformation*, 792. Fortunately, Scott achieved notable successes before Polk dismissed him.

[585] Mark Neely, "War and Partisanship: What Lincoln Learned from James K. Polk," *Journal of the Illinois State Historical Society* 74 (1981): 199–216.

[586] Howe, *Transformation*, 800. Trist had impeccable Democratic credentials. He had served as a companion to and protégé of Thomas Jefferson and had married his granddaughter. Polk sought unsuccessfully to keep the mission secret.

[587] Potter, *Impending Crisis*, 1.

[588] Greenberg, *A Wicked War*, 239.

[589] Trist was "savvy enough" to lop $5 million from the original figure of $20 million. Greenberg, *A Wicked War*, 259.

[590] Van Deusen, *Jacksonian Era*, 239.

to acquire all of Mexico.[591] Polk had little choice but to accept the treaty, submitting it to the Senate where it passed easily on March 10, 1848, 38 to 14, in a vote that was "neither partisan nor sectional."[592] Mexico accepted it in May. Polk proclaimed the end of the war on July 4, 1848.

Nicholas Trist had to face the wrath of a vindictive Polk. He was "bodily removed from the headquarters of the army in Mexico and escorted to Vera Cruz."[593] Polk "did everything in his power" to prevent Trist from receiving payment for his services or future government employment.[594] It is arguable that "never was a reward for services to a man's country more unjustly withheld or more nobly deserved."[595] He experienced twenty years of "biting poverty" while working as a paymaster for a railroad company.[596] Congress finally voted him back pay with interest in 1870. Charles Sumner supported his cause in Congress, and President Grant appointed him postmaster of Alexandria, Virginia.[597]

Polk's presidency, and indeed his life, were coming to an end.[598] But the problems which he had bequeathed to the nation were only beginning. The vast land acquisition which ended the war came about "by the acts of a dismissed emissary, a disappointed president, and a divided Congress"; it was an "ironic triumph of 'Manifest Destiny'" and an ominous harbinger of what was to come.[599] Perhaps the most convincing defense of Polk involves considering the long-term consequences. George P. Garrison concluded that "there are few in this day, even of those who condemned the methods, that would be willing to see the work undone."[600] But the long view was not a luxury which the men of Polk's own time could enjoy.[601] The issue of slavery in the territories was a Damoclean sword under which the whole nation sat uneasily. The issue of slavery expansion had become unavoidable; the Whig

---

[591] Most proponents were "wide-eyed northern Democratic imperialists." Most Southerners objected on racial grounds. Howe, *Transformation*, 788–89.

[592] Schroeder, *Mr. Polk's War*, 158.

[593] Greenberg, *A Wicked War*, 262.

[594] Greenberg, *A Wicked War*, 264.

[595] Van Deusen, *Jacksonian Era*, 245.

[596] Greenberg, *A Wicked War*, 264.

[597] Grant had "bitterly opposed" the Mexican War; he regarded it as "one of the most unjust ever waged by a stronger against a weaker nation." Quoted from *Personal Memoirs*, Greenberg, *A Wicked War*, 264.

[598] His health had deteriorated dramatically, and he died of cholera on June 15, 1849.

[599] Potter, *Impending Crisis*, 6.

[600] Quoted in Merk, *Slavery and the Annexation of Texas*, 106, from his book *Westward Extension, 1841–1850* (1906).

[601] In the short view, the Mexican War was lethal—one in ten died—12,518 in all. Over 88 percent died of disease. Also, the war cost around $100 million. Howe, *Transformation*, 752.

Party had grave doubts about this, while Democrats had become committed to it.

There were four basic approaches to the issue of slavery in the territories being debated in the context of the Mexican War: the Wilmot Proviso, geographical division (as in the Missouri Compromise), popular sovereignty, and the Calhoun Resolutions claiming an unbreakable constitutional right of slaveholders to take slaves into territories being organized for statehood.[602] Both the Proviso and the Resolutions had the potential to sever the Union. Incessant debate during Polk's presidency had failed to achieve sectional peace, and so the nation embarked on the presidential campaign of 1848 with the issue of slavery expansion unresolved.[603] Perhaps the best overall perspective regarding the campaign of 1848 is contained in the title of Joel H. Silbey's treatment *Party Over Section: The Rough and Ready Campaign of 1848* (2009). Both major parties sought to defuse the sectional issue. They both sought to deal with slavery by the simple, unheroic expedient of "obfuscating the issue."[604] But the issue of expansion, the legacy of the Mexican War, was unavoidable.

The Whig solution to the problem was to nominate Zachary Taylor, an apolitical war hero. The other Whig frontrunners all had various liabilities, but Taylor had essentially a clean political slate. He was also a Southern slaveholder. The Whigs wanted a candidate who could win the election, "the most important qualification."[605] Taylor was nominated by the Whigs at a convention which deliberately failed to draft a party platform.[606] The party could not make up its collective mind about expansion in general.[607] The Democrats also sought a middle-of-the-road candidate, someone who could heal the divisions within the party.[608] Both parties maintained their traditional stances on economic issues such as the tariff, internal improvements, banking, and monetary policy. The difference was that, unlike the Whigs, the Democrats "actively pursued a program of territorial expansion."[609] The proslavery position lurked beneath the issue of expansion. There were

---

[602] Potter, *Impending Crisis*, 154–62.

[603] The Free Soil and Liberty Parties also participated in the campaign.

[604] McPherson, *Battle Cry of Freedom*, 62.

[605] Schroeder, *Mr. Polk's War*, 141

[606] The Whigs nominated Millard Fillmore, a New York Whig, for vice president.

[607] Henry Clay's speech of November 13, 1847, which disavowed any new territory and "walked a tightrope on the slavery issue," divided Whigs. Schroeder, *Mr. Polk's War*, 140. The slaveholder Clay also advocated gradual compensated emancipation and colonization.

[608] The divisions were most dramatically revealed by the decision of Martin Van Buren to be presidential candidate of the Free-Soil Party

[609] Joel H. Silbey, *Party Over Section: The Rough and Ready Campaign of 1848* (2009), 20.

profound and ominous differences between the parties which were barely concealed as the campaign unfolded.

The Democrats also tried to finesse the issue by nominating Lewis Cass of Michigan, whose solution was popular sovereignty.[610] They hoped that all Democrats could unite behind it. What could be more democratic than simply letting the people themselves decide the issue? Unfortunately, it was not so simple because of the unavoidable question of timing. When, exactly, could the people decide for themselves? Southerners, led by Calhoun, argued that the territories were the common property of the nation as a whole and, as such, slavery could not be excluded prior to statehood. But if slavery could be introduced into the territories prior to statehood, how likely would it be that an entrenched slave system would be voted down after statehood had been achieved? Cass himself made no attempt to deal with this issue.[611] The long-running crisis that led to the Civil War was the work of the Democratic Party, which simply could not abandon slavery expansion, hidden as it sometimes was behind the reassuring rhetoric of popular sovereignty and other smokescreens.[612]

The campaign of 1848 was a "normal" election so far as the major parties were concerned. Taylor won the electoral vote 163 to 127 and took 47.4 percent of the popular vote to 42.7 percent for Cass. Neither candidate had "a slave or non-slave state vote advantage."[613] Despite the presence of the Free Soil Party, the most striking aspect of the campaign was "the persistence of traditional party loyalties among most of the electorate."[614] The Free Soil Party did drain some support from the Whigs but not enough to change the outcome.[615]

Although the issues of slavery and expansion dominated the narrative throughout this period, the Democrats remained wedded to their traditional neo-Jeffersonian agrarianism in opposition to the dynamic Whig vision of an America willing to develop its full economic potential in industry, banking, internal improvements, and commerce. The Democrats remained chained to

---

[610] Cass had been the zealous enforcer of Indian Removal, a "superimperialist" who advocated unlimited expansion. Howe, *Transformation*, 830.

[611] Howe, *Transformation*, 831.

[612] The Young America movement was largely a Democratic movement of nationalistic expansion. It was more open to transportation improvements, but it kept the slavery expansion issue very much alive.

[613] Silbey, *Party over Section*, 135–36. Van Buren got no electoral votes and only 10.1 percent of the popular vote, while Gerrit Smith of the Liberty Party was nearly invisible with 2500 votes. The Democrats did regain control of the House 113 to 108 and kept control of the Senate 33 to 25.

[614] Silbey, *Party over Section*, 140.

[615] The Free-Soil vote would have gone to the Whigs who, despite Taylor's slave ownership were "viewed as the antislavery party." Schweikart and Allen, *Patriot's History*, 265.

an increasingly outmoded static economy linked to agriculture and slavery. The particular issues of 1848, while seemingly less important only because of the divisive power of slavery and expansion, were nonetheless of vital importance for the future of the country. The economic progress of the United States was almost entirely due to the impetus of the Whig Party and the Republican Party which retained the economic philosophy of its Whig antecedent. But the immediate question for the people in the aftermath of the campaign of 1848 was whether these particular issues would remain dominant or whether there would be a "sectional upsurge."[616] The answer was not long in coming, for it turned out that nobody, neither Whigs nor Democrats, knew what they were getting in Zachary Taylor, the seemingly apolitical war hero.

Taylor was "a free-soil wolf in the clothing of a states'-rights sheep."[617] He pledged to lead an army into a defiant South if necessary, "a straight-forward Jacksonian response," unexpected but also unmistakable.[618] Emerson's arsenic began to exert its toxic effect on the political system, producing a crisis which was resolved, only partially and temporarily, by the Compromise of 1850. The crisis was triggered by the new lands acquired from Mexico. But these lands were a catalyst for something far more dangerous. The South, its appetite whetted by the land acquisition, had also developed a siege mentality. In January 1849, John Calhoun's "Address of the Southern Delegates in Congress to their Constituents" was a sweeping denunciation of all the alleged aggressions against the South, including the acquisition of Oregon as free territory.[619] Despite all the concessions the South had received, beginning with the three-fifths compromise, Southern Democrats increasingly saw themselves as "chronically endangered by radical fanatics and conniving Yankee politicians" who were always ready to "betray the nation's founding principles—that is protection of slavery—in return for a few abolitionist votes."[620]

Southerners faced a stark political reality. The North was inexorably growing in population and economic strength. Southerners were already outnumbered in the House and faced the prospect of falling behind in the Senate if California, along with the New Mexico and Utah territories, entered the Union as free states. They feared that the loss of political strength would put them under the control of abolitionists, whom they resisted "as if they

[616] Silbey, *Party over Section*, 146.
[617] McPherson, *Battle Cry of Freedom*, 66, 69.
[618] Potter, *Impending Crisis*, 95.
[619] Elbert B. Smith, *The Presidencies of Zachary Taylor & Millard Fillmore* (1988), 91.
[620] Fergus M. Bordewich, *America's Great Debate: Henry Clay, Stephen A. Douglas, and the Compromise that Preserved the Union* (2012), 12.

were resisting the holocaust itself."[621] In December 1849, Taylor in his annual message urged that California and New Mexico be admitted immediately as free states. For Taylor, this was simply a matter of facing the reality of "geography, climate, existing law, and customs."[622] But the South had what it thought was the appropriate response when Henry S. Foote simultaneously announced the determination of Texas to claim enough land from New Mexico to carve out four more slave states. For Taylor this was "just another example of greed and lawlessness" which he was resolved to resist.[623]

This is the impasse that led to the agonizing process of hammering out the Compromise of 1850. Henry Clay, whose reputation as a master compromiser stemmed from his actions during the Nullification and Missouri crises, stepped forward on January 29, 1850, with his proposals. They involved the admission of California as a free state and the organization of the New Mexico and Utah territories without any Congressional conditions regarding slavery. Texas would relinquish its claim to New Mexican territory in return for additional land in the Panhandle and the federal assumption of its 10-million-dollar state debt. Slave-trading, though not slavery itself, would be banned in the District of Columbia, and a stricter fugitive slave law would be enacted.[624]

Congress wrangled over these proposals for months until September 1850. They were packaged into an Omnibus Bill which could not pass because it contained provisions which nearly everyone, on one side or the other, opposed. The most dangerous aspect of the crisis was the Texas threat to New Mexico territory. Both Taylor, who died July 9, 1850, and the new president Millard Fillmore, vowed to defend New Mexico, by force if necessary. Fortunately, this resolution led Texas to back down. An exhausted Clay left Washington in August to regain his shattered health. Stephen A. Douglas, Democratic senator from Illinois, presented Clay's proposals, which he rewrote, one by one, in September 1850; one by one, they passed.[625] There were just enough senators willing to compromise to tilt each proposal toward acceptance, while the extremists on both sides approved or disapproved as they saw fit.

But once the sectional sound and fury faded away, what did it all mean? The crisis was the result of the ongoing aggression of slaveholding Democrats who, not content with the ironclad Constitutional protection of

---

[621] Potter, *Impending Crisis*, 94.

[622] Smith, *Presidencies*, 102

[623] Smith, *Presidencies*, 98.

[624] For a good overview, see Holman Hamilton, *Prologue to Conflict: The Crisis and Compromise of 1850* (1964; repr., 2005).

[625] Hamilton, *Prologue to* Conflict, 187.

slavery, kept insisting on their right to seek new slave territory.[626] While the Compromise was "the product of Northern Democrats' looking to please the Southern party leaders," the end result was "Southern aggression and Northern acquiescence."[627]

The Compromise of 1850 did not produce a genuine meeting of minds. It avoided the divisive implications of the Wilmot Proviso on the one hand and a denial of the right of territorial legislatures to deal with slavery on the other. The affirmation of popular sovereignty was enough to lay the issue to rest temporarily.[628] The Compromise did buy time—ten years, in fact— during which the North became even stronger in comparison with the South. But then the war came, so in retrospect the Compromise only the prologue to armed conflict. The problem was that it demanded "an unusual degree of sustained skill, anticipation, delicacy, and elevation of outlook in the White House," but these qualities "were not forthcoming."[629] The compromise would have worked only if the South had abandoned its increasingly vociferous demands for more slave territory. Ultimately, not all the concessions of Northern Democrats would be sufficient to satisfy these demands. With the passing of Henry Clay and Daniel Webster, the remaining leader of stature was Stephen A. Douglas, who had shepherded the Compromise through Congress. Yet Douglas, by an act of colossal misjudgment, soon negated the benefits of the Compromise he had labored so assiduously to enact. The United States was soon to become a House Dividing.

---

[626] Smith, *Presidencies*, 192.

[627] Michael Todd Landis, *Northern Men with Southern Loyalties: The Democratic Party and the Sectional Crisis* (2014), 36.

[628] There has been some confusion regarding the right of territorial legislatures to deal with slavery. However, Robert B. Russel's close study of the acts for the New Mexico and Utah territories clearly shows that Congress had conferred that right on the legislatures. Russel, "What Was the Compromise of 1850?" *Journal of Southern History* 22 (1956): 292–309. The problem was that these acts were not regarded as definitive, so the issue remained unresolved. Potter comments that the acts gave the territories "as much control over slavery as Congress could constitutionally delegate" without spelling out the legal extent of such delegation. Potter, *Impending Crisis*, 270.

[629] Hamilton, *Prologue to Conflict*, 187.

CHAPTER NINE: HOUSE DIVIDING, 1850–1860

During the 1850s, Southern Democrats made increasingly aggressive proslavery demands with the ultimate goal of nationalizing slavery, a goal apparently made feasible by the increasing capitulation of Northern Democrats.[630] But all the capitulation was ultimately to no avail. As Winston Churchill admonished Neville Chamberlain in the aftermath of the Munich Agreement of 1938: "You were given the choice between war and dishonor. You chose dishonor, and you will have war."[631] Northern Democrats anticipated this choice by over eighty years. They chose dishonor in the 1850s and got the war in 1861.

The Compromise of 1850 bought time but no sectional concord. Whatever relief anyone, North or South, might have felt during the sputtering remains of Millard Fillmore's caretaker administration was quickly dispelled by the election of 1852 and the ensuing presidency of Franklin Pierce. This election campaign was dominated by the determination of both parties to say as little as possible about slavery; the silence had a surreal quality. Most people knew that the next crisis was imminent.

---

[630]Chapter title: The title alludes to Abraham Lincoln's "House Divided" speech which was delivered in Springfield, Illinois, on June 16, 1858. The phrase is itself an allusion to Jesus' saying in Mark 3:25 regarding the fatal effects of disunity.

Northern Democrats consistently sought "to please the South" by combatting the rise of Northern antislavery sentiment. In doing so, they "helped produce the legislation and policies that tore the nation apart." Landis, *Northern Men*, 6. In a brief historiographical survey, Landis also notes that this topic has received "shockingly scant attention" (6).
[631]www. goodreads. com/quotes /614924.

The presidential nominations of both parties indicate how unprepared they were to deal with the looming crisis. Seen from one angle, the differences between the parties seemed fairly benign. They were non-ideological, based as much as possible on "consensus rather than divisiveness."[632] The Democrats had "a generalized and mildly populistic orientation" while the Whigs had "an equally mild orientation toward property values."[633] There was also some convergence on economic issues, particularly on internal improvements; more and more Democrats were willing to accept them, given the realities of western expansion. But this Pollyannish consensus theory works only if slavery is ignored.[634]

The Whig convention of 1852 reinforced this conclusion. The party was teetering on the edge of extinction. It was running out of leaders. Just beneath the surface was a growing tension between antislavery Conscience Whigs of the North and the Cotton Whigs of the South.[635] The way out was to avoid the whole question and just win the election. On the fifty-third ballot, the Whigs chose Winfield Scott, a slaveholder. Because he enjoyed the backing of New York Whig William Seward, many Southern Whigs distrusted him, so he went into the campaign as a badly compromised candidate.[636] The Democrats in 1852 faced a similar problem, a decade-long search for reliable "doughfaces"—Northern men with Southern loyalties.[637] The Democrats did have one advantage. They could count on the reliable support of Southern Democrats, so they were able to be more forthright in support of slavery. Even so, they cautiously couched their support under the banner of states' rights. They would resist "all attempts" to review the slavery issue wherever it surfaced by following a states'-rights course.[638]

At the Democratic convention, Lewis Cass, James Buchanan, and Stephen A. Douglas, all perceived to be reliable doughfaces, cancelled each

---

[632] Potter, *Impending Crisis*, 226.

[633] William E. Gianapp, *Origins of the Republican Party, 1852–1856* (1987), 35. Generally speaking, the Whigs won the argument on economic policy, and it was a good thing for the benefit of a burgeoning nation in the throes of a market revolution.

[634] The Democratic Party can be construed as nonideological only if a relentless proslavery agenda is nonideological. Behind the democratic façade of the Jacksonians crouched "a deeper, darker agenda" of proslavery activism. See Landis, *Northern Men*, 3.

[635] Whigs had always "reacted against slavery much more strongly than did Northern Democrats." Potter, *Impending Crisis*, 226.

[636] Seward's speech during the Compromise of 1850 debates on March 1, 1850, evoking "a higher law than the Constitution" as the basis for his opposition to slavery, made him anathema to a South increasingly outraged by any moral objections to slavery. His support of the slaveholder Scott reflected the lack of other viable candidates.

[637] In 1820, John Randolph introduced the term in a speech in which he was denouncing men without principles. Over time, the term "became a synonym for 'northern men with Southern principles.'" Richards, *Slave Power*, 85–86.

[638] Michael F. Holt, *The Political Crisis of the 1850s* (1983), 72.

other out. On the forty-ninth ballot, the party chose Franklin Pierce of New Hampshire, who turned out to be "a magnificent presidential candidate" but "a catastrophically weak president." He was "an empty page upon which each Democratic faction could project their own views."[639] The result of the election of 1852 was a foregone conclusion with Pierce cruising to an overwhelming victory in the Electoral College 254–42 and carrying twenty-seven of the thirty-one states. The fate of the Free-Soil Party confirms this point. Its major campaign position was to urge the federal government to adopt an antislavery agenda, which was the equivalent of asking the nation to sit on a keg of dynamite and light the fuse. The campaign with John P. Hale heading the ticket was "lifeless," and for a time "political antislavery was in eclipse."[640]

The election was significant for several reasons. It brought an inept man into the White House as the nation hovered on the brink of a daunting resurgence of the slavery controversy. It was the last election before the Civil War in which two national political parties competed. The Whig Party crumbled and died.[641] Scott was a terrible candidate, wandering ineffectually over the country making "blundering speeches and impulsive comments."[642]

Any Whig candidate would have faced formidable obstacles in addition to the question of slavery. The mid-1850s saw the rise of powerful ethno-cultural issues, primarily temperance, nativism, and anti-Catholicism, which found political expression in the rise of the American or Know-Nothing Party.[643] For a time, this party seemed unstoppable. It was a powerful factor in the demise of the Whig Party and in the dissolution of the second party system. The party complicated the emergence of the Republican Party after 1854.[644]

But the Democrats had little time to savor Pierce's victory before the onset of many problems. The ticking time bomb menacing Democrats is conveyed by one compelling statistic—for every vote Pierce received in the free states,

---

[639] Elbridge B. Smith, *The Presidency of James Buchanan* (1975), 238. Physically impressive, Pierce was inclined to depression and alcohol. His Mexican War service was dismissed by Whigs because of his reputation as the "Hero of many a well-fought bottle." Landis, *Northern Men*, 72.

[640] Mayfield, *Rehearsal for Republicanism*, 181, 183.

[641] Gienapp, *Origins of the Republican Party*, 32.

[642] Larry Gara, *The Presidency of Franklin Pierce* (1996), 38.

[643] Gienapp, *Origins of the Republican Party*, 66.

[644] Lincoln commented that "When the Know-Nothings get control, [The Declaration of Independence] will read 'All men are created equal except Negroes and foreigners or Catholics.'" Schweikart and Allen, *Patriot's History*, 276. Yet since the Catholic Church was conservative on social issues, opponents of slavery saw the issue as "freedom, temperance, and Protestantism against slavery, rum, and Romanism." McPherson, *Battle Cry*, 137.

one copy of Harriet Beecher Stowe's antislavery bestseller *Uncle Tom's Cabin* (1852) was sold.[645] Yet it is at this point that the demands of Southern Democrats began a steady escalation which led to greater antislavery resistance in the North. The death blow which the Whig Party had received in 1852 meant that the only viable national party left was the Democratic Party, but it was a highly factionalized party under growing sectional strain.

The Pierce administration witnessed a resumption of Southern aggressiveness which began with the expansionism of Polk.[646] Pierce's inaugural address of March 4, 1853, had a schizophrenic quality. With an incredibly tin ear, he pledged to support strict enforcement of the Fugitive Slave Act, which in the North was obviously the most unpopular aspect of the Compromise of 1850 because it "brought to life the plight of human beings who had escaped from slavery."[647] But then he expressed "a fervent hope that the slave question was at rest."[648] His immediate problem, fitting irony for a Democratic president, was the perennial issue of patronage. Here things went wrong through good intentions. Pierce tried to manage patronage to please everyone, but he wound up pleasing no one. Spreading patronage around the various Democratic factions "proved an unmitigated disaster," primarily because Southern Democrats opposed anyone they could remotely brand as antislavery.[649] Pierce quickly learned that he could obtain unity only by following "a solidly pro-Southern, unassailably proslavery course."[650]

Pierce's handling of economic issues reflects his subservience to Southern interests. Despite what had been a bipartisan convergence on economic issues, Pierce assumed the mantle of Democratic economic orthodoxy, even though many rank-and-file Democrats were open to greater flexibility. Pierce consistently voted against internal improvements and lower land prices, showing a "callous indifference to the needs and interests of the Midwest."[651] He also supported lowering the historically low Walker Tariff as part of an effort to keep the Democrats from being "shivered to atoms" by

---

[645] Potter, *Impending Crisis*, 143. Lincoln described Harriet Beecher Stowe as "the little woman who wrote the book that made this great war."

[646] The Mexican War was "an unabashed grab for more slave territory." Landis, *Northern Men*, 5.

[647] Gara, *Presidency of Franklin Pierce*, 48; Potter, *Impending Crisis*, 130. Abolitionists quickly grasped its propaganda value and "focused all the energies . . . upon the fugitive question" (132).

[648] Gara, *Presidency of Franklin Pierce*, 48.

[649] Holt, *Franklin Pierce*, 67. His patronage policy was "lacking in success, if not an absolute failure." Roy Nichols, *Young Hickory of the Granite Hills* (1958), 292.

[650] Landis, *Northern Men*, 89.

[651] Holt, *Franklin Pierce*, 25. Southerners feared that lower land prices would cause an influx of antislavery, free-soil white settlers.

factionalism.[652] He gave only "qualified approval" to a transcontinental railroad.[653] His Jacksonian orthodoxy even extended to his veto of a bipartisan bill sponsored by the reformer Dorothea Dix, providing funds for the hospitalization of the indigent insane, because the government should not be the "almoner of public charity."[654]

Pierce was always a reliable doughface who did not perceive any moral issue regarding slavery, which involved no "moral or ethical question" because slaves "had no rights at all."[655] Since he denied any ethical dimension to the issue, he could not understand the antislavery movement. His bitterness against abolitionists "amounted to hate."[656] Pierce was incapable of providing any judicious leadership for the nation as a whole when the slavery controversy was dramatically rekindled during his presidency.[657] The trigger for this rekindling was an acceleration of expansionism and its powerfully disruptive connection to the acquisition of slave territory. There were two dimensions to the issue: continental and transcontinental. The Democratic Party was the driving engine behind both. Only a few years after the enactment of the Compromise of 1850, it resurfaced dramatically in connection with Kansas and the Caribbean. Territorial aspirations in the Caribbean were more grandiose, but westward expansion in Kansas–Nebraska was far more dangerous.

Pierce was an eager advocate of both kinds of expansion. In his inaugural address, he described the Mexican War as "just and proper," asserting that he would "not be controlled by any timid forebodings of evil from expansion."[658] The Democrats denounced Whig caution regarding expansion as a "failure to uphold the national honor." Pierce was also a proponent of the Young America movement, a coterie of mostly younger Democratic expansionists, which was always demanding that "territory must be acquired."[659] The most flamboyant expression of Caribbean ambition was articulated by the Knights of the Golden Circle, an expansionist group organized in the mid-1850s. The issue was a projected "golden circle of slave states" running from the American South through Mexico and Central America to the rim of South

---

[652] Holt, *Franklin Pierce*, 70–71.

[653] Holt, *Franklin Pierce*, 53–54.

[654] Gara, *Presidency of Franklin Pierce*, 78.

[655] Gara, *Presidency of Franklin Pierce*, 78

[656] Nichols, *Franklin Pierce*, 488.

[657] The depth of Pierce's pro-Southern extremism was fully revealed during the Civil War. He was in "open opposition" to the Union war effort and "became increasingly bitter" during its course. Nichols, *Franklin Pierce*, 521–22.

[658] Potter, *Impending Crisis*, 181.

[659] Nichols, *Franklin Pierce*, 330. Nichols denounced Pierce's "almost unbelievable stupidity" in granting the group such influence (544).

America and through the West Indies to Key West.[660] Thomas Jefferson's vision of an empire of liberty had been transmogrified into a nightmarish empire of human bondage expressed by the desire to "plant American liberty with Southern institutions upon every inch of American soil."[661]

The Caribbean ambitions of the South started with Cuba. Reflecting the views of Southern slavery expansionists, Pierce very much wanted to acquire it, but he could not settle on a coherent policy to do so effectively. Pierre Soule, his minister to Spain, was a volatile Louisiana Frenchman whose reckless temperament was matched by poor judgment. He exceeded his instructions by acting as though his mission was to acquire Cuba "by hook or crook."[662] Pierce had not authorized purchase negotiations, but Soule had been told that the administration "hoped" that Cuba would "release itself or be released" from Spanish control.[663] The result of Soule's erratic behavior and the murkiness of the intent of the Pierce administration was not so much a policy as a series of spasmodic actions which ended badly.[664]

Because the Spanish were reluctant to sell Cuba, various filibustering expeditions, primarily one headed by John A. Quitman of Mississippi, were planned. He had met with Pierce in July 1853 and announced his intention to "strike with effect" in Cuba "after the fashion of Texas."[665] Quitman proceeded to raise men and money in preparation for an invasion. However, by the spring of 1854, the winds had shifted. Pierce signed the Kansas–Nebraska Act on May 30, 1854, and, sensing the gathering storm, he decided that one big fight was enough. He struck at Quitman's filibustering project by upholding the nation's neutrality laws, sending a clear warning to him. This may well have been "the most decisive step that Pierce took during the four years of his presidency."[666]

But this was not yet the end of the comic-opera aspects of the Cuban issue, because Soule "characteristically contrived to terminate it with one more bang."[667] In August 1854, he arranged a meeting in Ostend, Belgium, with two other American ministers in Europe—James Buchanan, minister to Great Britain, and James M. Mason, minister to France. In October 1854, he somehow managed to get his diplomatic peers to put their names on the so-called Ostend Manifesto, which asserted that Cuba was "necessary"

---

[660] McPherson, *Battle Cry of Freedom*, 116.

[661] McPherson, *Battle Cry of Freedom*, 116.

[662] Potter, *Impending Crisis*, 185.

[663] Potter, *Impending Crisis*, 185.

[664] Potter, *Impending Crisis*, 184–86, especially footnote 20, 185–86.

[665] McPherson, *Battle Cry of Freedom*, 108–9.

[666] Potter, *Impending Crisis*, 188–89.

[667] Potter, *Impending Crisis*, 189.

to the "North American Republic."[668] Soule had not bothered to keep the meeting secret, and when the story broke there was widespread consternation. Abolitionists, already mobilized over Kansas, were outraged, and "the shell-shocked administration forced Soule's resignation and abandoned all schemes to obtain Cuba."[669]

While the Ostend Manifesto had its buffoonish aspects, it was significant nonetheless because Northern opponents of slavery saw the whole episode as yet another effort by an insidious Slave Power to create a slave empire and, in conjunction with the issue of Kansas, it greatly accentuated sectional distrust. Both the struggle over Kansas and the Ostend Manifesto represent ill-considered overreaches by proslavery Southern expansionists who seemed to vindicate the most extravagant Northern fears of Southern aggression. But for all the bluster of Young America activists, the only land acquired from a foreign power during the 1850s was the Gadsden Purchase, acquired from Mexico in December 1853. James Gadsden, the U.S. ambassador to Mexico, negotiated the purchase of 38,000 square miles in what are now the southern parts of Arizona and New Mexico for $15 million in order to provide a Southern route for a transcontinental railroad. In normal times, the treaty would have sailed easily through the Senate, but it was rejected on April 17, 1854. Then, after a reduction of 9,000 square miles, the Senate approved the purchase for $10 million. Even so, the treaty "squeaked through" because of Northern fears of the acquisition of additional slave territory.[670]

It is in this atmosphere of deepening sectional distrust that the crisis of "Bleeding Kansas" unfolded. There has probably never been a greater gap between the intentions behind a piece of legislation and the actual results achieved. The Kansas–Nebraska Act released the coiled spring of the slaveholders' obsession with the expansion of slave territory which Northern opposition made even more virulent. It was the "most divisive piece of legislation that Congress passed before the Civil War—and maybe the most divisive in the entire history of the nation."[671] Its impact on the political parties was transformative. It "killed the Whig party, divided and weakened the Democrats, and sparked the rise of the Republicans."[672] It created the political party system which, by destroying the two national parties, led directly to the Civil War. The most important politician in this unfolding saga was Illinois senator Stephen A. Douglas, who did *not* intend to precipitate a

[668] McPherson, *Battle Cry of Freedom*, 110.

[669] McPherson, *Battle Cry*, 130.

[670] Potter, *Impending Crisis*, 183.

[671] Richards, *Slave Power*, 184.

[672] Schweikart and Allen, *Patriot's History*, 293.

national crisis. Rather, he was acting on his belief that the West was "the balance wheel of the Republic" and "the hope of this nation."[673]

But there was also a partisan issue involved. Douglas was interested in pushing Kansas because he was casting about for an issue to "reignite inter-party combat" by uniting Democrats.[674] But, paradoxically, he sought to do this by using an issue with some Whiggish overtones. He was committed to both commercial and geographical expansion because only this could prevent the growth of "an unpropertied class, the bane of democracy."[675] His record was mixed on specific issues. He opposed "banks of all kinds," especially a national bank.[676] He also supported tariffs for revenue only. However, his Whiggish side emerged with his consistent approval for Federal support for internal improvements, a stance which brought opposition from Southerners.

The most important internal improvement was a transcontinental railroad. Even though the railroad would benefit Douglas personally and politically, most historians do not ascribe his actions to "ignoble motives."[677] Even so, it is not possible to absolve him of catastrophically bad judgment. Both Douglas and the Democratic Party leadership used terrible judgment during the entire crisis period. Democratic politicians continued to make "short-term calculations of partisan, factional, and personal advantage" rather than focus on the well-being of the country and "the very preservation of the Union."[678]

In the deceptive calm after the Compromise of 1850, even experienced politicians might be excused for failing to anticipate the looming explosion. But once Douglas introduced the Kansas–Nebraska bill in January 1854, all illusions should have been blown away. Regarding the central issue of slavery, two things were occurring simultaneously. While the majority of Northerners were not and never became out-and-out abolitionists, there certainly were growing misgivings about slavery and a growing reluctance to acquiesce to its continuing extension.[679] But at the same time, many South-

---

[673] Gerald M. Capers, *Stephen A. Douglas: Defender of the Union* (1959), 87.

[674] Holt, *Franklin Pierce*, 73.

[675] James L. Huston, *Stephen A. Douglas and the Dilemmas of Democratic Equality* (2004), 45.

[676] A national bank was "more to be feared" than "the great Nahant Sea-Serpent." Johannsen, *Douglas*, 121.

[677] Martin H. Quitt, *Stephen A. Douglas* (2012), 119.

[678] Michael F. Holt, *The Fate of Their Country: Politicians, Slavery Extension, and the Coming of the Civil War* (2004), 97.

[679] Like all zealous reformers, abolitionists could easily become insufferable. Particularly objectionable was their use of the politics of personal destruction. They were all too ready to attack defenders of slavery not merely as mistaken but as "vicious, dishonest, and evil." But this tactic was effective only in producing greater estrangement. Potter, *Impending Crisis*, 163–64.

erners were becoming more and more anxious not merely to defend slavery in the states where it existed but also to see it expand into new western territories.

Shrewd and perceptive as he often was, this is the key point which Douglas missed completely. The measure which he intended to help unify the Democratic Party wound up shattering it. At least part of the problem was Douglas's own opinion regarding slavery. "In his private and personal thinking," he may well have been "an antislavery man."[680] But it is also clear that he lacked any fundamental sense of the moral evil of slavery, so he stood by the essential idea of popular sovereignty as the democratic way of coping with slavery expansion. However, he also had a personal connection with slavery after his wife inherited a Mississippi plantation of 2500 acres and a hundred slaves, which became one of his most dependable sources of income. He always said that he wanted to end this link with slavery, but, like so many ostensibly reluctant slaveholders, he never did, a fact which affords "a deep understanding of why slavery endured and so easily conquered idealism."[681] Douglas clearly had no wish to see slavery expand into Kansas. On the slave issue, he regarded himself as a realist who did not think the Midwest was suitable for slavery. But this kind of realism was ill-equipped to deal with profound moral issues, and it was the moral aspect of the question which had been growing inexorably more intense. The South was an increasingly isolated slave enclave. Southerners responded with an aggressive defense, touting slavery as a positive good.[682] The central divide was the moral issue for which political solutions were inadequate.

The issue might have been manageable, in the short term at least, but for the destabilizing impact of territorial expansion. When Douglas introduced the Kansas–Nebraska Act on January 23, 1854, in order to facilitate statehood for Kansas, he quickly learned that he had produced a crisis. The Kansas–Nebraska Territory lies north of the 36° 30' Missouri Compromise line, making it free territory. Southerners demanded an explicit repeal of the Missouri Compromise with an intensity that boded no good for sectional peace. Douglas added a section to the bill that left slavery up to the people of the territories by virtue of popular sovereignty—a section which, the

---

[680] Potter, *Impending Crisis*, 329–30. He also believed in the inferiority of blacks, stating this belief "with brutal frankness" (340).

[681] Huston, *Stephen A. Douglas*, 54. He had supported the Gag Rule and had "a deep repugnance" for abolitionists. Johannsen, *Stephen A. Douglas*, 237.

[682] In a speech to the Senate on February 6, 1837, John C. Calhoun asserted, "Never before has the black race of Central Africa, from the dawn of history to the present day, attained a condition so civilized and so improved, not only physically but morally and intellectually." So in his eyes, slavery was, in fact, "a positive good."

cover story went, had been omitted through "clerical error."[683] This was not enough. The next demand was for an explicit repudiation of the Missouri Compromise. With his back to the wall, Douglas made a virtue of necessity: "By God, Sir, you are right. I will incorporate it in my bill, though I know it will raise a hell of a storm."[684] Blustering while in full retreat, Douglas sent this bill to Congress, where it provoked a three-and-a-half-month struggle "of unprecedented intensity."[685] The ferocity of the debates made the debates of 1850 "seem like a gentle shower."[686]

But if Douglas seemed oblivious to the magnitude of the crisis, Pierce appeared even less aware of political reality. Although he had not even mentioned Kansas in his first annual message, the issue had become a high priority by the end of 1853. Pierce was not only a doughface but a dough-face desperate to regain leadership of the party. He signed off on Kansas at a fateful meeting on January 24, 1854, and made support for the Kansas bill the primary test of party loyalty. He agreed to proclaim the Missouri Compromise to be "inoperative and void." A key factor in this crisis was the growing division between the Northern Democratic leadership, committed to party unity by placating the South, and many Northern Democratic voters who were increasingly alarmed over the expansion of slavery. It was one thing to dismiss what could be seen as the predictable rantings of abolitionist fanatics, but it was not so easy to dismiss the steady shift of Northern public opinion.

The Missouri Compromise had acquired an iconic status as a symbol of sectional compromise. Then suddenly it was repudiated, which led to a sense of betrayal attributable to the malevolent actions of the Slave Power. Perhaps the most dramatic evidence of this growing sentiment was the Appeal of Independent Democrats by six antislavery Democratic congressmen which "foreshadowed a bitter fight by the free-soil Democrats against the bill and against the administration."[687]

Despite mounting opposition, the bill passed the Senate on March 5, 1854, by a comfortable 37–14 margin. In the House, the majority of congressmen opposed the measure, so only the most strenuous effort, strengthened by the Pierce's zealous use of patronage, enabled it to squeeze through on May 22, 1854, by a vote of 113–100. It passed only because of the three-

---

[683] Potter, *Impending Crisis*, 158–59.
[684] This explicit repudiation was included in the January 16 version of the bill which went to Congress. Potter, *Impending Crisis*, 160.
[685] Potter, *Impending Crisis*, 165.
[686] McPherson, *Battle Cry*, 123.
[687] Potter, *Impending Crisis*, 163.

fifths boost to Southern representation.[688] Pierce signed the bill on May 30, 1854, "expressing the hope that the slavery agitation was forever allayed."[689] Everyone conceded that Douglas's tireless leadership contributed significantly to the outcome. [690] But Douglas could not see what would become the bitter fruit of his success. Popular sovereignty had acquired the status of Douglas's own version of a "higher-law philosophy" which could justify the abandonment of the Missouri Compromise.[691]

Southerners had moved from resistance to the Wilmot Proviso to the embrace of popular sovereignty. But then another issue emerged. Southerners claimed the right to take slaves into the territories. Slavery could be restricted only when a territory applied for statehood. This was to ensure that the territories would certainly become slave states. This position was to "contaminate the doctrine of popular sovereignty by employing it as a device for opening free territory to slavery."[692] The Democratic Party adopted this position in its 1856 party platform.[693] The result was that popular sovereignty proved to be no defense against the expansion of slavery into the West.

The first dramatic sign of the political upheaval caused by the Kansas question was 1854 elections. Voters rebelled "against what they saw as the arrogant demands of the slave power."[694] The Democrats suffered "crushing defeats" because a large number of disillusioned Democrats did not even bother to vote.[695] Only seven of the forty-five Northern Democrats who voted for the Kansas–Nebraska Act won reelection. While this outcome alarmed Northern Democratic leaders, it did not compel them to change their policy of appeasement of the South. The Kansas issue had other significant political effects. The damage did not stop with Democrats in Congress. The Pierce administration was "a second casualty of the elections," while the election was fatal for the Whigs.[696] The growing division between the Conscience and the Cotton Whigs became irreparable. The result was that most Southern Whigs "slithered" into the Democratic Party where "their proslavery principles found a more appropriate home."[697] One of the two

---

[688] Richards, *Slave Power*, 184.

[689] Johannsen, *Stephen A. Douglas*, 434; Nichols, *Franklin Pierce*, 338.

[690] Nichols, *Franklin Pierce*, 338.

[691] Johannsen, *Stephen A. Douglas*, 421.

[692] Potter, *Impending Crisis*, 173.

[693] Capers, *Stephen A. Douglas*, 148

[694] Gara, *Presidency of Franklin Pierce*, 100.

[695] Holt, *Franklin Pierce*, 83.

[696] Gara, *Presidency of Franklin Pierce*, 99–100.

[697] Landis, *Northern Men*, 121. After the election of 1854, Whigs comprised less than 20 percent of the House; 75 percent of them were from the South. Gara, *Presidency of Franklin Pierce*, 99.

great national parties was murdered by the Kansas–Nebraska Act, and the second had received a paralyzing body blow.

Two new parties appeared in this turbulent situation. The American (Know-Nothing) Party seemed very strong in 1854 and for several years afterward. It reflected the powerful opposition to the mass immigration of the 1840s and 1850s. It also derived much strength from the longstanding animus against Catholicism since colonial times by an overwhelmingly Protestant America. The party had nationwide aspirations, but it was strongest in the North. However, it also split along sectional lines, suffering "a remarkable eclipse" after 1854.[698] The Republican Party never had any realistic national ambitions, being a Northern party from its beginning, and yet it "surged" in strength in the mid-1850s.[699] The reason was simple—many Northerners had concluded that "the slave power was after all a much greater threat to republican liberty than the Pope was."[700] The emergence of the Republican Party, which was not abolitionist but which opposed the expansion of slavery, triggered vicious anti-black racism by the Democrats who thereafter stigmatized Republicans as "Black Republicans."[701]

The spectacle of "Bleeding Kansas" was the primary cause of this political upheaval. The signing of the Kansas–Nebraska Act was not the end of the slavery agitation but the prelude to a much more intense phase. Despite the ostensible commitment to popular sovereignty, there was a bitter struggle of pro- and antislavery activists to seize control of Kansas which extended from the remainder of the Pierce administration into that of a yet another doughface, James Buchanan. There were two underlying realities. The first is that the proslavery forces, buttressed by invaders from Missouri known as "Border Ruffians," were determined to impose slavery on Kansas. The second is that Pierce reflexively supported the proslavery side, however egregious its actions proved to be.

The furor over the Kansas–Nebraska Act galvanized an obscure Whig ex-congressman from Illinois. In the fall of 1854, Abraham Lincoln delivered three speeches in opposition to the Kansas–Nebraska Act which catapulted him into the political arena. The most substantive of these, a three-hour oration, was delivered at Peoria, Illinois, on October 16, 1854, with Douglas in attendance. Lincoln's "Speech on the Repeal of the Missouri Compromise" is a closely reasoned, sustained analysis of what he clearly understood to be a new intensity of slaveholder aggression. Lincoln clearly saw the signifi-

---

[698] McPherson, *Battle Cry*, 144.
[699] McPherson, *Battle Cry*, 144.
[700] McPherson, *Battle Cry*, 144.
[701] Gara, *Presidency of Franklin Pierce*, 78.

cance of violence in Kansas, where one sees "bowie-knives and six-shooters" but "never a glimpse of the ballot-box."[702] In a haunting passage, he asked, "Will not the first drop of blood be the real knell of the Union?" It very nearly was. Lincoln's dissection of the Southern assault on any limitation of slave expansion is infused with a profound sense of the evil of slavery. Slavery for Lincoln could never be anything other than an inherited evil and a national tragedy.[703] It was an evil to be contained until its final disappearance. Southerners could dismiss the often-extravagant rhetoric of the abolitionists as unhinged. But it was not so easy to escape the quiet yet resonant power of Lincoln's eloquence. His speech was both a critique of what would make the 1850s the decade of Southern aggression and a prescient analysis of how events would unfold in "Bleeding Kansas."

The bowie-knives and six-shooters Lincoln alluded to were very much in evidence in Kansas. The election for the territorial legislature in March 1855 was marred by armed proslavery intimidation. This, in turn, triggered an antislavery convention in September 1855, a free-state legislature, and a free-state Topeka constitution in the fall of 1855. In January 1856, a free-state governor and legislature were elected. There were two governments in Kansas in 1856, leading to a civil war which extended from May 1856 through the end of the year. The worst month was undoubtedly May which saw the "sack" of Lawrence by proslavery forces, the Pottawatomie Massacre by the violent abolitionist John Brown, and the spill-over in the Senate with the caning of Senator Charles Sumner by Congressman Preston Brooks.[704]

In his final annual message, Franklin Pierce blamed "antislavery fanatics" for the troubles in Kansas; they had given the South "cause of war."[705] Nevertheless, Southerners turned against him because he had been "proslavery in intent, but not proslavery enough in product."[706] Kansas was in turmoil; Cuba had not been acquired, and Northern Democrats had been crushed in recent elections. Southern Democrats were blaming Pierce for the failure of their own policies. Undeterred, they began casting about for his replacement. Since they knew that a Southerner could not win in 1856, they turned to the

---

[702] Abraham Lincoln, "Speech on the Repeal of the Missouri Compromise."

[703] Lincoln argued that the Founders also regarded it so as evidenced by the Northwest Ordinance and the abolition of the foreign slave trade.

[704] Each of these events had the effect of deepening the sectional estrangement. The so-called "sack" of Lawrence was undoubtedly exaggerated, but it certainly inflamed Northern public opinion. Southerners were outraged by the cold-blooded murder of proslavery settlers by John Brown. The near-fatal assault on Sumner was widely regarded by Northerners as evidence of a Southern proclivity to violence.

[705] Landis, Northern Men, 141.

[706] Landis, Northern Men, 142.

doughface James Buchanan with his "untarnished proslavery reputation."[707] His nomination was a "resounding triumph for the South."[708] But the real enablers of the Southern slaveholding aggression of the 1850s were the Northern Democratic leaders who "did all they could to make their conservative, proslavery agenda appealing to the free-state voters."[709] The rise of the Republican Party, which appeared suddenly and nearly full grown, demonstrated the limitations of this strategy. Like a slow political virus, the venerable proslavery alliance forged by Martin Van Buren was bringing the Union to the brink of destruction.

The most significant political factor in 1856 was not the Democratic selection of Buchanan. It was not the American Party candidacy of Millard Fillmore.[710] It was the dramatic emergence of the Republican Party, fueled by the fallout from the Kansas–Nebraska Act, which caused a portentous realignment of the two-party system. For Democrats, the selection of Buchanan was a foregone conclusion. Both Pierce and Douglas, each with significant liabilities, withdrew. Buchanan was the safest doughface candidate, with the additional advantage that he was undamaged by the Kansas imbroglio.[711] The Democratic platform encompassed the "old Jacksonian chestnuts" in its domestic program—limited government and opposition to a national bank and internal improvements.[712] Their domestic program had been fossilized despite a dynamically changing economy. The Republicans, by contrast, offered a free-labor philosophy which reflected its commitment to small-scale capitalism. Its identification with "the aspirations of farmers, small entrepreneurs, and craftsmen" gave their program "its dynamic, progressive, and optimistic quality."[713]

On the issue of slavery in the territories, the contrast was clear. The Democrats wanted all the slavery they could get by whatever means. Democrats paid lip service to popular sovereignty which was meaningless in light

---

[707] Landis, *Northern Men*, 143.

[708] Landis, *Northern Men*, 152.

[709] Landis, *Northern Men*, 152. As early as 1842, James Buchanan proclaimed that "All Christendom is leagued against the South upon the question of domestic slavery," so slaveholders "have no other allies to sustain their constitutional rights except the Democracy of the North." The *Congressional Globe*, August 19, 1842, quoted in Howe, *Transformation*, 524.

[710] The American Party had already peaked in 1854–55; it was beset by sectional division and overshadowed by the Republicans.

[711] He had served as U.S. ambassador to Great Britain.

[712] McPherson, *Battle Cry*, 157.

[713] Eric Foner, *Free Soil, Free Labor, Free Men: The Ideology of the Republican Party before the Civil War* (1970), 316. Foner gives an excellent account of the dynamic Republican free-labor position. This was basically "the ancient Whig program." See also McPherson, *Battle Cry*, 155.

of their denial of the right of the people in a territory to restrict slavery until they applied for statehood. The position of Republicans was simple—they opposed slavery in the territories. The expansion of slavery was seen as a betrayal of the promise of America as an exemplar of freedom and democracy. For many Republicans, Southern insistence on expanding slavery in the territories was merely a prelude to what Lincoln feared as the ultimate nightmare—"a paramount common danger" of the "spread and nationalization of slavery."[714] In taking this stance, the Republicans saw themselves as "one part of a worldwide movement from absolutism to democracy."[715]

The emergence of the Republican Party would have been greatly enhanced by the selection of a viable presidential candidate in 1856, but this was not to be. Lincoln was still several years from national prominence. The logical choice was William Seward of New York. However, Thurlow Weed, the emerging Republican kingmaker, was convinced that the Republicans could not win in 1856. He decided not to "waste" Seward in a hopeless contest. The choice then fell upon John C. Fremont, a well-known military officer and western explorer. He was regarded as "young and vigorous, a great popular hero."[716] Unfortunately for the Republicans, his nomination represented the "triumph of image over achievement."[717] He was a bad candidate whose "ineptitude left a leadership void."[718]

Seen from one angle, the election results were not surprising. Buchanan won the electoral vote easily 174–114, but he received only 45 percent of the popular vote.[719] The election did show "the completeness of sectionalization" because, with the exception of Ohio, all eleven Fremont states were farther north than Buchanan's twenty states.[720] Buchanan enjoyed the advantage of the fear factor. Democrats dropped broad hints that a Fremont victory would mean disunion.[721] There was also the race card. Buchanan urged that "the Black Republicans must be . . . boldly assailed as disunionists, and this charge must be reiterated again and again."[722] Seen from another angle, the result was surprising. A brand-new party, poorly organized and running an inferior candidate, had nonetheless become a national political force within

---

[714] Quoted by Gianapp, *Origins of the Republican Party*, 448. Lincoln also feared that the slaveholders would try to use the Fifth Amendment to force a nationwide acceptance of slavery by means of a Supreme Court decision. Potter, *Impending Crisis*, 349–51.

[715] Foner, *Free Soil*, 72.

[716] Gianapp, *Origins of the Republican Party*, 321.

[717] Gianapp, *Origins of the Republican Party*, 341.

[718] Gianapp, *Origins of the Republican Party*, 411.

[719] Schweikart and Allen, *Patriot's History*, 298. Fillmore carried only Maryland.

[720] Potter, *Impending Crisis*, 364–65.

[721] McPherson, *Battle Cry*, 158; Potter, *Impending Crisis*, 263.

[722] McPherson, *Battle Cry*, 158.

two years of its inception. The election revealed the ongoing process of political sectionalization. The Democratic success was an "ominous victory."[723] The Republican failure was a "victorious defeat," demonstrating that it was the party of the future.[724]

At the beginning of Buchanan's presidency, there was an earthquake of a Supreme Court decision. The efforts of Dred Scott, an obscure slave, to secure his freedom with the aid of sympathetic whites on the basis of temporary residence in free territory powerfully contributed to the sectional tensions. After a complicated history of judicial wrangling, the case finally landed in the Supreme Court.[725] It seemed initially that the case might be decided only on narrow jurisdictional grounds with little political impact. But the election of Buchanan changed this. Everything suddenly shifted between February 14 and February 19, 1857. Buchanan put his thumb on the judicial scale by urging Justice Robert C. Grier of Pennsylvania, at the suggestion of Justice John Catron of Tennessee, to go along with "a comprehensive judgment" to settle the issue of slavery in the territories once and for all.[726] Buchanan exerted "highly improper but efficacious influence."[727] The Supreme Court in 1857 consisted of five Southerners and four Northerners. The acquiescence of Grier provided the desired political cover for a far-reaching proslavery decision.

Buchanan's meddling enabled Chief Justice Roger B. Taney to write "an opinion he had long wanted to write."[728] Although Taney, a Jacksonian Democrat from Maryland, had freed his own slaves, he was primarily interested nonetheless in the "defense of slavery" and was deeply angry at what he saw as "Northern aggression."[729] The result was a seven-to-two decision which both by the timing of its delivery and its content generated an immense political storm. In his inaugural address of March 4, 1857, Buchanan slid glibly over the issue of when the people of a territory could decide the issue of slavery for themselves as "a matter of little practical importance." He predicted that the issue will "be speedily and finally settled."[730] Three days later, the shockingly proslavery decision was announced.

---

[723] Schweikart and Allen, *Patriot's History*, 277.

[724] Holt, *Franklin Pierce*, 110.

[725] The best source on all ramifications of the case is Don E. Fehrenbacher, *Slavery, Law, and Politics: The Dred Scott Case in Historical Perspective* (1981).

[726] Jean H. Baker, *James Buchanan* (2004), 84.

[727] McPherson, *Battle Cry*, 173; see also Potter, *Impending Crisis*, 274.

[728] McPherson, *Battle Cry*, 173–74.

[729] McPherson, *Battle Cry*, 173–74.

[730] Inaugural Address, March 4, 1857, American Presidency Project. The phrase "finally settled" indicates that he knew what was coming.

But if the timing of the decision was suspicious, its content was devastating. Taney seized the opportunity to "solve" the problem of slavery in the territories once and for all. The Court ruled that since blacks were not, and could not be, citizens, they did not have the right to sue. Furthermore, Congress had no power to regulate slavery in the territories; any attempt to do so (such as the Missouri Compromise) was unconstitutional. So "in essence," the Court ruled that "slavery could spread anywhere prior to statehood and that the government was powerless to stop it—the ultimate vindication of the Slave Power."[731] Lurking in the background was the specter of the nationalization of slavery. The willingness of Taney to invoke the Fifth Amendment in defense of property rights meant that the fear of nationalization was a realistic one. Soon after the decision was announced, Lincoln asserted that Republicans had been drawn together by "a paramount danger" which he defined as "the spread and nationalization of slavery."[732]

Both William Seward and Lincoln described the decision in conspiratorial terms which "hit uncomfortably close to the mark."[733] It was evidence of the growing hyperaggression of slaveholders to absolutize their right to take their slaves anywhere, which would convert the American "charter of freedom into a safeguard of slavery."[734] The decision was unacceptable to Republicans; it undercut their reason for existence. Lincoln's attitude can be taken as representative; he did not believe that the decision should be regarded as final. He argued that the Supreme Court on occasion had overturned its own decisions, and in general he denied the doctrine of "unqualified judicial supremacy."[735]

The *Dred Scott* decision undercut Stephen Douglas's support of popular sovereignty. His response to the decision has become known as the Freeport Doctrine. Douglas argued that, *Dred Scott* decision or not, the people of a territory could effectively block slavery by the simple expedient of refusing to enact the support legislation essential to its maintenance.[736] Douglas had lost control of the Kansas issue and had been "crashing and hurtling about, caught like a rock in gush of lava."[737] But the Freeport Doctrine was a kind of

---

[731] Landis, *Northern Men*, 170.

[732] "Fragment of the formation of the Republican Party," c. February 28, 1857, quoted in Gianapp, *Origins of the Republican Party*, 448.

[733] McPherson, *Battle Cry*, 178–79.

[734] Potter, *Impending Crisis*, 293.

[735] Fehrenbacher, *Slavery, Law, and Politics*, 243. Lincoln denounced the *Dred Scott* decision as a "burlesque upon judicial decisions." Quoted in Eric Foner, *Fiery Trial: Abraham Lincoln and American Slavery* (2005), 95.

[736] Douglas outlined this position during the Lincoln–Douglas debates at Freeport, Illinois, on August 27, 1858. What slaveholder would take valuable slaves into a territory where there was no provision for the recovery of runaways?

[737] Nichols, "Kansas-Nebraska Act," 212

"residual popular sovereignty."[738] It affirmed the ability of settlers to control slavery in their territories by avoiding the ambiguities of the *Dred Scott* decision. His Freeport Doctrine put him under "fierce Southern attack."[739]

The end result was that the decision which Buchanan had hoped would settle everything actually settled nothing. The *New York Tribune* expressed the attitude of the ever-growing number of Northern antislavery voters by dismissing it as a "dictum" handed down by "five slaveholders and two doughfaces."[740] Emboldened by the *Dred* Scott decision, Buchanan set the tone of his administration at the very outset by appointing a cabinet consisting of "four Southerners and three doughfaces." This was perceived as "an insult to the North."[741] This cabinet was also "among the most corrupt in American history."[742]

The corruption of the Buchanan's administration was not merely in the service of ordinary vices. Buchanan was also using the immense patronage power of his doughface faction to maintain its control, to get his way in Kansas, and to push through his pro-Southern policies. By 1858, Buchanan, having "bribed newspapers and colonized voters," nevertheless discovered that "the impact of federal spoils clearly reached its limit."[743] Buchanan was a mostly orthodox Jacksonian Democrat who supported "strict construction and limited government."[744] The growing problem of his administration is that he became progressively identified with only the doughface faction. He vetoed a Homestead Act and a bill to establish land-grant colleges in the West; both measures were popular among many western Democrats.[745] Many Democrats also opposed any transcontinental railroad that did not follow a southern route. In doing this, they were doing what they had always done; they were resisting economic progress."[746] But at the same time, Buchanan was "one of the most aggressive, hawkish chief executives in American history" in the service of the expansionist ambitions of the South.[747]

The clearest indication that Buchanan had fatally divided the Democratic Party in subservience to the South was his break with Douglas, who had

---

[738] Fehrenbacher, *Slavery, Law, and Politics*, 259.

[739] Fehenbacher, *Slavery, Law, and Politics*, 247.

[740] *New York Tribune*, March 7, 1857, quoted in McPherson, *Battle Cry*, 177; Richards, *Slave Power*, 199.

[741] Baker, *James Buchanan*, 79.

[742] Baker, *James Buchanan*, 114.

[743] Richards, *Slave Power*, 210–11.

[744] Michael J. Birkner, ed., *James Buchanan and the Political Crisis of the 1850s* (1996), 23.

[745] See Baker, *James Buchanan*, 117–18. Both measures were later passed by the Republicans during the Lincoln administration.

[746] Potter, *Impending Crisis*, 392.

[747] Baker, *James Buchanan*, 110.

"campaigned vigorously" for him. Now Buchanan rejected him and all his friends.[748] His perfunctory thank-you after the election was addressed to "The Hon. Samuel A. Douglas." Buchanan permitted his hatred of Douglas to make himself "the chief architect of the Democratic ruin."[749] Douglas was a rival for Democratic leadership, but Buchanan was the president and controlled all the levers of patronage; despite this, Buchanan forced the break. Douglas had a genuine, stubborn commitment to popular sovereignty. After the *Dred Scott* decision, he was driven to uphold it by the desperate expedient of the Freeport Doctrine. But by 1858 at the latest, popular sovereignty had become unacceptable to many Democrats, including Buchanan. So the break came which fractured the united party.

The catalyst for this course of events was the notorious Lecompton Constitution in Kansas.[750] By the fall of 1856, territorial governor John W. Geary had been able to lower the level of violence significantly. However, he was not able to rein in the actions of a virulently proslavery legislature which had been fraudulently elected with the votes of Missouri Border Ruffians in 1855. His efforts to secure genuinely free elections and self-government failed. He resigned and was succeeded by Robert J. Walker of Mississippi, a Buchanan appointee, in early March 1857. Walker pledged that any constitution would be submitted to a fair vote, but the Lecompton constitutional convention, meeting between October 14 and November 8, 1857, ignored his promise. The result was the disastrous Lecompton Constitution, a proslavery "heads I win, tails you lose" document. The only part of the constitution submitted to a popular vote was a special article on slavery. But a no vote on slavery would not negate the right of existing slaveholders to keep their slaves.

This was too much for Walker, who left Kansas on November 8, 1857, "never to return."[751] In Washington, he urged Buchanan to reject the Lecompton Constitution. It was a hopeless mission. Buchanan decided to support it, and Walker, repudiated, resigned on December 17, 1857. The Lecompton Constitution was approved in Kansas on December 21, 1857, with the antislavery men refusing to participate in what they regarded as a rigged election. The Kansas legislature then approved the proslavery constitution on January 4, 1858.

---

[748] Smith, *Presidency of James Buchanan*, 21.

[749] George Fort Milton, *The Eve of Conflict: Stephen A. Douglas and the Needless War* (1934), 506.

[750] Potter's chapter on Lecompton is entitled "Lecompton: The Descent Grows Steeper," *Impending Crisis*, 297-327.

[751] Potter, *Impending Crisis*, 307. Walker was a friend of Douglas and, like him, was committed to an untrammeled exercise of popular sovereignty.

On December 3, 1857, Douglas had a tempestuous interview with Buchanan in which Douglas "became furious" at Buchanan's support of Lecompton, warning that it would "most likely kill the Northern Democracy."[752] Buchanan threatened to "destroy" Douglas if he persisted in his opposition. So "the gage was down," because of Buchanan's folly, "for a duel that would split the Democratic Party and assure the election of a Republican in 1860."[753] Only five days later, Douglas gave the "most significant speech of his career" against the Lecompton Constitution, leaving his future in the Democratic Party "a matter of speculation."[754]

The issue then came before Congress. Despite Douglas's strenuous opposition, the Lecompton bill passed the Senate 33–25 on March 23, 1858. Then it was defeated in the House 120–112 on April 1, 1858. The pro-Lecompton Democrats then resorted to a farcical bit of legislative bribery known as the English Bill.[755] The people of Kansas could approve of the Lecompton Constitution and receive around four million acres of public land; rejection would delay statehood until the population reached the 90,000 required for Congressional representation. Douglas opposed the bill; it squeaked through the Senate 31–22 and the House 112–103 on April 30, 1858. However, the people of Kansas had the last word. On August 2, 1858, they rejected it 11,300 to 1,788. This vote finally put the longstanding upheaval in Kansas to an end.[756] It did not, however, prevent the bitter consequences of the whole Kansas fiasco. Buchanan was in total denial. His annual message of December 6, 1858, had a surreal quality to it.[757] He soared with Olympian serenity over the whole sordid imbroglio which his own policies had done so much to foment. He took credit for resolving a crisis, largely of his own making "with the insouciance that often masked his failures."[758] But very few people on all sides of the issue shared his rosy outlook. Many Northern voters were "appalled at the Lecompton Constitution" and considered it to be a "swindle" and "a grand fraud."[759]

The most dramatic indication of the political fallout from Kansas was the election of 1858. The Democrats had suffered back-to-back debacles in 1854 and 1856. At the time of the Kansas–Nebraska bill, there were ninety-

[752] Landis, *Northern Men*, 179.

[753] McPherson, *Battle Cry*, 166.

[754] Johannsen, *Stephen A. Douglas*, 592-93.

[755] It was introduced by William H. English of Indiana.

[756] Kansas eventually entered the Union as a free state in 1861.

[757] See https://www.presidency.ucsb.edu/documents/second-annual-message-congress-the-state-the-union

[758] Baker, *James Buchanan*, 105.

[759] Landis, *Northern Men*, 179. They were supported in this judgment by an eyewitness, Robert W. Walker, who denounced it as "a vile fraud." McPherson, *Battle Cry*, 165.

three Democrats in the House; by the time of Lecompton, there were only fifty-three. After the election of 1858, the number plummeted to thirty-three. So the Northern wing of the Democratic Party had been "decimated," indicating that "the day of the doughface had passed."[760] Voters were expressing their disapproval of the Lecompton Constitution. Only 7 percent of the pro-Lecompton Democrats were reelected.[761] Buchanan's last year in office was "the worst time in his life," but it was also a bad time for Northern Democrats who were being destroyed by his policies.[762] The venerable Van Buren coalition was crumbling as the Democratic Party, the "one pillar of the old order," was disintegrating.[763] This was happening at the same time that the Republican Party was becoming the majority party.

The most important race in 1858 was the Lincoln–Douglas Illinois senatorial contest. Douglas won the election, but his victory was hollow because his stance on slavery in the territories—the Freeport Doctrine—caused Southern Democrats to repudiate him. Senate Democrats stripped him of his chairmanship of the Committee on Territories. This Southern vendetta against Douglas had obvious and ominous implications for the election of 1860. Lincoln's loss, while painful at the time, was another "victorious defeat" which spurred his rapid rise to national prominence, putting him in a position to warrant serious consideration as a presidential candidate in 1860.

The debates revealed the sharp contrast between the Republicans and Democrats on slavery expansion. To his credit, Douglas courageously supported popular sovereignty, though the Dred Scott decision compelled him to espouse the desperate expedient of the Freeport Doctrine as a way of sidestepping its implications. The Republicans simply and unapologetically opposed expansion. The most fundamental issue of all, always present in either implicit or explicit fashion, was the morality of slavery. On this question, the contrast was stark. Douglas never expressed the slightest degree of moral qualms on the issue. With Lincoln, it was quite the opposite. He firmly believed that if slavery was not wrong, nothing was wrong.[764] For him, the bedrock conviction was simply his belief that African Americans were human beings. While most Northerners never became abolitionists, they were also expressing growing uneasiness about the morality of slavery.

The countdown to the presidential election of 1860 was characterized by an explosive convergence of Northern resistance to the expansion of slavery

---

[760] Richards, *Slave Power*, 208.

[761] Nine anti-Lecompton Democrats switched to vote for the English Bill; only three were reelected. Landis, *Northern Men*, 213.

[762] Baker, *James Buchanan*, 106.

[763] Richards, *Slave Power*, 211.

[764] Lincoln letter to A. G. Hodges, April 14, 1864, *Collected Works of Abraham Lincoln*, volume 7.

with an ever-growing Southern aggressiveness. By 1859, Southern Democrats had completely repudiated Douglas. On February 23, 1860, Jefferson Davis, speaking for Southern Democrats, began a push for a Federal slave code for the territories. Popular sovereignty, he announced, was "full of heresy."[765] Douglas was denounced "in language usually reserved for Black Republicans."[766] The ensuing debate revealed "an irrepressible conflict within the Democratic Party."[767] Even as the presidential election loomed, Southern Democrats raised the dreaded specter of the nationalization of slavery.[768]

The Democratic convention in April 1860 occurred in Charleston, South Carolina. It was "the worst possible place" for the convention because of the "fevered atmosphere of 1860."[769] The omens were menacing at the outset. Buchanan had abandoned "any desire for reelection," which was just as well since his chances were close to zero.[770] Many Democrats wished to break new ground by selecting someone who was not a doughface; the forerunner was Douglas. When the Democratic convention met on April 23, 1860, the irrepressible conflict within the Democratic Party quickly erupted. Many Southern Democrats went to Charleston with "one overriding goal: to destroy Douglas."[771] The flash point was the issue of slavery in the territories, and the specific point was the question of a Federal slave code guaranteeing slaveholder rights. Neither side gave any quarter. Finally, angry Southern delegates withdrew from the convention, which adjourned in acrimony; they then reassembled in Baltimore on June 18. After another bitter struggle, Douglas was nominated.

The result was a second withdrawal by Southern delegates who met again in Charleston where they nominated John C. Breckinridge of Kentucky for president. The Democratic Party, taken as a whole, had entered into what amounted to a suicide pact, ensuring a Republican victory in the fall. Why did they do this? One theory holds that ultra-radical Southerners wanted the Republicans to win so that they could exploit that victory to secede from

---

[765] McPherson, *Battle Cry*, 195.

[766] McPherson, *Battle Cry*, 195.

[767] Fehrenbacher, *Slavery, Law, and Politics*, 266. The conflict within the Democratic Party may have been irrepressible, but Southern Democrats clearly held the upper hand.

[768] Not even the abolition of the slave trade was sacrosanct. During the Buchanan administration, the slave trade, particularly with Cuba, "was allowed to flourish." Buchanan refused to cooperate with the British in attempts to suppress it. Landis, *Northern Men*, 174–75.

[769] McPherson, *Battle Cry*, 214.

[770] Smith, *Presidency of James Buchanan*, 101.

[771] McPherson, *Battle Cry*, 213.

the Union. This may have been the motive for some, but the Democrats had "been drifting toward this debacle ever since the Lecompton contest."[772]

In the midst of the slow-motion disintegration of the Democratic Party, the Republican Party met in Chicago on May 9, 1860. Since Democratic divisions meant that the Republican nominee would probably win the election, the decision at Chicago was of paramount importance. The Republican nomination of Lincoln shows how quickly the Republican Party had grown in political sophistication. The Republicans, while remaining strongly opposed to slavery expansion, moderated their rhetoric. Their bedrock position had been articulated by Lincoln in his Cooper Union speech in New York City on February 27, 1860. He argued that the Founders had always regarded slavery as an evil and even "marked [it] as an evil not to be extended, but to be tolerated and protected only because of and so far as its actual presence among us makes that toleration and protection necessary."[773] William Seward was the frontrunner when the convention opened, but his strong views on slavery, expressed in his "higher law" and "irrepressible conflict" speeches, gave him "a radical reputation that daunted old Whig conservatives."[774] The key calculation in Lincoln's favor was his strength in the Lower North battleground states, such as Pennsylvania, Ohio, Indiana, and New Jersey. For many Republicans, Lincoln "combined moderation and antislavery in the most attractive combination possible."[775]

But the Republicans had not only chosen their strongest candidate; they had also crafted a strong Whig domestic program with broad appeal, which called for a protective tariff, free homesteads of 160 acres, and internal improvements, including a transcontinental railroad. An additional inducement was that free land was to be available even for immigrants who were not yet citizens. This platform plank "went far to clear the Republicans of the stigma of nativism."[776] The Republicans went into the campaign with a clear advantage, but it was a complicated race with four candidates: Lincoln, Douglas, Breckinridge, and John Bell of Tennessee.[777] The danger was that the race would be thrown into the House, precipitating a constitutional crisis during an even larger national crisis.

---

[772] Potter, *Impending Crisis*, 415.

[773] Quoted in Potter, *Impending Crisis*, 421.

[774] McPherson, *Battle Cry*, 216.

[775] Potter, *Impending Crisis*, 427.

[776] Potter, *Impending Crisis*, 418–19.

[777] Bell ran as a candidate for the ephemeral, border-state Constitutional-Union Party, a fusion of the remnants of Whig and American parties which could only offer an appeal for peaceful coexistence.

Douglas, though "severely weakened by illness and alcoholism," campaigned courageously, even in the South where he had almost no chance of success.[778] The Democrats instinctively resorted to their "old standby": branding Republicans as "racial egalitarians" and by using the crudest racial epithets.[779] Although such attacks "wilted a good many Republicans," Lincoln kept on his message, pushing through such vitriol.[780] Lincoln may have underestimated the danger of secession. Donn Piatt, a contemporary journalist, recalled that Lincoln "could not be made to believe that the South meant secession and war."[781] But what could he have done beyond disavowing any intent to interfere with slavery in the slave states?

The election result was not surprising. Lincoln received only 39 percent of the popular vote, but he garnered 180 electoral votes, 27 more than he needed. The election revealed a starkly sectional character. He carried all eighteen free states except New Jersey where he won four of the seven votes. Furthermore, Lincoln "did not receive a single recorded vote in ten slave states."[782] The best-case vote for the South, combining the vote for Bell and Breckinridge, totaled only 31 percent of the total. This was a "shocking comeuppance" for a South long accustomed to dominating the Federal government.[783]

The result of the election was interpreted by opposing sides in an ironically similar fashion. An editorial in the *New Orleans Crescent* branded "the black Republican party" as "essentially a revolutionary party."[784] Charles Francis Adams concurred, saying that "the great revolution had taken place . . . the country has once and for all thrown off the domination of the slaveholders."[785] The key question in the immediate aftermath of the election was how would the South respond to its loss of the political dominance it had enjoyed since the 1790s? Alexander Stephens counseled patience, urging the South to play a long political game to regain control.[786] But it was not to be. Through a decade of Southern proslavery aggression, Northern Democrats, led by doughface presidents, had chosen dishonor; soon enough they and the nation they had betrayed would have the war.

---

[778] Landis, *Northern Men*, 239.
[779] McPherson, *Battle Cry*, 224.
[780] McPherson, *Battle Cry*, 224.
[781] Quoted in Potter, *Impending Crisis*, 432.
[782] Schweikart and Allen, *Patriot's History*, 298.
[783] Schweikart and Allen, *Patriot's History*, 298.
[784] McPherson, *Battle Cry*, 232–33.
[785] McPherson, *Battle Cry*, 233.
[786] See Richards, *Slave Power*, 214.

Chapter Ten: House Divided, 1861–1865

In the aftermath of victory, neither Lincoln nor the Republican Party ever threatened to interfere with slavery in the states where it existed. The effort to reassure Southerners reached its apex with the "other Thirteenth Amendment," introduced by William H. Seward and Thomas Corwin, which would bar any Congressional interference with slavery in the slave states. This measure passed both houses of Congress with Lincoln's approval in early March 1861.[787] But this measure did not halt the inexorable movement of the Deep-South states to secession. Here were the fruits of that fateful course pursued by Northern Democratic leaders—they did choose dishonor; they, and the nation, got the war. The Southern drive to secession was the culmination of a process set in motion by the Mexican War. The election of Lincoln signaled that the political balance of power was shifting away from the South. But what did Democrats think would happen after the split in the party in 1860? Their last chance for peace was to support Stephen Douglas in 1860. But virtually all Southern Democrats and all too many Northern Democrats spurned this opportunity; the result was secession and war.

It was unfortunate that the reins of government during the agonizing interregnum from November 1860 to March 1861 were in the hands of James Buchanan, the quintessential doughface. But why, in the light of all these reassurances, did the South continue its headlong plunge into secession and war? The answer clearly lies in the reality of slavery. To be sure, the mythologizing began almost immediately after the war with the comforting moonshine-and rose-water of the Lost Cause mythology. An idealized South

---

[787] For a book-length treatment, see Daniel W. Crofts, *Lincoln & the Politics of Slavery: The Other Thirteenth Amendment and the Struggle to Save the Union* (2016).

and its noble way of life was overwhelmed by a grasping, materialistic North headed by a ruthless President Lincoln who "remains the ultimate monster."[788] As time passed in the postwar period, a vision of reconciliation emerged in which "romance triumphed over reality, sentimental remembrance won over ideological memory" so that "devotion alone made everyone right, and no one truly wrong."[789] There is also an ongoing Lost Cause, neo-Confederate perspective in which the war was fought by a heroic South to defend a constitutionally sanctioned state sovereignty against a lawless Northern assault. The extreme version of this view is that the Civil War would have been fought had not a single slave labored on a Southern cotton plantation.[790] The common factor is the refusal to confront the central issue of slavery, but an aggressively proslavery South did not secede and then take up arms in defense of a constitutional abstraction.[791]

Secession was no abstraction, but it was bafflingly extra-constitutional. Buchanan's rationale for doing nothing was his belief that although secession was wrong, he was powerless to stop it.[792] However, Buchanan, even in the midst of an unprecedented crisis, continued his professions of sympathy for the South. His annual message of December 3, 1860, came dangerously close to defending the Southern position, while he "completely ignored the Northern side of the argument."[793] There was also the issue of the off-shore

---

[788] By contrast, Forrest A. Nabors argues that the central motive of the Southern planter class was to create and maintain an oligarchy in which both slavery and the subordination of poor whites were embedded. They had "repudiated the lofty ideals of their nation's birth" and "finally aspired to install themselves as permanent suzerains over a great empire, whether within the American Union or outside of it." See Allen C. Guelzo's review of Nabors, *From Oligarchy to Republicanism: The Great Task of Reconstruction* (2017) in the *Claremont Review of Books*, Summer 2018, 46–48 (quote 47). In this view, the Radical Republicans were a "Jacobin band" which represented "the extreme left of Civil War politics." George Fort Milton, *Abraham Lincoln and the Fifth Column* (1942), 118.

[789] David W. Blight, *Race and Reunion: The Civil War in American Memory* (2001), 4.

[790] See H. W. Crocker III, *The Politically Incorrect History of the Civil War* (2008). Of the 337 pages in this book, only 142 are devoted to any sort of analysis. The remaining pages simply present a straightforward military history in which his pro-Confederate bias is clearly evident.

[791] The rationalization began very soon after the war. Jefferson Davis himself, one of the most zealous proponents of slavery expansion in the 1850s, asserted in his self-serving *The Rise and Fall of the Confederate Government* (1881) that the South was resisting the despotic power of the Federal government and that slavery was "in no wise the cause of the conflict but only an incident." Quoted in Blight, *Race and Reunion*, 259.

[792] Andrew Jackson, although a Democrat and a Southerner, had no problem in asserting Federal authority in the Nullification Crisis. However, whether he would have done so had the issue been slavery instead of the tariff seems very unlikely.

[793] Smith, *Presidency of James Buchanan*, 148. He angered Southerners by failing to concede their right of secession. Republicans denounced him as a "Pharisaical old hypocrite" who was "bristling with the spirit of a rabid slaveocracy." McPherson, *Battle Cry of Freedom*, 251.

Federal forts, especially the indefensible Fort Sumter in the Charleston harbor. In late December 1861, rumors circulated that Buchanan was about to surrender Fort Sumter. "If that is true," Lincoln is reported to have exclaimed, "they ought to hang him."[794] Buchanan remained unhanged, but it appeared to have been a close call. When the *Star of the West*, a Federal steam-ship, attempted a peaceful resupply of the fort, Confederate shore batteries opened fire, forcing it to turn back. Louis T. Wigfall, a Confederate from Texas, gloated: "[Your] flag has been insulted; redress it if you dare."[795] The Buchanan administration limped to its inglorious end, and Buchanan had come "closer to committing treason than any other American president."[796] Retirement, with its opportunity for reflection, produced no wisdom. In his memoir he blamed the whole crisis primarily on "the malign influence of the Republican Party."[797]

Lincoln inherited the worst crisis in American history. It was a crisis without a solution simply because key Southern leaders were bent on secession. They felt an urgency to take the irrevocable step before Lincoln "had come into office and been given a chance to show his Whiggish moderation."[798] The Confederate States of America came into existence on February 18, 1861. This story "shines a damning light on the late antebellum political leaders" who rejected all calls for compromise; they "spurned the proffered constitutional amendment [Seward–Corwin Amendment], fractured the Union, and started a war."[799] The final irony is that it was secession itself that destroyed slavery. Had the South been content only to maintain its independence, Lincoln would have been confronted with an extraordinarily difficult problem. To do nothing would have been to acquiesce in secession, yet to attack would stigmatize the North as the aggressor. His dilemma was resolved by the Confederate leadership which loudly laid claim to the remaining off-shore Federal forts, particularly Fort Sumter. Lincoln's policy was to engage in peaceful resupply of nonmilitary essentials—"food for hungry men."[800]

The Confederate response to this peaceful resupply was to open fire on Fort Sumter on April 12, 1861, forcing its surrender. The tactic of peaceful

---

[794] Quoted in Potter, *Impending Crisis*, 558.

[795] Quoted from the *Washington Globe*, January 1861, in Jean H. Baker, *Affairs of Party: The Political Culture of the Democratic Party in the Mid-Nineteenth Century* (1998), 139.

[796] Baker, *Affairs of Party*, 142. It may well have been that only the strenuous objections of his own Cabinet dissuaded him from surrendering Fort Sumter.

[797] *Mr. Buchanan's Administration on the Eve of the Rebellion* (1866), quoted in Baker *Affairs of Party*, 143.

[798] Potter, *Impending Crisis*, 500.

[799] Crofts, *Lincoln & the Politics of Slavery*, 9.

[800] McPherson, *Battle Cry*, 271.

resupply was "a stroke of genius," an early sign of "the mastery that would mark Lincoln's presidency."[801] News of the bombardment of the fort "galva-nized the North," so Lincoln called 75,000 militiamen into service to put down the insurrection.[802] He was unconditionally determined to defeat the Confederacy and save the Union. For Lincoln, fidelity to the Union involved "loyalty to the Declaration of Independence as the moral foundation of Amer-ican republicanism and the Constitution as its legal foundation."[803] This involved the "promise of liberty to all" which gave hope to people around the world in search of freedom. But there were those who were so impatient with Lincoln's deliberate pace that they denied he was committed to emancipa-tion at all. This extreme position is exemplified by the abolitionist Wendell Phillips who, angered by Lincoln's earlier refusal to call for the repeal of the Fugitive Slave Act, had called him the "Slave Hound of Illinois."[804]

Central to Lincoln's position was the Constitutional protection of slavery in the four loyal border states—Missouri, Kentucky, Maryland, and Delaware. Their allegiance was vital to the Union cause. Lincoln memorably observed: "I hope to have God on my side, but I must have Kentucky."[805] This political reality explains the caution with which Lincoln approached the issue of slavery. On the question of the Union, however, Lincoln enjoyed what initially seemed near-universal support in the North. Initially, Democrats generally joined "in the eagle scream of patriotic fury" and supported the war "for a year or more."[806] Stephen Douglas energetically supported the Union cause until his untimely death on June 3, 1861, at age forty-eight, asserting that "a man cannot be a true Democrat unless he is a loyal patriot."[807]

Opposition parties are essential to a functioning democracy, even in wartime. There were legitimate issues on which debate could be helpful. The war was not going at all well, particularly in the East.[808] The draft represented an unwelcome extension of Federal authority which was often resented.[809]

---

[801] McPherson, *Battle Cry*, 271–72. But it was a mastery that was made evident at this point only by the foolishness of the Confederate leadership.

[802] McPherson, *Battle Cry*, 274.

[803] Joseph R. Fournieri, *Abraham Lincoln's Political Faith* (2004), 153–54.

[804] Quoted in McPherson, *Battle Cry*, 247. A grotesque recent version of this perspective is represented by Lerone Bennett who achieved the remarkable feat of writing an unreliev-edly negative 624-page book about him. See Lerone Bennett, *Forced into Glory: Lincoln's White Dream* (2000).

[805] Quoted by William E. Gienapp, "Abraham Lincoln and the Border States," *Journal of the Abraham Lincoln Association* 13 (1992): 13.

[806] McPherson, *Battle Cry*, 274.

[807] Phillip S. Paludan, *A People's Contest: The Union and the Civil War, 1861–1865* (1994), 85.

[808] George M. McClellan had consistently mismanaged the Army of the Potomac. After being dismissed by Lincoln, he became the Democratic presidential candidate in 1864.

[809] Historians differ in their evaluations of the measure. McPherson thinks that it gener-ally worked fairly well, while George F. Milton argues that the law was not at all well

But the most ominous aspect of the political situation was the violent resistance in some areas where "virtually all those who denounced and resisted the militia were Democrats."[810] These Democrats also reached into their toolbox for the ever-reliable use of class-warfare rhetoric, making conscription "a partisan and class issue."[811] A much broader issue was the question of civil liberties, made urgent by the nature of the civil conflict. Lincoln summed up the dilemma: "Must a government, of necessity, be too strong for the liberties of its own people, or too weak to maintain its own existence?"[812] Lincoln took the strong option, and, so his critics charged, endangered the freedom of the people. Early in the war, the case of John Merryman went to the heart of the issue. Merryman, a member of a secessionist military organization in Maryland, was arrested in May 1861 for destroying some railroad bridges. Lincoln then suspended habeas corpus over an area extending from Philadelphia to Washington, DC.

This action provoked a vigorous response from Roger B. Taney, acting in his capacity as the presiding judge of the Maryland Circuit Court. In *Ex parte Merryman* (1861), he demanded that Merryman be released and lectured Lincoln on his suspension of habeas corpus. Lincoln ignored him, so Taney "was left to soothe his outrage . . . [by ruling] against every Union government action regarding civil liberties."[813] While it is undoubtedly the case that the Republican Party and the Federal government at various times and in various places overreached, started at shadows, and engaged in unwarranted accusations, it seems clear that, owing to the unprecedented danger to the Union, Lincoln had the better of the argument.[814]

Since the Union was in great peril, Lincoln invoked "the doctrine of implied powers" as well as "the plenary authority of his position of commander-in-

---

framed and so "much of the criticism of it would seem justified." See McPherson, *Battle Cry*, 605–7; Milton, *Lincoln and the Fifth Column*, 127.

[810] Paludan, *People's Contest*, 493. In some areas, signs appeared reading "We won't fight to free niggers" (493). This theme was to emerge as the main thrust of all Democratic opposition to the war.

[811] McPherson, *Battle Cry*, 608. It is not always easy to distinguish between understandable complaints based on the predictable instances of government inefficiency and bureaucratic bungling and efforts intended to cripple the Union war effort. Mark E. Neely, who generally argues for the loyalty of wartime Democrats, admits that on the issue of the draft they engaged in a "desperate search for constitutional objections to the administration's war effort." The party "branched out into areas of constitutional complaint well beyond the bounds of good sense." This was, he concluded, the "hidden tragedy of the Civil War Democratic Party." Mark E. Neely, *Lincoln and the Democrats: The Politics of Opposition in the Civil War* (2017), 160.

[812] First Message to Congress at the Special Session, July 4, 1861.

[813] Kelly and Harbison, *American Constitution*, 439–40.

[814] The Democratic Party acted as though the war should be fought as though the unprecedented danger did not exist.

chief."[815] He also claimed authority based on Article I, section 9 of the Constitution which allows for the suspension of the "Writ of Habeas Corpus" when "in Cases of Rebellion or Invasion the public Safety may require it."[816] The general consensus is that Lincoln curtailed civil liberties reluctantly and only by necessity.[817] Yet opposition to Lincoln's actions regarding civil liberties "became the cornerstone for every argument conservatives [i.e., Democrats] made during the rest of the war."[818] George McGovern claims that the suspension of habeas corpus was Lincoln's "most questionable judgment," while conceding that there was "a horde of Confederate spies and saboteurs" who were "operating within the shadow of the U.S. capitol."[819] Lincoln's record is good "when measured against the far vaster civil liberties violations levied on German Americans and Japanese Americans in America's twentieth-century wars."[820] Lincoln was fighting a civil war against a rebellious South and enemies in the North. Our twentieth-century wars, led by liberal Democratic presidents, were against enemies who were oceans away.

The Union confronted a network of Confederate sympathizers which actively plotted against the government. In January 1863, Lincoln expressed concern of what he called "the fire in the rear."[821] Northern opponents of the Union war effort were branded as "Copperheads."[822] This is an important topic with an evolving historiography. Some historians have implied that Lincoln was wrong to fear any danger from rumors of various Confederate plots in the North.[823] The most thoroughgoing recent skeptic regarding

---

[815] Milton, *Lincoln and the Fifth Column*, 236

[816] Lincoln and Taney differed as to whether this section applies to Congress or to the Executive. The issue remained undetermined. In 1863, Congress passed the Habeus Corpus Indemnity Act which justified Lincoln's actions.

[817] See Jennifer L. Weber, *Copperheads: The Rise and Fall of Lincoln's Opponents in the North* (2006), 32.

[818] Weber, *Copperheads*, 29–30. The unanimity of these objections while the Union was fighting for its life inevitably raises the question of motivation. When Lincoln banished Clement Vallandigham, a notorious Confederate sympathizer, to the Confederacy, he received "an eruption of attack and abuse from Northern Democrats." Allen C. Guelzo, *Fateful Lightning: A New History of the Civil War and Reconstruction* (2012), 229.

[819] George S. McGovern, *Abraham Lincoln* (2009), 8–9. He cannot bring himself to criticize any major aspect of the behavior of the Democratic Party during the course of the Civil War.

[820] Guelzo, *Fateful Lightning*, 230.

[821] Quoted by Jennifer L. Weber, "Lincoln's Critics: The Copperheads," *Journal of the Abraham Lincoln Association* 32 (Winter 2011): 33–47.

[822] In use since July 1861, it has proved to be "one of the most effective epithets in American history." Wood Gray, *The Hidden Civil War: The Story of the Copperheads* (1942; second edition, 1964), 141.

[823] These plots were engineered by Northern sympathizers acting in concert with Confederate agents. There was a constantly shifting set of groups, such as the Knights of the Golden Circle (a proslavery expansionist organization before the war), the Order of

Northern Confederate plots is Frank L. Klement. A degree of skepticism regarding plots and conspiracies is justifiable, but Klement overdoes it. His extended discussion demonstrates a consistent bias which he reveals by denouncing Republicans for "waving the bloody shirt."[824] Klement laments the success of the Republicans in pushing their own partisan narrative by which "legends and myths nurtured by nationalism and based upon wartime political propaganda remain a part of consensus history."[825] He rejects the findings of earlier historians who pushed what he calls "the nationalistic line."[826]

Klement, however, not only rejects the findings of earlier historians, but he also refuses to accept even an account by Thomas Henry Hines of a plot in Indiana which he headed, claiming that Hines had "concocted a fanciful tale" based on flawed sources rather than "his own personal knowledge and experiences."[827] One of the "flawed sources" Klement says Hines relied on was the Holt Report on the subject by Lincoln's judge advocate general, Joseph Holt, a Unionist Democrat from Kentucky.[828] On the basis of this investigation, Holt came to believe in "a hellish conspiracy of virulent Copperheads in the West."[829] According to Klement, we are to believe neither the findings of contemporary historians nor the memories of actual participants.

But there is substantial evidence of Confederate clandestine agents active in the North, particularly in the Midwest. A significant number of Midwesterners, in some places as high as 40 percent, were "of southern birth or parentage," making the region fertile soil for Confederate opera-

---

American Knights, and the Sons of Liberty; opinions vary as to their size, strength, and efficiency.

[824] This was a postwar Republican tactic, at times overdone, of extracting political gains by invoking the shedding of Union blood.

[825] Frank L. Klement, *Dark Lanterns: Secret Political Societies, Conspiracies, and Treason in the Civil War* (1984), 244.

[826] Klement, *Dark Lanterns*, 242–43. A. James Fuller dismisses Klement as a Progressive-era historian who "believed that economic issues and class conflict dominated history." A. James Fuller, "Oliver P. Morton, Political Ideology, and Treason in Civil War Indiana," *Ohio Valley History* 13 (Fall 2013): 28–29.

[827] Klement, *Dark Lanterns*, 239. Klement gives no reason why he thinks Hines would have done this.

[828] Published on October 8, 1864, by Edwin Stanton, Lincoln's secretary of war and another Unionist Democrat, as a pamphlet entitled *Report of the Judge Advocate General on the Order of American Knights*.

[829] Elizabeth D. Leonard, *Lincoln's Forgotten Ally: Judge Advocate General Joseph Holt of Kentucky* (2011), 186. Leonard expresses no reservations regarding the contents of the report. The report was published as a campaign document for the 1864 presidential campaign and it "helped Lincoln in his November reelection effort." Stephen E. Towne, *Surveillance and Spies in the Civil War: Exposing Confederate Conspiracies in America's Heartland* (2015), 286. This does not mean, however, that the report was compiled for political reasons.

tions and consequently the most studied area.[830] Recent research is based in larger part on archival sources of the army along with "scattered records of the secret groups and individuals."[831] While private papers have often been purged of potentially incriminating material, some memoirs cast additional light on the activities by ex-Confederate soldiers; this has in turn cast light on various aspects of clandestine operations.[832]

Confederate agents developed ambitious plans for various operations. They plotted "a fantastic variety of activities."[833] One aspect of the conspiracies was a scheme by Harrison H. Dodd of the Order of the American Knights to liberate Confederate prisoners of war from Camp Morton in Indianapolis in late May 1863. His plan was "unique in that it had serious aspirations as a regional uprising."[834] Meanwhile, Hines was deeply involved in an ambitious plan, along with the Sons of Liberty, to free thousands of Confederates from Camp Douglas on the outskirts of Chicago on the opening of the Democratic National Convention meeting there on July 4, 1864. He also planned to raid Federal arsenals, creating a major distraction which would force the Federal government to pull troops away from other fronts to confront a newly emerging threat.[835]

The most important reason why some scholars have downplayed these plots is that many were never even launched. There are two reasons for their failure. Federal intelligence agents penetrated the organizations and learned of their plans. There were major "military-intelligence activities in the lower Midwestern states of Ohio, Indiana, and Illinois."[836] In addition, the Confederate organizations suffered from poor planning, general incompetence and, at key times, a lack of nerve. Some plotters "simply lacked the courage of their convictions."[837] They "ran into problems that characterized the entire

---

[830] Stephen Z. Starr, "Was There a Northwest Conspiracy?," *Filson Club History Quarterly* 38 (1964): 324. This was the "principal seat" of Confederate conspiracies. Gray, *Hidden Civil War*, 219.

[831] Towne, *Surveillance and Spies*, 309–11.

[832] Among others, see Thomas Henry Hines, "The Northwest Conspiracy," *Southern Bivouac*, 2, nos. 7–9, II (1886–87), 437–45 and John B. Castleman, *On Active Service* (1917).

[833] McPherson, *Battle Cry*, 764. They met with some Peace Democrats. Clement Vallandigham, the most prominent member of that group, was aware of at least some of these plots in his capacity as a "Supreme Commander" of the Sons of Liberty. Weber, *Copperheads*, 150.

[834] Weber, *Copperheads*, 149. Jefferson Davis was kept informed of this plot.

[835] Starr, "Northwest Conspiracy," 332–33. The size and identity of the Sons of Liberty, the Order of American Knights, and the Knights of the Golden Circle are not always clear. Some Confederate agents were inclined to vastly overestimate the size of the groups which also shifted in identity.

[836] Towne, *Surveillance and Spies*, 9.

[837] Starr, "Northwest Conspiracy," 333.

---

antiwar movement: shoddy organization and loose lips."[838] It seems clear that there really was a potentially dangerous fire in the rear; however, it never burst into flames. The evolution of contemporary historiography has been to take the Confederate plots seriously despite their ultimate failure.[839] But it is also true that the threat of fire in the rear was only part of a much broader threat posed by the Northern Democratic Party.

There was one longstanding area of partisan disagreement which had triggered powerful confrontations in the past but seemed almost innocuous, given the more urgent issues of the war. This was a debate over economic policy—a normal debate in an abnormal time. Republicans saw their victory in 1860 as a chance to implement their economic program. Lincoln had described himself as "always a Whig in politics." His lifelong commit-ment to self-improvement "found the Whig program appealing."[840] In many ways, Lincoln was the last Whig president as well as the first Republican president; his presidency marked "the triumph of most of Henry Clay's old 'American System' over the political legacy built up since 1800 by successive Democratic administrations."[841] The success of Republicans in implementing their economic agenda was aided by the absence of Southern Democrats from Congress.[842] Republicans in the 37th Congress were able to pass major pieces of their economic program, often quite easily. The Homestead Act, which provided 160 acres of free Federal land for bona fide settlers, passed in February 1862. The Morrill Land Grant College Act, which Buchanan had vetoed earlier, passed in June 1862. By establishing support for agricultural colleges, the act encouraged "new approaches to public land utilization."[843]

Congress passed the Pacific Railroad Act in July 1862. This major project, long stymied by sectional division, "made possible the breaking of

---

[838] Weber, *Copperheads*, 149. Towne also notes that the failure of the Camp Douglas plot "owed much to luck"—the timely arrival of troop reinforcements. Towne, *Surveillance and Spies*, 275.

[839] James McPherson illustrates this shift. He asserted that the Sons of Liberty was a "shadowy organization" whose "vast army" was "in reality a mere phantom." McPherson, *Battle Cry*, 762–64. *Battle Cry* was published in 1988. However, in his foreword to Weber's *Copperheads* (2006), he praises her "splendid new study" which challenges the "reigning interpretation" by demonstrating the "genuine and dangerous threat" posed by the Copperheads in all phases of their activities, including efforts to ignite the fire in the rear. McPherson, Foreword to Weber, *Copperheads*, ix–x.

[840] Eric Foner, *Fiery Trial: Abraham Lincoln and American Slavery* (2005), 34.

[841] Guelzo, *Fateful Lightning*, 231.

[842] Northern Democrats tried to maintain their traditional opposition to the Whig program, but they could not successfully resist without Southern Democrats. Weber, *Copperheads*, 29.

[843] Leonard P. Curry, *Blueprint for Modern America: Non-Military Legislation of the First Civil War Congress* (1968), 115.

---

the Great Plains transportation barrier."[844] Another key piece of the Republican agenda was the passage of the Morrill Tariff, which raised the average level of duties to 37 percent. Its longstanding rationale was the protection of domestic industry from foreign companies. The legislation stirring up the greatest degree of partisan debate was the National Banking Act, which passed in late February 1863. Democrats railed against "this Monstrous Bank Bill" as evidence of a "wartime conspiracy" by "the money monopoly of New England."[845]

These are the major pieces of legislation which achieved the long-delayed implementation of Henry Clay's American System. The effects of this program persisted long after the cannon of the Civil War had fallen silent. The 37th Congress had "been active in drafting the blueprint for a new social order" which laid the foundation for modern America.[846] The retrograde economic program of the antebellum Democratic Party, which had long retarded progress, then finally suffered a decisive defeat. There has never been a significant retreat from this blueprint for modern America. The shift in economic philosophy, for all of its profound implications for the future of America, was inevitably overshadowed by the existential threat to the Union posed by the Democratic Party, North and South.

Northern Democrats soon settled into what was at best an obstructionist stance during the struggle for national survival. There was a small, honorable group of what may be called War Democrats who were willing to prosecute the war to final victory. Such men as Secretary of War Edwin M. Stanton and Judge Advocate General Joseph Holt made significant contributions to the Union war effort.[847] Nevertheless, it is symptomatic that such Democrats have to be singled out for praise against the backdrop of the Northern Democratic Party in general. The two major factions of the Northern Democratic Party were the War Democrats and the much larger faction of Peace Democrats. But there was a range of opinion among Peace Democrats. There were the hard-core Copperheads and those simply favoring peace at all costs. But it is difficult "all things considered" to find "much good in the leaders of the peace movement."[848] They seemed willing to sacrifice the Union itself. There was a deep vein of dishonesty in their rhetoric. By 1864, they had come to espouse "peace at any price," despite the Confederate insistence

---

[844] Curry, *Blueprint*, 136.

[845] McPherson, *Battle Cry*, 136.

[846] Curry, *Blueprint*, 244.

[847] Had he lived, Stephen Douglas would have been in the first rank of Unionist Democrats.

[848] Gray, *Hidden Civil War*, 224.

that "the recognition of Confederate independence was a precondition for negotiations."[849]

Their prevailing slogan was: "The Constitution as it is, the Union as it was."[850] The slogan had some validity before the war; it was essentially the position of the border-state Constitutional Union Party. But once the war started, and the longer it continued, the less sense it made. By the time of the off-year election of 1862, it had become a blueprint for capitulation. With increasing thousands dead, the plan to restore the Union "as it was" meant returning to the condition which had triggered the war in the first place. What the nation most needed in 1862 was a Northern Democratic Party fully committed to winning the war, restoring the Union, and destroying slavery But this commitment never occurred. The greatest threat posed by the Civil War was not that the South would win but that Northern Democrats would be able to force a peace on the Union which would have perpetuated slavery indefinitely. The greatest crisis in American history was posed by the twin menace of Southern and Northern Democrats.

But surely the War Democrats would help. The key question is what did it mean to be a War Democrat? Obviously, it meant some level of commitment to fighting the war. The War Democrats were not Copperheads; they did not believe in peace at any price. They were committed to fighting the war, and, up to a point, they were even willing to cooperate with Lincoln. Lincoln's fully developed plan was simple: win the war, restore the Union, and end slavery. But the War Democrats could never subscribe to this. Their level of commitment was always uncertain, vacillating, and tentative. The real sticking-point was the question of war aims. Even while helping fight the war, the War Democrats, never stopped seeking "to turn the country from its revolutionary course," meaning anything having to do with ending slavery and extending rights to freedmen.[851]

Many questions about the War Democrats remain unanswered. Joel Silbey claims that "they remain an elusive group" which "was never numerous enough to affect the fortunes of the party to any significant extent."[852] A very different perspective is offered by Christopher Dell who argues that they

---

[849] Weber, *Copperheads*, x.

[850] To which many added "and the Negroes where they are," even though that it is implicit in the first two provisos. Jules Witcover, *Party of the People: A History of the Democrats* (2003), 217.

[851] Joel Silbey, *A Respectable Minority: The Democratic Party in the Civil War Era* (1977), 61. Silbey seeks to support the thesis contained in the title of his book, but he presents a wealth of evidence calling it into question, particularly regarding the issues of race, slavery, and emancipation.

[852] Silbey, *Respectable Minority*, 56, 58. This perspective is significant, given Silbey's intent to defend the Democratic Party.

were indispensable to the Union war effort at a time when "without their aid the country might well have been shot into oblivion."[853] This means that "seldom in history" has there been "so important an alliance as that between Lincoln and the War Democrats."[854] But the irony of this position is that even if it is true, it says more about the desperate state of the Union than it does about the "respectable minority" that was the Democratic Party. Lincoln and the Unionists needed all the help they could get and help from the War Democrats could well have made the difference. Yet what does it say about an American political party which can garner praise for simply supporting the nation at a time when its very survival was at stake?

But what was it which constituted the deepest root of Northern Democratic Party opposition? Wars are not fought or supported on behalf of constitutional abstractions. The easy answer is slavery. But it is deeper than that. Emancipation—even deeper. The bedrock issue was race. The ugly open secret is the inveterate racism of the Northern Democratic Party, acting in tandem with the Southern defenders of slavery. This is the central motivation behind all the Democratic disloyalty, intransigence, and obstruction that dogged the Union war effort, ultimately thwarting the achievement of postwar racial justice. And this is also the reality which must be kept out of popular histories and mainstream American history textbooks.[855]

There is an instructive contrast in the narrative of race, politics, and the Civil War in reference to Lincoln and the Republican Party. Lincoln's path from secession to emancipation, to black soldiers, and to the Thirteenth Amendment was slow and at times tortuously complex. It was a path complicated by the need to retain the indispensable border states, the constitutional protection of slavery in those states, and Northern political reality. By contrast, there is the simplicity of the Democratic response. Whatever policy was proposed against slavery, for emancipation, or for any

---

[853] Christopher Dell, *Lincoln and the War Democrats: The Grand Erosion of Conservative Tradition* (1975), ll.

[854] Dell, *Lincoln and the War Democrats*, 20

[855] Howard Zinn cannot bear to link slavery and racism to the Democratic Party, so neither do the multitude of college students who have been assigned his textbook by leftist professors. His thesis is that "the American government" fought the war "not to end slavery but to retain the enormous national territory and market and resources." Zinn, *People's History*, 193. The Democratic Party also disappears almost entirely from the Civil War chapter of Sean Wilentz's Bancroft-prize-winning *The Rise of American Democracy: Jefferson to Lincoln* (2005). The near-complete disappearing act of the Democratic Party is symptomatic. Wilentz does briefly reference "southern Master Race democrats" (778), a bizarre circumlocution. He also alludes to "a small number of northern antislavery Democrats" who "bolted the party in disgust" (792). By contrast, the ugly secret is freely discussed in the specialized monographs cited in this chapter, even in books by scholars who attempt to salvage something of the reputation of the Democratic Party. See particularly Silbey, *Respectable Minority* and Neely, *Lincoln and the Democrats*.

other initiative favorable to blacks, the Northern Democratic response was always vociferous opposition. Wars often produce unintended, even revolutionary, consequences, and the Civil War was no exception. Lincoln's first task was to find ways to win the war, and this proved to be a difficult task because of an enormous disparity in military leadership between the Union and Confederate generals, particularly in the eastern theater where Robert E. Lee had no equal. Lincoln's second task was finding a way to deal with slavery as a military issue quite apart from any humanitarian considerations. The starting point was the obvious fact that slave labor was a Confederate military resource. The first attempt to deal with this reality was the passage of two confiscation acts, the first on July 12, 1862, and the second on August 12, 1862. The clear intent was to seize the slaves of disloyal slaveholders. These acts freed "thousands of slaves immediately and without compensation." Even while justified as a war measure, it is "hard to imagine how emancipation could have begun any sooner."[856]

The Democratic Party was almost unanimously opposed. The act passed the Senate 24-11 in a party-line vote. In the House only six Republicans opposed it, while only three Democrats supported it. This opposition was a foretaste of things to come, for Democrats "would fight Republicans throughout the war," although they "usually supported bills that supplied and armed the soldiers."[857] The confiscation acts were not effective; the second act, which was supposed to remedy defects in the first was itself complicated and "ambiguous in places."[858] A better approach was needed, along with an exquisite sense of timing. There was also the issue of slavery in the border states, where the confiscation acts did not apply. It is important to remember an aspect of slavery in America which is so obvious that it is easy to overlook its implications. American slavery differed from "all other forms of slavery that western civilization had known. This time slavery was based on race."[859] So emancipated slaves, unlike the earlier indentured servants, could never simply blend into the general population; this simple fact fueled fears that freeing the slaves would result in chaos and race war.

This unsettling reality is what lay behind one of the enduring chimeras related to slavery—colonization, a policy which bemused many otherwise

---

[856] The second act limited confiscation to the lifetime of the owner without encumbering his estate. But even the first act "was generally acknowledged to be ineffective and unworkable." Curry, *Blueprint*, 99.

[857] Republicans did control the 37th Congress 105–43 in the House and 31–10 in the Senate. Secession had "cost the Democrats almost half of their voting strength." Paludan, *People's Contest*, 88.

[858] Oakes, *Slavery National*, 236.

[859] Guelzo, *Fateful Lightning*, 29. "Slave" is derived from the word Slav, evidence for the white slavery practiced in early-medieval Europe.

astute American leaders, including Jefferson, Clay, and even Lincoln who believed that it was "the best way to defuse much of the anti-emancipation sentiment."[860] However, the policy had no chance of success. Another equally futile policy, which was intended to deal with slavery in the border states, was "gradual, compensated emancipation."[861] Congress adopted a resolution from Lincoln in April 1862; however, 85 percent of Democrats and border-state Unionists opposed it. This was "a discouraging sign."[862] Despite the consistent resistance he encountered, Lincoln maintained his interest in compensated emancipation because he was keenly aware of the constitutional protections for slavery in the border states. He never gave up on the idea, even after the move to enact the Thirteen Amendment had begun. At the Hampton Roads Conference in early February 1864, he continued to support "his longstanding idea of compensated emancipation."[863] He offered to provide $400 million in government bonds to secure Southern ratification of the Thirteen Amendment, but after the Cabinet expressed "united opposition," the plan "never saw the light of day."[864] Both colonization and compensated emancipation were dead ends. The ways to deal with the unresolved issues of slavery and emancipation were the Emancipation Proclamation and the Thirteenth Amendment. But it was at best a complicated, halting process. Emerson, unlike many of his fellow abolitionists, realized this, observing that "Liberty is a slow fruit."[865]

The war had been going so badly that Lincoln was concerned lest any move toward emancipation would seem to foreign powers to be a desperate ploy to gain respectability for the Union cause. He needed a victory to put this perception to rest. Finally, on September 17, 1862, he got as close to a victory as he was likely to get at the battle of Antietam with McClellan leading the Army of the Potomac. It was a bloody draw, but Lee pulled back from Maryland to Virginia. The battle established a measure of military credibility for the Union cause and discouraged England and France from recognizing the Confederacy. Five days later, on September 22, 1862, shortly before

---

[860] McPherson, *Battle Cry*, 508. The number of slaves was staggering; the cost would be astronomical, and the slaves did not want to be shipped back to what was for them an alien environment.

[861] Foner, *Fiery Trial*, 272.

[862] McPherson, *Battle Cry*, 498–99. In an earlier meeting, border-state congressmen voiced comprehensive objections, resisted "federal coercion," and "deplored the race problem that would emerge with a large black population" (499).

[863] Lincoln and William Seward met with Alexander Stephens and other Confederates in an unsuccessful attempt to negotiate an armistice. Foner, *Fiery Trial*, 315.

[864] Paul Escott, *What Shall We Do with the Negro? Lincoln, White Racism, and Civil War America* (2009), 215–16.

[865] *Atlantic Monthly*, November 1862, quoted in Louis P. Masur, *Lincoln's Hundred Days: The Emancipation Proclamation and the War for the Union* (2012), 7.

the election, Lincoln issued his Preliminary Emancipation Proclamation. He announced that all slaves in areas still in rebellion against the Federal government would, after January 1, 1863, be "then, thenceforward and forever free."[866] Lincoln justified the measure on the basis of his "war power to seize enemy resources."[867] Many commentators have observed that Lincoln freed the slaves in areas where he had no power and left them enslaved in the areas under his control. But what else could he have done?

The Emancipation Proclamation "faced withering criticism," virtually all of it from Northern Democrats.[868] The issuance of the Proclamation started what was to become an all-too-familiar pattern. Any steps taken by the Union favorable in any way to blacks were subject to denunciation, usually accompanied by vicious racist rhetoric. Jefferson Davis set a high bar for such rhetoric by calling the Proclamation "the most execrable measure in the history of guilty man."[869] But Northern Democrats were not far behind. The Proclamation gave them additional antiwar ammunition by turning a war for the Union into what they denounced as "a nigger crusade."[870]

On the one hand, the emancipation of slaves was only "a means to victory."[871] It rested on "military necessity" and not "on the rights of mankind."[872] Yet, on the other hand, its long-term effect was revolutionary. As became increasingly obvious over time, the Proclamation turned Union armies "into armies of liberation."[873] It removed the prohibition of entice-ment and instead "made it the explicit policy of the Union army in the disloyal states."[874] The longer the war continued, the more revolutionary its impact became. The Proclamation began as a war measure but became an engine of race liberation which raised inescapable questions about the future of slavery in general. No wonder that Northern Democrats attacked it "from every direction."[875] It also led to perhaps the worst nightmare for the defenders of slavery, North and South—black soldiers.[876] The Proclama-tion was certainly "sending the war and the country down a very different

---

[866] Lincoln's Preliminary Emancipation Proclamation, September 22, 1862.
[867] McPherson, *Battle Cry*, 558.
[868] Masur, *Lincoln's Hundred Days*, 7.
[869] Quoted in McPherson, *Battle Cry*, 566.
[870] Edward Chase Kirkland, *The Peacemakers of 1864* (1927), 28–29.
[871] Escott, *What Shall We Do?*, 29.
[872] Foner, *Fiery Trial*, 242.
[873] McPherson, *Battle Cry*, 558.
[874] Oakes, *Freedom National*, 370.
[875] Gray, *Hidden Civil War*, 98.
[876] Altogether around 179,000 black soldiers, 10 percent of the total, served in the Union armies. This service "offered self-empowerment" for black soldiers and "transformed the thinking of white soldiers." Masur, *Lincoln's Hundred Days*, 232.

road" than some people thought should be taken.[877] It seems clear that the Proclamation and its consequences contributed to the growing conviction of many in the North that slavery could not and should not be permitted to survive the war. It does not seem surprising that Lincoln came to define the Emancipation Proclamation as "the central act of my administration and the great event of the nineteenth century."[878]

In December 1862, just before the Proclamation was to go into effect, the Democrats denounced it as "a high crime against the Constitution."[879] This was absurd, but the charge did raise an important issue. The Proclamation was a war measure; what would happen when the war ended? Would the slaves of the Confederacy be returned to slavery? Would they remain free, while blacks in the loyal border states remain enslaved? Could a Congress controlled by Democrats rescind the order? The Supreme Court was still controlled by Southern sympathizers, so the Proclamation theoretically could be subject to judicial disaster like the Dred Scott decision. The Proclamation was at best only a temporary expedient, not a permanent solution. It did put the nation on the road to general emancipation, but it could not accomplish this by itself.

The fragility of the Proclamation was graphically demonstrated by the results of 1863 election. It is to Lincoln's credit that he announced the Preliminary Emancipation Proclamation in 1863 shortly before the election, even though such elections usually go against the party in power. This year was no exception. The war was not going well for the Union, and there were few reasons to hope for any immediate improvement. Both Lincoln and the Republicans seemed strangely disengaged at a time when the stakes were uniquely high for the future of the Union.[880] In contrast to Republican complacency, the Democrats, sensing victory, made an all-out effort to gain control of Congress. They did gain thirty-five Congressional seats held by Republicans and also won gubernatorial races in New York and New Jersey. Even so, Republicans retained control at a time when everything seemed to favor the Democrats.[881]

---

[877] Guelzo, *Fateful Lightning*, 184. It also forced Lincoln to "confront for himself the full implications of some of the issues of black freedom and black equality" (184).

[878] Guelzo, *Fateful Lightning*, 172. Quoted from Francis Bicknell Carpenter, *Six Months at the White House* (1866).

[879] McPherson, *Battle Cry*, 562.

[880] Harold Holzer believes that his uncharacteristic behavior could have cost him "his ability to govern his fractured country and imperiled the war to preserve the Union and destroy slavery." See his review of Neely's *Lincoln and the Democrats* in the *Wall Street Journal*, March 17, 2017.

[881] Perhaps the biggest single factor was the failure of Republicans to energize their base, so "Republicans stayed home." Paludan, *People's Contest*, 101. Lincoln attributed the result,

However, there was another political factor which was reassuring in the long run. The Democrats waged an intense racist campaign against the "black Republicans."[882] They made emancipation "the main issue in their quest for control of Congress."[883] The Emancipation Proclamation was "a proposal for the butchering of woman and children, for scenes of lust and rapine, and of arson and murder." The Democrats had really nothing to offer the American people besides racism and an outworn economic program.[884] Racism was "the most compelling of the weapons in the Democratic arsenal."[885] So the contrast was between the Republican economic program, the blueprint for modern America, and the old laissez-faire shibboleths. It was also between a revolution in race relations and "the Constitution as it was." These dichotomies validate Ralph Waldo Emerson's contrast between the party of memory and the party of hope.[886] The Union, and not just the Republican Party, needed a great deal of hope between the election of 1862 and the presidential contest of 1864.

The longer the war continued, the more difficult it became to see how restoration of the status quo antebellum would even be possible. But it was also true that the longer the war continued, the greater became the threat of Northern war-weariness, on which Northern Democrats and the Confederacy increasingly pinned their hopes. By the end of July 1863, with the Confederate defeats at Gettysburg and Vicksburg, a Union victory was inevitable. But not even this reality dissuaded Democrats from persistent tactics of obstruction and resistance. Even so, Unionists were able to draw comfort from the 1863 state elections. Prominent Copperheads Clement Vallandigham in Ohio and George W. Woodward of Pennsylvania were both defeated "by Lincoln's nonpartisan coalition."[887] The core of the Unionist

---

in part, to the loss of the soldier's vote (remedied in time for the presidential election in 1864) and "ineligible foreign voters." Holzer, *Wall Street Journal*, March 17, 2017.

[882] The details are given in specialized monographs. Mainstream textbooks and popular historical accounts give highly sanitized versions. McPherson, commenting on Democratic behavior in the campaign of 1864, observes that "the vulgarity of their tactics almost surpasses belief." McPherson, *Battle Cry*, 789.

[883] McPherson, *Battle Cry*, 560.

[884] They continued to live "on the ideals of laissez-faire." Paludan, *People's Contest*, 91.

[885] Paludan, *People's Contest*, 95. Mark Neely attempts to deny the centrality of Democratic racism, but he has to admit that "the plow of emancipation had to be pulled through a heavy and recalcitrant soil of racism." Neely, *Lincoln and the Democrats*, 49.

[886] Paludan, *People's Contest*, 91.

[887] Dell, *Hidden Civil War*, 261. This broad-based Unionist approach was carried on throughout the presidential race in 1864. Dell also acknowledges the important contributions of prominent generals who were War Democrats, including Ulysses S. Grant, Henry Halleck, Ambrose Burnside, and George H. Thomas. Perhaps the most important War Democrat was Secretary of War Edwin M. Stanton who "shut down newspapers, imprisoned Democratic editors and dissidents, persecuted army officers he suspected

coalition was the Republican Party. It was also helped by the violence of the antidraft riots in New York City in July 1863 as well as by the gallant performance of the black 54th Massachusetts Infantry Regiment at Fort Wagner, South Carolina, in the same month. Republican newspapers made the point that "black men who fought for the Union deserved more respect than white men who fought against it."[888]The period between the election of 1863 and the presidential campaign of 1864 was a period of ever-greater political polarization between the Republican and Democratic parties, essentially a polarization between the opponents and defenders of slavery. The longer the war continued and the more obvious the momentum for emancipation became, the more the Democrats doubled down on their defense of slavery.

By early 1864, a "powerful antislavery consensus within the [Republican] party emerged" which viewed a constitutional amendment as the only sure guarantee for the destruction of slavery.[889] But this was met by a "full-scale defense of slavery" by Democrats.[890] Lincoln remained somewhat disengaged from the first effort at passage. In June 1864, the amendment passed the Senate easily, but it failed in the House in a party-line vote with near-unanimous Democratic opposition; one Republican voted against it and four Democrats supported it.[891] Disheartening as it was, this setback did not dissuade Republicans from their steady commitment to the passage of the amendment. To the extent that Democrats attempted any defense of slavery, they based their argument on "the Constitution as it is" which simply meant property rights. But their main strategy, particularly in 1864 as the presidential election loomed, was to rely on open racism. This continued until it reached a crescendo during the campaign itself. It is instructive to deal briefly with the efforts of two contemporary historians—Mark E. Neely and Joel Silbey—to defend the party. But in an oddly paradoxical way, their efforts seem counterproductive. The very weakness of their defenses makes the indictment even stronger.

---

of favoring the opposition, seized control of the nation's telegraph and railroad lines, replaced civil courts with military tribunals, and sent soldiers home to vote—a novelty in the era before absentee ballots—often to provide decisive electoral margins for Republicans." Harold Holzer, review of Walter Stahr, *Stanton: Lincoln's War Secretary* (2017), *Wall Street Journal*, August 5–6, 2017.

[888] McPherson, *Battle Cry*, 687. The regiment was led by Colonel Robert Gould Shaw who was killed in action. When a request was made for the return of his body, a Confederate officer is reported to have replied, "We have buried him with his niggers."

[889] Oakes, *Slavery National*, 438.

[890] Oaks, *Slavery National*, 446.

[891] For all the congressional votes on the Thirteenth Amendment, see Michael Vorenberg, *Final Freedom: The Civil War, the Abolition of Slavery, and the Thirteenth Amendment* (2004), 251–52.

Joel Silbey argues that during the war years, the Democratic Party func-tioned as a "respectable minority." But he undercuts his own thesis almost at the outset. In his preface, he concedes that Democrats "forcefully challenged the government's policies, particularly the administration's determination to use whatever means necessary to destroy the South and inflict blows against its social system [i.e. slavery] in the name of winning the war." In doing so, they "carped, nagged, and viewed with alarm all in the provocative and bitter style." So, he concludes, the Democrats "did not acquiesce in or celebrate the government's effort even to win the war." [892] This raises the inevitable question: what would a disrespectable minority have done? He claims that most scholars have been "camp followers of the successful army," so the Democratic Party "has not been well served by historical scholarship."[893] But then he acknowledges Democratic faults, particularly in regard to racial issues. Without commenting on the persistent Democratic use of the racial epithet "black Republicans," he concedes that Democrats "reserved their violent abuse for the antislavery policies of the administration." So, after conducting his readers through a Democratic chamber of racist horrors, he concludes that they were "perhaps wrong-headed."[894] Finally, Silbey resorts to the cop-out of moral relativism. He derives the phrase "respectable minority" from an 1864 letter from Jefferson Coolidge to George McClellan asserting that Democrats "were respectable in what they advocated in terms of the times in which they lived." In other words, their racism was accept-able simply because it "was congruent with many of the political and social rhythms of the day."[895]

Mark Neely begins by claiming that much of the apparent conflict was "deafening rhetoric" which "all but deafened historians to the low murmur of steady nonpartisan work for victory."[896] His description of Democrats is puzzling. They were "loyal" but "not at all helpful, upbeat or cheering."[897] So during a time when the Union was fighting for survival, Democrats were "not at all helpful." This is an odd variety of loyalty, but he plunges on to claim that they have been "poorly understood," in fact "consistently misunderstood because of their partisanship and more recently because of their racism," which was "nearly universal among white people at the

---

[892] Silbey, *Respectable Minority*, x.
[893] Silbey, *Respectable Minority*, xii–xiii.
[894] Silbey, *Respectable Minority*, 4, 82, 245.
[895] Silbey, *Respectable Minority*, 244–45. The issue of moral judgments in history is a compli-cated one. But even supposing that slavery could in some way be defended, how could the vile racist rhetoric be excused? The truth is that blacks had to be dehumanized in order for the system to be justified. Dehumanization is always the first resort of exploiters.
[896] Neely, *Lincoln and the Democrats*, 44.
[897] Neely, *Lincoln and the Democrats*, 1.

time."[898] Another odd line of defense occurs when he deals with the issue of white supremacy. Racism became "much more powerful and pernicious" after the war "when Southern voters [i.e. Democrats] returned to the Union." The party "exploited racism," but it was "not yet the party of white supremacy."[899] Finally, Neely's estimate of the overall achievements of the parties is revealing. The Republicans were successful in "saving the Union and freeing the slaves" while the Democrats' achievement was "the survival of the idea of a loyal opposition through the war."[900]

The culmination of the Democrats' racist strategy in 1864 was the publication and dissemination of a 74-page pamphlet entitled *Miscegenation*. It was a "hoaxing pamphlet" written by two Democratic operatives, David G. Croly and George Wakeman of the *New York World*.[901] It was purportedly written by abolitionists who were recommending a deliberate policy of race-mixing by means of interracial marriage. Democrats disseminated it with enthusiasm to prove "the perverse and hidden agenda of the Lincoln administration."[902] The pamphlet anticipated the strategy of the anti-Semitic *Protocols of the Elders of Zion* (1903) in "revealing" the nefarious schemes of a hated minority. It made a significant contribution to the all-out racism of the 1864 Democratic campaign strategy.[903]

But while the Democrats agreed on the centrality of race as a campaign weapon, they were divided into factions of Peace Democrats and War Democrats, a division with significant implications for the 1864 campaign. The election of 1864 was the most consequential in all of American history; the fate of the Union hung in the balance. The Republicans had two goals—to win the war and pass the Thirteenth Amendment.[904] They were rightly convinced that losing to "any Democrat" would mean that "slavery would almost certainly survive the war."[905] The basic problem was simply

---

[898] Neely, *Lincoln and the Democrats*, 2.

[899] Neely, *Lincoln and the Democrats*, 3.

[900] Neely, *Lincoln and the Democrats*, 82. He claims that Democrats "pretty much invented the idea" (82). But how disloyal were the Whigs during the Mexican War?

[901] Neely, *Lincoln and the Democrats*, 245. The title was a newly coined word. The *Merriam-Webster Dictionary* gives 1863 as the year of its appearance. The pamphlet first appeared in December 1863.

[902] Weber, *Copperheads*, 160.

[903] Neely is inclined to treat the whole thing as almost a harmless prank. He admits its racism but dismisses its importance, stating that the hoax came to "a laughable end" in the fall of 1864. Neely, *Lincoln and the Democrats*, 112.

[904] There were brief flurries of interest in Salmon Chase and John Fremont as alternatives to Lincoln, but neither man really posed a serious, enduring challenge, although McPherson asserts that Lincoln's nomination and reelection were "by no means assured." McPherson, *Battle Cry*, 713.

[905] Oakes, *Freedom National*, 472.

that only "a smattering of War Democrats" supported emancipation.[906] The Peace Democrats were a mixed bag, and the best outcome they could offer was peace and reunion with slavery—the status quo antebellum. But clearly there were those, like Vallendigham, who were "unconditionally and reflexively antiwar."[907] They were willing to renounce the entire Union war effort, though they were cautious about saying so openly. This group was itself divided, with "much tension . . . during the war: anger, bitterness, and internal sniping."[908]

A badly fragmented Democratic Party went to its convention in late August 1864. Democrats did agree on one important thing. George McClellan was the hands-down choice to be the pre Wade sidential nominee. But what did that mean? The Peace Democrats were unhappy with the choice; after all, he was, ostensibly at least, a War Democrat. His popularity easily carried the day, but what were the policy implications? Even Neely concedes that the party platform was "disastrous."[909] The key passage was a call for "immediate efforts to be made for a cessation of hostilities with a view of an ultimate convention of States, or other peaceable means, to the end that, at the earliest practicable moment, peace may be restored on the basis of the Federal Union of the States."[910] But to end the fighting without conditions except the hope of ultimate reunion was a recipe for disaster. The call for "an immediate armistice" was to put peace first "and Union a distant second."[911] It was also hardly reassuring that the Democrats also nominated George H. Pendleton, "a notorious antiwar man," for vice president.[912]

Despite McClellan's ostensible position as a War Democrat, some in the party were uneasy and feared that he would be stigmatized as a peace-at-all-costs candidate. The result was that "older and possibly wiser heads" insisted that a recognition of the Union by the Confederacy should be "an indispensable preliminary to the cessation of hostilities."[913] Finally in response to a letter from August Belmont, McClellan produced a letter which gave "an impression of crisp, terse Unionism."[914] So the Democrats went into the

---

[906] Vorenberg, *Final Freedom*, 96.

[907] Silbey, *Respectable Minority*, 99.

[908] Silbey, *Respectable Minority*, 110.

[909] Neely, *Lincoln and the Democrats*, 4. Weber has a darker view, calling it "a Copperhead manifesto." Weber, *Copperheads*, 1.

[910] 1864 Democratic Party Platform.

[911] McPherson, *Battle Cry*, 772.

[912] Weber, *Copperheads*, 1.

[913] Charles R. Wilson, "Changing Views of the Peace Plank of 1864," *American Historical Review* 38 (1933): 499.

[914] Wilson, "McClellan," 504. George McGovern concedes that McClellan "did not support emancipation in any way." McGovern, *Lincoln*, 107.

campaign of 1864 with a popular candidate whose basic convictions were unknown. The Republican Party convention met in early June 1864 as the National Union Party. It was hoped that the Union label would appeal to a broad base of Unionists outside the Republican Party. The most dramatic evidence of this strategy, besides the party label, was that Vice President Hannibal Hamlin was replaced by Andrew Johnson, a War Democrat and Southern Unionist from Tennessee.

The presidential campaign began against the backdrop of the military campaign. Events on distant battlefields would decide the election. From the Union perspective, it was a race against time. From a purely military standpoint, the Union had won the war, but the Northern war-weariness could easily prove decisive. In late summer 1864, Lincoln, with good reason, thought that he would lose the election. But even so, he continued to insist that "the end of slavery serve as a precondition for peace and readmission to the Union."[915] The only hope of the Confederacy was that the North, understandably appalled by never-ending casualty lists, would seek an immediate end to the endless slaughter. The "violence and gruesomeness" of the military campaign "stunned the North."[916] Lincoln and his generals were acutely aware of the danger. This is why Grant pounded remorselessly at Lee's army at this stage of the war, accepting the enormous cost to his own troops.[917] But finally, it was the dramatic twin victories of David Farragut and William T. Sherman that carried Lincoln to victory. Farragut closed off Mobile, Alabama, the last Confederate port on the Gulf of Mexico, in August 1864. In early September, Sherman captured Atlanta and regrouped for his March to the Sea. At last, with the end in sight, the people of the North could vote their political convictions, freed of the nightmare of endless war.

The most remarkable thing about the election of 1864 is the one thing we most take for granted—that it was held at all. How many nations hold elections in the midst of civil war? If ever there was a case for declaring a national emergency and suspending elections and civil liberties, this was it. Yet for all the Democratic carping, elections were held and civil liberties were honored during an unprecedented national emergency. The election result constituted a clear vindication of Lincoln and the Republican Party. Lincoln overwhelmed McClellan in the electoral vote 212–21, carrying all but three states—Delaware, Kentucky, and New Jersey, and he won the popular

---

[915] Joseph R. Fournieri, *Abraham Lincoln's Political Faith*, 165
[916] Weber, *Copperheads*, 139.
[917] Grant's reputation as a butcher is based primarily on these late-war attacks which were undertaken in a uniquely dangerous political context: there was no time to spare.

vote 55 percent to 45 percent.[918] The result showed that the people of the North to an encouraging degree were committed to both the Union and emancipation.

Another significant aspect of the election was the soldiers' vote. Lincoln had learned from his negligence in 1862, so he was careful to ensure that the soldiers were able to vote. Democrats opposed this, to the extent that they dared, with good reason for the soldiers were generally Unionist if not Republican.[919] They were not spilling their blood for the status quo ante-bellum; they resented Democratic obstruction of the war effort. Democrats ran "the most explicitly virulent racist campaign in American history."[920] But despite this, white soldiers were grateful for the help of black soldiers and generally repudiated Democratic racism. The decisive victory in 1864 enabled Lincoln and the Republicans to push ahead with winning the war and securing the passage of the Thirteenth Amendment, realizing that it was the only sure means of securing permanent emancipation against Democratic congressional repudiation or a Supreme Court reversal.[921] Despite earlier hesitations, Lincoln had come to regard the Thirteenth Amendment as "a king's cure for all the evils."[922] After his election victory, "no piece of legislation during Lincoln's presidency received more of his attention than the Thirteenth Amendment."[923]

Although there was powerful momentum after the victorious election in support of the Thirteenth Amendment, passage was by no means certain because of determined Democratic opposition and the high bar required for constitutional amendments. Lincoln wanted it to be approved in a bipartisan fashion, but that was not to be. Most Democrats "preferred to stand on principle in defense of the past. Even if the war killed slavery, they refused to help bury it."[924] The outcome was so uncertain that the Republicans were compelled to resort to "vote swapping and patronage deals" to secure passage.[925] The amendment passed the Senate in April 1864 and the House in January 1865. The amendment enjoyed overwhelming Republican

---

[918] It is also true that the Democrats received almost 450,000 more votes than in 1860; in several key states Lincoln's margin of victory was only around 5 percent.

[919] McPherson, *Battle Cry*, 804.

[920] Foner, *Fiery Trial*, 309.

[921] The Supreme Court situation improved from the Republican perspective with the death of Roger B. Taney, Lincoln's inveterate enemy, in October 1864. Lincoln appointed Salmon Chase to the Supreme Court in December 1864.

[922] Foner, *Fiery Trial*, 314.

[923] Vorenberg, *Final Freedom*, 180.

[924] McPherson, *Battle Cry*, 839.

[925] Vorenberg, *Final Freedom*, 201.

support and overwhelming Democratic opposition.[926] It was a splendid triumph, which vindicated the Republican commitment to end slavery. The triumph was completed when twenty-seven of the then-existing thirty-nine states approved the amendment. Many Republican congressmen regarded its passage as "the crowning moment of their careers."[927] Lincoln was so pleased that he insisted on signing it though his signature was not legally required. Ironically, this supreme triumph may well have cost Lincoln his life. It was the nightmarish prospect of black freedom and civil rights that led John Wilkes Booth, a pathologically embittered Democrat, to kill Lincoln on Good Friday, April 14, 1865.

Over the years, Lincoln's death has spawned seemingly endless speculations about what might have been. Such speculation is inevitable but fruitless. The issue which emerged after the passage of the Thirteenth Amendment came to be known as Reconstruction. There had been various tensions between Lincoln and congressional Republicans on how the Southern states would rejoin the Union after the war. But if the Republicans and Lincoln had grappled with differences and complexities, it was all very simple for the South. All Southerners wanted was simple reunion with no questions asked, no requirements imposed, and no social reform attempted. But if the Republicans had not yet definitely decided on what they wanted, they clearly did not want that. After all, if even the Northern Democrats had gone into the ditch defending slavery, how likely was it that Southern Democrats would evince any regard for the Thirteenth Amendment or for any other measure designed to secure civil rights for the blacks in their midst?[928] Mark Neely certainly had one thing right in his attempted defense of the Democratic Party when he observed that racism became "much more powerful and pernicious" after the South rejoined the Union.[929] He admits that Democrats became the party of white supremacy during the Reconstruction era, endangering Lincoln's hope for "new birth of freedom."[930]

---

[926] There was a smattering of votes of Unionist and Unconditional Unionists congressmen who split a small number of yes and no votes. See Vorenberg, *Final Freedom*, appendix, 252. See also Chapter Eleven for a more detailed partisan breakdown of the vote.

[927] Vorenberg, *Final Freedom*, 208, 210.

[928] During the war and Reconstruction period, for some historians Democrats mysteriously vanish; they become Southerners, states-rightists, ex-Confederates, whites, or even conservatives. According to Robert Rutland postwar Southern blacks suffered violence at the hands of "desperate whites." Rutland, *Republicans*, 71. For a definitive overview of the stance of the Democratic Party on all issues related to black civil rights during the middle period of American history, see Glenn Linden, *Politics or Principle: Congressional Voting on Civil War Amendments and Pro-Negro Measures, 1838–1869* (1977), especially the voting on the three civil-rights constitutional amendments, 1864–1869, 9–28.

[929] Neely, *Lincoln and the Democrats*, 3.

[930] Abraham Lincoln, Gettysburg Address, November 19, 1863.

CHAPTER ELEVEN: MASSIVE RESISTANCE: RECONSTRUCTION, 1865–1877

The long, bitter war ended at Appomattox with the scruffy, victorious Grant offering generous terms to the impeccably accoutered Lee, whose gratitude was no less profound for being restrained. It was a generosity which Lee received by saying, "This will have the best possible effect upon the men and will also do much toward conciliating our people."[931] When news of the surrender spread among the Union troops, a spontaneous celebration erupted in the firing of salutes. Grant ordered them to stop "immediately," saying that, "the war is over; the rebels are our countrymen again."[932] But this soulful scene was deceptive. The survivors of the Army of Northern Virginia were doubtless grateful for the twenty-five thousand rations, their horses, and their sidearms. But there has been a "mighty myth" regarding Appomattox. The Confederate soldiers returned "home from fighting still fighting" and launched "a powerful insurgency" against the soon-to-be enacted Reconstruction policy.[933] It is almost axiomatic that civil wars end badly; in this case, at least, there was to be no American exceptionalism. Appomattox was no prelude to national reconciliation.

Discussions of Reconstruction often start with "What Would Lincoln Have Done?" It is difficult not to get drawn into the issue but impossible

---

[931] See among many retellings, Ronald C. White, *American Ulysses: A Life of Ulysses S. Grant* (2017), 413.

[932] White, *Grant*, 413.

[933] Gregory P. Downs, *After Appomattox* (2015), 9. Reconstruction refers to the Republican policy regarding the terms of the reunion of the Southern states. The absolute minimum requirements were an affirmation of loyalty to the Union and the abolition of slavery. But even this was too much for some Democrats, North and South, to accept.

to ever resolve it. Lincoln clearly hoped for a quick, generous method of restoring the Union, best exemplified by his 10 percent plan presented in early December 1863.[934] It reflected Lincoln's hope for a relatively painless restoration of the Union based on the reemergence of strong Unionist sentiment in the South before ominous signs of Southern intransigence had appeared.[935] Ominous signs were not long in appearing. The bedrock consequence of the long, bloody Civil War was the end of slavery, and the bedrock guarantee of its demise was a constitutional amendment. The Thirteenth Amendment passed the Senate on April 8, 1864. Republicans approved it unanimously 30–0, while Democrats voted 5–4 against it. There were three votes in the House. In a test vote on the antislavery resolution on February 15, 1864, the Republican vote was 97 percent in favor; the Democratic vote was 98 percent opposed. When it failed on June 15, 1864, the Republican vote was 99 percent in favor and the Democratic vote was 94 percent opposed. When it finally passed on January 31, 1865, the Republican vote was 100 percent in favor; the Democratic vote was 77 percent opposed.[936]

In response to Democratic resistance, exasperated Republicans passed the Wade–Davis Bill, a more stringent Reconstruction measure, on July 2, 1864. Much to the consternation of Congressional Republicans, Lincoln pocket-vetoed it.[937] At the time of the assassination in April 1865, the only real certainty was the ratification of the Thirteenth Amendment. The myriad details of Reconstruction were yet to be worked out.

Perhaps the principal reason Lincoln failed to sign the Wade–Davis Bill was that it clearly intended to assert a Congressional role in the process of Reconstruction.[938] This vital issue was unresolved at the time of the assassination. His last speech, delivered on April 11, 1865, indicated that he was not prepared to make a "statement of settled Reconstruction policy."[939]

---

[934] If 10 percent of the 1860 electorate in any Southern state took a loyalty oath and accepted emancipation, it could form a new state government and apply for readmittance to the Union.

[935] Lincoln greatly overestimated Unionist sentiment in the South before the war began. His reference for a minimalist approach to Reconstruction was predicated on this optimistic but false estimation.

[936] Vorenberg, *Final Freedom*, 251–52; see also McPherson, *Battle Cry*, 706. The cumulative vote totals were Republicans 526 in favor, out of 536; Democrats 329 opposed, out of 362. Linden, *Politics or Principle*, 13. This intense Democratic opposition validated the realization of Republicans that, in the absence of this amendment, "once the Southern Democrats were allowed to rejoin their Northern brethren, there was nothing to stop them from reimposing slavery." Randy E. Barnett, "Free at Last," *Claremont Review of Books*, Winter, 2015/16, posted, February 23, 2016.

[937] This bill required that a majority of the electorate in each state take a loyalty oath.

[938] Douglas Egerton, *The Wars of Reconstruction: The Brief History of America's Most Progressive Era* (2013), 62.

[939] Eric Foner, *Reconstruction: America's Unfinished Revolution, 1865–1877* (1988), 74.

Before the election, Lincoln had dropped "his capable vice president, the abolitionist Hannibal Hamlin," for Andrew Johnson of Tennessee, a strongly Unionist War Democrat.[940] In anticipation of what promised to be a close election, this decision was understandable. Lincoln might have chosen an ex-Whig, but he was "appealing to Northern War Democrats" on a Unionist ticket.[941] Johnson was an energetic War Democrat who "waged a valiant struggle against secession."[942] In 1862, he became military governor of Tennessee, serving as "virtually the dictator," using "high-handed" tactics to establish a "pro-Union civil government."[943] During the campaign of 1864, he was "merciless in his condemnation of the southern rebels."[944] But, nevertheless, signs of trouble were not long in coming. Johnson delivered a meandering inaugural speech while intoxicated to a "horrified" audience.[945] But the problem went far deeper than this public gaffe.

Fredrick Douglass provided a piercing insight into the problem. At Lincoln's swearing-in ceremony on March 4, 1864, Douglass recalled seeing Lincoln pointing him out to Johnson whose first expression, "the true index of his heart," was "one of bitter contempt and aversion." After realizing that Douglass was looking at him, his expression changed to the "bland and sickly smile of the demagogue." Douglass concluded that, "whatever Andrew Johnson is, he is no friend of our race."[946] The replacement of Lincoln with Johnson was a devolution from a man who manifested charity for all in the worst of times to a man whose dominant traits in the moment of victory were "preternatural stubbornness and racism."[947]

Several of Johnson's early statements seemed reassuring. In October 1864, he promised to be a "Moses" who would lead blacks "through the Red Sea of war and bondage to freedom."[948] In an interview with Grant soon after becoming president, Johnson vowed to "make treason odious" by punishing

---

[940] Fergus M. Bordewich's review of Egerton's *Wars of Reconstruction* in the *Wall Street Journal*, January 18/19, 2014.

[941] Thomas B. Alexander, "Persistent Whiggery in the Confederate South, 1860–1877," *Journal of Southern History* 27 (1961): 315.

[942] Albert Castel, *The Presidency of Andrew Johnson* (1970), 8.

[943] Castel, *Andrew Johnson*, 9.

[944] Annette Gordon-Reed, *Andrew Johnson* (2011), 78.

[945] Hans L. Trefousse, *Andrew Johnson: A Biography* (1989), 189.

[946] Gordon-Reed, *Andrew Johnson*, 2. Quoted from Frederick Douglass, *The Life and Times of Frederick Douglass* (1881).

[947] Gordon-Reed, *Andrew Johnson*, 5. Johnson believed that Douglass was "just like any nigger & he would sooner cut a white man's throat than not." Quoted in Allen Guelzo, *Fateful Lightning*, 494.

[948] Gordon-Reed, *Andrew Johnson*, 80; Trefousse, *Andrew Johnson*, 183. Only a short time later, he reinvented himself as Pharaoh.

Lee and other Confederate leaders.[949] He had the poor-white resentment of the great planters, relishing having them come to him hat-in-hand seeking pardons.[950] Johnson's popularity peaked in May 1865, culminating in a great victory parade. Even the hard-line Republicans, by no means easily satisfied, had high hopes for him, but the warning signs were quick to materialize. There were three major issues confronting the nation in the spring of 1866: the status of the Confederate states; the status of the freedmen; and the unresolved issue of who was in charge—Congress or the president? On all three issues, Johnson took flagrantly antagonistic positions.[951]

Johnson denied that the Southern states could secede, and if they could not secede, they were still in the Union. Lincoln had dismissed the secession issue as a "pernicious abstraction."[952] While this may well have been true in a constitutional sense, the on-the-ground political implications were vast. If the Southern states were still in the Union, Johnson was in charge, no Reconstruction was possible, and these states could immediately assert their presence in Congress. But then the Southern states, in conjunction with Northern Democrats, could regain control of Congress.[953] This would mean that the only thing the Civil War victory would actually have accomplished would have been the abolition of slavery, a hollow victory in light of the obvious intentions of Southern whites toward the freedmen.

Johnson's proclamation admitting Virginia into the Union did not mention black suffrage. It is not surprising that Northern Democrats welcomed the presence of "a fellow Democrat in the White House." The Northern Democrats wanted the "immediate and unconditional return of the Southern states to the Union."[954] Republicans of all the various persuasions from conservative to moderate to radical resisted, so their Reconstruction policy was taking shape in the middle of an ongoing and increasingly bitter confrontation with Johnson, culminating ultimately in the ill-fated impeachment effort. But to see the struggle only in this context would be a simplistic

---

[949] Jean Edward Smith, *Grant* (2002), 418. Grant refused to violate the terms of the surrender at Appomattox, threatening to resign over the issue. Johnson, knowing "when he was overmatched," gave way, but this incident was a harbinger of a troubled relationship.

[950] He made "a great show of this" but, nonetheless, issued many pardons "with great alacrity" and restored as many ex-Confederates as possible to their old positions. Gordon-Reed, *Andrew Johnson*, 25.

[951] See Guelzo, *Fateful Lightning*, 484–85.

[952] Gordon-Reed, *Andrew Johnson*, 104. The quote is from Lincoln's last speech on April 11, 1865.

[953] The math was daunting. Instead of blacks increasing Southern voting strength by the three-fifths ratio, the entire black population would be counted.

[954] Castel, *Andrew Johnson*, 21. Castel says that while "most" Democrats supported the Union, "a large portion of them had sympathized with the Confederacy."

distortion of the fundamental dynamic. Everything Frederick Douglass had said about Johnson could be said with equal accuracy about the Democratic Party as a whole.[955] But even this does not completely get to the heart of the matter. This is yet another instance of what may be called the Van Buren Curse, that longstanding linkage which has put the Northern Democratic Party in thrall to the Southern extremists—extremists in defense of slavery, then extremists in defense of black peonage.

Republicans experienced an ever-deepening disillusionment with Johnson, who had quickly turned from making treason odious to encouraging Southern resistance to even modest efforts at Reconstruction. However, there is one charge against him which should be quickly dismissed. This is what might be called the myth of the lost opportunity, the idea that the South immediately after the war was so shattered by defeat that it would have accepted Republican demands, so Johnson's recalcitrance enabled "a small but determined cadre of aggressive reactionaries to seize control."[956] But the whole burden of Southern history dictated a different response. The most one could reasonably expect would have been a short period of stunned acquiescence followed by the dogged resistance which did appear. The behavior of Southerners at times bordered on the unbelievable. They resisted black rights, "repealed" rather than "repudiated" secession, and even resisted the implications of the Thirteenth Amendment.[957]

Nothing indicated the intensity of Southern resistance more clearly than the enactment of black codes throughout the South. These codes had both political and economic implications. They were intended to keep the freedmen in a condition as close to slavery as possible by binding them to contract-labor servitude. The result was both political and economic peonage. It is no exaggeration to say that the goal was "to restore slavery in all but name."[958] Therefore, the codes "became a lightning rod for Northern criticism."[959] These codes seemed to many Northerners to contest the whole purpose of the Civil War with all of its immense sacrifices; they were "deeply infuriating" because the "moral victory" which the North had "imagined itself to have won had come to nothing."[960] The result of all these factors was that

---

[955] Annette Gordon-Reed refers to "the white supremacist Democratic Party." *Andrew Johnson*, 111. Some historians are reluctant to make any explicit reference to the Democratic Party.

[956] See Egerton, *Wars of Reconstruction*, 18.

[957] Guelzo, *Fateful Lightning*, 491

[958] Egerton, *Wars of Reconstruction*, 180.

[959] Michael W. Fitzgerald, *Splendid Failure: Postwar Reconstruction in the American South* (2008), 33.

[960] Eric L. McKitrick, *Andrew Johnson and Reconstruction* (1960), 38–39, 41.

by the end of December 1865 there were "poisons in the Northern bosom."[961] The black codes strengthened "the resolve of Republicans to keep the South on probation" until they could find ways to protect the freedmen.[962] The attitude of many Southerners contributed to a sense of a complete impasse as when Garrett Davis, a Kentucky Democrat, denounced what he called the Republican "tyrannical and despotic faction in Congress."[963]

The Radical Republican faction had an ambitious agenda for a top-to-bottom reformation of the South. But the term has been used with baffling imprecision. Some historians and Southerners called all Republicans Jacobins.[964] Some mainstream history textbooks, while avoiding the Jacobin label, seem to regard every Republican measure as part of a Radical Reconstruction, as though efforts to ensure equal rights for the freedmen should be characterized as radical.[965] The truly Radical faction, led by Thaddeus Stevens and Charles Sumner, did advocate a Radical program centering on "general confiscation" of land, primarily from the great planters, and its redistribution to the freedmen.[966] This program would be linked to black suffrage and an open-ended period of "territorial status" for Southern states before their readmittance to the Union.[967] But for all of the frenzied attention it received, this group was never in control. These aspects of the Radical program were never implemented because they called for "a striking departure in American public life."[968]

It was never probable that such an agenda would ever have been implemented. The Republican agenda during 1866 was a moderate one. The Republicans supported the creation of the Freedmen's Bureau to aid their transition from slavery to freedom, a civil-rights bill, and, finally, the Fourteenth Amendment to confer full citizenship on them. The state governments "erected under Johnson's authority" had "only to accept the [Fourteenth] amendment and repeal laws which were discriminatory."[969] But even this minimalist agenda proved to be too much for either Johnson or the Democrats to accept. Minimalist it well may have been, yet it was ambitious enough in the context of what the Democratic Party as a whole was inclined to accept. In this narrow sense, it was a radical program; it can be "seen as

[961] McKitrick, *Andrew Johnson*, 41.

[962] James M. McPherson, *Ordeal by Fire: The Civil War and Reconstruction* (2001), 509.

[963] Quoted in Guelzo, *Fateful Lightning*, 493.

[964] T. Harry Williams, *Lincoln and the Radicals*; see McKitrick, *Andrew Johnson*, 384.

[965] See, for example, Alan Brinkley, *American History: A Survey*, 2 vols. (10th ed., 1999), vol 1, 512–17.

[966] McKitrick, *Andrew Johnson*, 333.

[967] Michael L. Benedict, *The Impeachment and Trial of Andrew Johnson* (1999), 17.

[968] Foner, *Reconstruction*, 237.

[969] Benedict, *Impeachment and Trial*, 15.

the last great crusade of the nineteenth century romantic reformers."[970] The Democratic response was total rejection. Both the Freedmen's Bureau bill and the Civil Rights Act of 1866 had been crafted by Lyman Trumbull, a prominent Republican moderate from Illinois. Johnson's rejection of these bills meant that "the possibility of compromise was finally withdrawn" and the break with Congress was "open and explicit."[971]

The Freedmen's Bureau had been created in March 1865. Efforts to renew it in 1866 had to run the gauntlet of Johnson's vetoes before finally passing in mid-July 1866. It passed with unanimous Republican approval against "the solid opposition of Democrats."[972] Johnson wrote "an abrasive, confrontational veto message" which was promptly overridden.[973] The full name of the bureau, which indicates something of its mission, was the Bureau of Refugees, Freedmen, and Abandoned Lands. It was an idealistic social-service agency, headed by General O. O. Howard, "the Christian general," with daunting responsibilities for helping the freedmen with land ownership, education, and racial justice.[974] The history of the agency reveals an ongoing contest between its laudable purposes and the withering hostility it endured throughout the South until its eventual demise in 1872. Hostility to the agency and its idealistic personnel quickly reached pathological proportions. Bureau agents directly encountered the "depths of racial antagonism and class conflict in the postwar South."[975]

Land ownership for the freedmen was at the heart of the mission of the Bureau, and here resistance was the strongest. Acting unilaterally, Johnson returned hundreds of thousands of acres to the planters.[976] Since the army was charged with sustaining the activity of the Bureau, he also sought to appoint Democrats to key army positions. The result was that only a "minuscule" amount of land was ever given to freedmen; "tens of thousands" of freedmen were displaced throughout the South. The result was "a deep sense of betrayal by freedmen" as the idea of promoting black landownership "came to an abrupt end."[977]

---

[970] Kenneth M. Stampp, *The Era of Reconstruction, 1865–1877* (1965), 101. True to their Whiggish roots, the Republicans held to "ideas of social betterment. Their story is the story of American progress." Hans L. Trefousse, *The Radical Republicans: Lincoln's Vanguard for Racial Justice* (1975), 33.

[971] McKitrick, *Andrew Johnson*, 11.

[972] Castel, *Andrew Johnson*, 65.

[973] Egerton, *Wars of Reconstruction*, 126.

[974] Foner, *Reconstruction*, 142.

[975] Foner, *Reconstruction*, 170.

[976] Egerton, *Wars of Reconstruction*, 127.

[977] Foner, *Reconstruction*, 161–64.

So the most promising effort to provide the freedmen with significant economic opportunity was largely unsuccessful. Sharecropping and tenant farming, rather than land ownership, kept blacks in economic servitude, and the Republican effort to establish landownership and a free-labor system failed.[978] By the end of 1866, "nearly all the arable land of the Freedmen's Bureau had been returned to its ex-Confederate owners."[979] Democratic critics of the Bureau "offered only widespread poverty as an alternative."[980] The end of slavery with its resulting economic chaos actually put the freedmen in even greater danger since they were no longer "the expensive chattel of politically influential planters."[981]

The other major purpose of the Bureau was the education of the freedmen. Here the Bureau did achieve a measure of success. By 1869, the Bureau had over a quarter of a million students in over three thousand schools throughout the South. The result was that there were "spectacular gains" in literacy which continued even after the end of Reconstruction. Dependable statistics are hard to come by, but one study shows that black illiteracy dropped from 90 percent in 1861 to 70 percent in 1880.[982] There was violent resistance. Many idealistic white teachers from the North, often employed by the American Missionary Society, an "evangelical abolitionist organization," went south on educational missions.[983] Yet they encountered "the bitterness of most Southerners" and a degree of "social ostracism" which often "escalated into vigorous campaigns of arson and murder."[984] In the face of such resistance, it is remarkable that Bureau teachers enjoyed any significant success at all. The Bureau lost most of its funding in 1869, coming to an abrupt, inglorious end in 1872 when Congress refused to renew the legislation required to maintain it.[985]

The Freedmen's Bureau was an attempt to prepare the freedmen, economically and educationally, for citizenship. The Civil Rights Act of 1866 attempted to confer the citizenship rights for which the Thirteenth Amendment was only a preparation.[986] The bill followed what was becoming an all-

---

[978] Planters detested even sharecropping because it gave blacks at least some measure of freedom. Egerton, *Wars of Reconstruction*, 152.

[979] McPherson, *Ordeal by Fire*, 505.

[980] Egerton, *Wars of Reconstruction*, 123.

[981] Egerton, *Wars of Reconstruction*, 205.

[982] Egerton, *Wars of Reconstruction*, 137, 166–67.

[983] Egerton, *Wars of Reconstruction*, 146.

[984] Egerton, *Wars of Reconstruction*, 155, 159. Southerners regarded the idea of public education for blacks as "nearly incomprehensible" (163).

[985] Its real work had "scarcely begun." Stampp, *Era of Reconstruction*, 135.

[986] It was intended to "give meaning to the Thirteenth Amendment" by granting the basic rights of citizenship to all Americans except Indians. Foner, *Reconstruction*, 243–44.

too-familiar trajectory. It passed Congress easily in February-March 1866. Virtually everyone expected Johnson to sign it; almost all of his Cabinet urged him to do so. But he was at this point committed to confrontation; he denounced it as "evil."[987] His veto was easily overridden in April 1866, and the bill became law. The veto really ended "all hope of cooperation with the president."[988] The Democrats as a whole were "once again united in opposition."[989] Some of the rhetoric was unhinged. Garrett Davis said that passage of the bill would compel him "to regard himself as an enemy of the Government and work for its overthrow."[990]

From a constitutional perspective, however, opponents of the bill had a point. The act implemented an "astonishing expansion of federal authority and black rights."[991] Republicans realized that the Democrats would immediately challenge its constitutionality. This led to the move toward the definitive solution of another constitutional amendment.[992] The amendment was crafted by moderate Republicans seeking to safeguard the basic intent of the Civil Rights Act. On the one hand, it was an indisputable legal remedy. But on the other hand, it "transferred vast areas of what formerly had been exclusive state responsibility to federal government control."[993] Yet what was the alternative? In an ideal world, the states, acting in good faith, would guarantee the basic rights of citizenship for all Americans. But on this volatile issue, good faith could not be assumed.

Johnson's reaction to the proposed Fourteenth Amendment revealed an abysmal sense of timing. He had persuaded himself that he had a viable political future, so he hurled himself into the 1866 Congressional elections. He patched together a National Unionist Convention as a vehicle for his campaign; it was an abortive effort to produce a coalition of conservative Republicans and Northern Democrats. The biggest problem was that Republicans were "conspicuously scarce."[994] It was evident that, despite the fusionist rhetoric, "the Democratic tail was growing faster than the Unionist dog."[995]

---

[987] Castel argues that this action was "one of the greatest blunders of his presidency—perhaps the greatest." Castel, *Andrew Johnson*, 71.

[988] Foner, *Reconstruction*, 250.

[989] Egerton, *Wars of Reconstruction*, 199.

[990] Quoted in Egerton, *Wars of Reconstruction*, 199.

[991] Foner, *Reconstruction*, 251. Passage of the act led to "renewed violence." Egerton, *Wars of Reconstruction*, 206.

[992] The Supreme Court declared the act unconstitutional in the *Civil Rights Cases* (1883). The Court became ever more reactionary on the issues of Reconstruction, ultimately culminating in the separate but equal doctrine of *Plessy v. Ferguson* (1896).

[993] Michael Stokes Paulsen and Luke Paulsen, *The Constitution: An Introduction* (2015), 181.

[994] Castel, *Andrew Johnson*, 85.

[995] McKitrick, *Andrew Johnson*, 407.

But if the preparations were faulty, the actual campaign was even worse. Almost always his own worst enemy, Johnson launched an ambitious speaking campaign, "the swing around the circle," which was marred by intemperate speeches made even more intemperate by vigorous heckling. The "all-dominant issue" was Reconstruction; the campaign was "a dismal fiasco"—marred by reckless language. Frequent recourse to alcohol made Johnson seem to be a drunkard, since "he talked and acted like one."[996] He wanted a quick, easy, no-questions-asked restoration of the Union, using the old Democratic slogan, "as it was." But the overwhelming number of Northerners, radical Republicans or not, wanted a "more perfect union" which would vindicate the immense sacrifices of the Civil War. The election was an unmitigated disaster for Democrats as the Republicans "swept state after state" on their way to a veto-proof majority in Congress.[997] Johnson's uncompromising support for the "immediate and unqualified admission of the Southern states" with its implicit acceptance of white supremacy had met with a powerful repudiation by Northern voters.[998]

Throughout this entire period Johnson pursued his course of single-minded obstructionism. At nearly any point in 1866, Johnson could have abandoned his collision course. The Fourteenth Amendment, which passed Congress in June 1866, was a predictable response to his rejection of the Civil Rights Act. It was an attempt to establish racial equality beyond Democratic rejection and presidential vetoes. It established "the primacy of national citizenship," and it "carried forward the state-building process born of the Civil War."[999] However, Johnson "quickly repudiated the entire process."[1000] For their part, the Southern states "reacted with almost unanimous opposition."[1001] The Republicans had "exhausted every means" of coming to an agreement with Johnson.[1002] They also "made every effort to retain moderate support."[1003] It is true that some Republicans had reservations about racial equality, particularly with regard to suffrage. So Congressional Republicans tried to avoid getting too far ahead of Northern public

---

[996] Castel, *Andrew Johnson*, 87, 94–95.

[997] Trefousee, *Radical Republicans*, 449. The Republicans "crushed Johnson's moderate and Democratic friends" with margins of 173–53 in the House and 43–9 in the Senate. Guelzo, *Fateful Lightning*, 497.

[998] McKitrick, *Andrew Johnson*, 449.

[999] Foner, *Reconstruction*, 260.

[1000] Foner, *Reconstruction*, 260; Stampp, *Era of Reconstruction*, 113.

[1001] Castel, *Andrew Johnson*, 101.

[1002] Trefousee, *Radical Republicans*, 332.

[1003] Trefousee, *Radical Republicans*, 345–46.

opinion. The Fourteenth Amendment did not contain an explicit reference to suffrage.[1004]

The amendment passed both houses of Congress easily in April 1866.[1005] Yet in "an unprecedented act" Johnson crafted a special message repudiating the action because the eleven ex-Confederate states had not yet been readmitted to the Union.[1006] White Southerners reacted to the Congressional passage of the amendment "with hysterical exaggeration" of its dire social effects.[1007] Ultimately, passage of the amendment occurred only when it was made a condition of the readmittance of the Southern states into the Union. Even so, 73 percent of Democratic senators voted against it; 93 percent of Republican senators supported it. In the House, 84 percent of Democrats opposed it, while 87 percent of Republicans supported it.[1008] The drama unfolding during the Republican effort to provide a legal basis for black citizenship in as moderate and noncoercive a way as possible played out in the context of two other developments, one hidden from the public eye and the other all too visible.

Johnson's dogged efforts to thwart every aspect of Republican policy became increasingly intense in the summer of 1866. Grant feared that Johnson, who wanted to dispatch him on a diplomatic mission to Mexico and replace him with the more compliant Sherman, was planning a coup to thwart an impending Republican landslide. But Sherman "wouldn't bite and Grant wouldn't budge."[1009] Grant, leaving nothing to chance, "quietly ordered the removal of weapons and ammunition from Federal arsenals in the South."[1010] Nothing happened, so it is nearly impossible to determine with any accuracy the extent of Johnson's intentions. But at the least, the incident is evidence of the profound distrust Johnson's actions had provoked.

There was a backlash of Southern violence in response to the Republican effort to secure black rights. Two Southern cities were rocked by riots

---

[1004] There was "much disagreement" among Republicans over an explicit reference to black suffrage, McKitrick, *Andrew Johnson*, 332. Nevertheless, Republicans supported it by "a large majority," while Northern Democrats "mounted an antisuffrage campaign that exploited race prejudice in the usual manner." McPherson, *Ordeal by Fire*, 499.

[1005] Senate, 33–11; House, 120–32.

[1006] Castel, *Andrew Johnson*, 75.

[1007] Dan T. Carter, *When the War was Over: The Failure of Self-Reconstruction in the South, 1865–1877* (1985), 243.

[1008] Linden, *Politics or Principle*, 11, 13. Many Democrats could not even bring themselves to repudiate slavery itself. Senate Democrats voted against the Thirteenth Amendment 60 percent of the time, while in the House they voted against it 91 percent of the time. Meanwhile, virtually all Republicans supported it in both houses of Congress.

[1009] Smith, *Grant*, 427.

[1010] Smith, *Grant*, 428. Smith finds evidence for this action in Grant's papers. Stanton may also have feared a possible coup attempt; Summers, *Ordeal of the Reunion*, 98.

in 1866. A riot occurred in Memphis in May. Grant, realizing that Johnson had no intention of acting, regretted that "his "hands were tied."" [1011] But an even more serious riot erupted in New Orleans at the end of July, occurring against the backdrop of a return of ex-Confederates to power and the Republican call for a constitutional convention. Fear of black suffrage sent "many whites into a sustained frenzy."[1012] General Philip Sheridan was dispatched to restore order; he said that the riot was "an absolute massacre by the police."[1013] Johnson did not utter "a single word of sympathy" for the victims of the violence.[1014] During one of his "swing around the circle" speeches, he launched into a "jumbled tirade against both the New Orleans radicals and Radical members of Congress."[1015] This had "the worst possible effect on Northern public opinion."[1016] In the face of such open violence, conducted with presidential approval, Grant feared that the Union was "slipping away."[1017] The "brutal response of white Southerners" in both Memphis and New Orleans proved to be the "final factor" in the emergence of "growing Northern anger and hostility."[1018]

The year 1866 was transitional. The minimalist approach to Reconstruction by moderate Republicans had failed.[1019] Republican frustration at the stubborn resistance of both Johnson and the Democrats peaked during the aftermath of the Republican Congressional landslide. This set the stage for even more ambitious efforts to reconstruct a stubborn South which was encouraged by Johnson's recalcitrance. Early in 1867, the Republicans passed a series of acts containing explicit coercion supported by army units scattered throughout the South.[1020]

The first Reconstruction Act passed on March 2, 1867; it was followed by supplementary measures on March 19, 1867, July 10, 1867, and March 11, 1868. The first act divided the South into five military districts, requiring

---

[1011] Smith, *Grant*, 424–25.

[1012] George C. Rable, *But There Was no Peace: The Role of Violence in the Politics of Reconstruction* (2007), 54–55.

[1013] Egerton, *Wars of Reconstruction*, 207.

[1014] Castel, *Andrew Johnson*, 84.

[1015] McKitrick, *Andrew Johnson*, 427.

[1016] McKitrick, *Andrew Johnson*, 427.

[1017] Smith, *Grant*, 425.

[1018] Carter, *When the War was Over*, 251.

[1019] The Radical Republicans, who favored the "conquered province" approach to the eleven ex-Confederate states complete with land confiscation and redistribution, were still in Congress, but they had never been in control. In the face of intense Southern resistance, moderate Republicans shifted toward stricter measures.

[1020] If the South refrained from enacting the black codes, tolerated the Freedmen's Bureau, and accepted the Fourteenth Amendment, Republicans would have been hard pressed to justify exclusion of the Southern states. Carter, *When the War was Over*, 233–34.

Southern states to call constitutional conventions elected by universal manhood suffrage. These new state governments were required to guarantee black suffrage and ratify the Fourteenth Amendment.[1021] Johnson dispatched a futile veto message; the Southern states did nothing regarding establishing new governments. The supplementary acts gave military commanders authority to set the process in motion, and they also prevented Southerners from obstructing the process by boycotting the vote.[1022] Southern resistance had the effect of requiring "the supervisory presence of swarms of Federal officials."[1023] Initially, Southern resistance was a "priceless" political asset because it appeared to vindicate Republican policy.[1024] The Republicans believed that, after initial resistance, the South would give in; they were slow to grasp the "vigor, variety, and viciousness." of the resistance.[1025]

Initially, the Reconstruction acts seemed to work. By virtue of an Omnibus Act in late June 1868, seven ex-Confederate states were readmitted.[1026] In 1870, the three remaining states were also readmitted.[1027] By September 1867, 735,000 blacks had been registered to vote to only 635,000 whites and another 25 to 30 percent failed even to register.[1028] Southern whites were attempting to sabotage the Reconstruction process. In the short term, they failed. The process proceeded, and new state governments came into existence on the basis of black suffrage, even with black representatives in state legislatures. But these governments had severe weaknesses. They ultimately depended on the army, scattered as it was, over the five military districts. They enjoyed a very limited base of support and were the targets of unremitting hostility. These governments have been the objects of constant, even vituperative, criticism. Furthermore, this criticism was sustained by an early generation of historians who were responsible for what might be called "the tragic era" view of Reconstruction.[1029]

[1021] The provisions are outlined in all standard historical monographs. See, for example, McKitrick, *Andrew Johnson*, 476–83.

[1022] A majority of votes cast, regardless of the number, would be sufficient.

[1023] McKitrick, *Andrew Johnson*, 484. The resistance of Northern Democrats was also intense; only one Democrat, Reveredy Johnson of Maryland, voted for any of the Reconstruction acts.

[1024] McKitrick, *Andrew Johnson*, 484.

[1025] Harold M. Hyman, *A More Perfect Union: The Impact of the Civil War and Reconstruction on the Constitution* (1973), 477.

[1026] Alabama, Arkansas, Florida, Georgia, Louisiana, North Carolina, and South Carolina

[1027] Mississippi, Texas, and Virginia

[1028] McPherson, *Ordeal by Fire*, 530–31.

[1029] Claude Bowers, *The Tragic Era: The Revolution after Lincoln* (1929). Bowers was an active Northern Democratic politician during the New Deal. He was "an important Democrat whose book reached a more popular audience." Roosevelt admired his work and gave him diplomatic appointments. Egerton, *Wars of Reconstruction*, 334.

According to this viewpoint, the Reconstruction state governments were oppressive disasters, inflicting grave damage to a long-suffering South groaning under harsh regimes of corrupt, incompetent blacks and repugnant white Republicans. The consensus is that these governments were far from perfect, but they appear to have been generally no worse than, and sometimes better than, state governments throughout the country as a whole. But it seems clear that beneath the contrived concern over corruption, the flashpoint of criticism is that they were Republican, often biracial, governments which took seriously the mandate to secure racial justice.[1030] This, it seems evident, constituted their fundamental offense. From 1867 on, these governments became the targets of unremitting hatred and opposition. Until well into the twentieth century, the historiography of Reconstruction was dominated by the Dunning School of William A. Dunning at Columbia University. Dunning and his disciples perpetuated the tragic-era viewpoint in which a defeated but noble South reeled under Negro–white Republican oppression.[1031]

The influence of the Dunning School persisted into the 1930s.[1032] W. E. B. Du Bois's book *Black Reconstruction in America* appeared in 1935.[1033] His last chapter, entitled "The Propaganda of History," is a critical analysis of the Dunning School. The *American Historical Review* did not review it; prominent Southern historian Avery Craven dismissed it as "abolitionist propaganda."[1034] Dunning-School historiography made any sober evaluation of the Reconstruction state governments difficult. Kenneth Stampp, one of the early critics of the Dunning School, noted that those who resisted the Civil Rights movement in the 1960s "evoked the hobgoblins of Reconstruction."[1035] Although this viewpoint has disappeared, it merits attention to "highlight the racist enormities of early twentieth-century historians."[1036] The struggles

---

[1030] McPherson observes that "seldom has the truth been so distorted." *Ordeal by Fire*, 554.

[1031] W. A. Dunning and another member of his school, James Ford Rhodes, were also Northern Democrats who denounced "black dominion." Egerton, *Wars of Reconstruction*, 327.

[1032] Allen C. Guelzo provides a good brief survey of Reconstruction historiography in which he takes issue not only with the Dunning School but also with some of its Marxist critics. Guezlo argues that Reconstruction was an attempted bourgeois free-labor revolution which ultimately succumbed to "the thousand-bale planters" who succeeded in turning "the Enlightenment clock backwards to medieval serfdom." See "Defending Reconstruction," *Claremont Review of Books*, Spring 2017, 77–81 (80).

[1033] Egerton, *Wars of Reconstruction*, 337–38. The "vast majority" of white historians "simply ignored his work" (330).

[1034] Egerton, *Wars of Reconstruction*, 330.

[1035] Stampp, *Era of Reconstruction*, vii. On the site of the infamous Colfax Riot of April 13, 1873, a historical marker was erected in 1951 which claimed that "this event . . . marked the end of Carpetbag misrule in the South."

[1036] Michael W. Fitzgerald, *Splendid Failure: Postwar Reconstruction in the American South* (2008), 213.

of these beleaguered governments provide the main narrative thread of the whole Reconstruction era. Unreconstructed Southerners manifested incessant resistance, even open defiance, toward them. The Reconstruction acts of 1867–1868 had established the framework for substantial reform. What was then needed from the Republican Party was determination and focus, neither of which was consistently forthcoming.

The Republican effort to impeach Johnson was, nevertheless, a serious blunder. The Founders, wisely, set the bar for impeachment very high.[1037] The Republicans justified their actions by citing Johnson's violation of the Tenure of Office of March 2, 1867, which was designed to prevent him from removing officials without the consent of the Senate. Johnson removed Secretary of War Edwin Stanton in February 1868, and the impeachment proceedings began almost immediately. He was impeached in the House by a vote of 126-47, and the Senate began its proceedings in mid-March. But Johnson had good reasons for questioning the constitutionality of the law. Many Republicans had doubts about the law themselves but pushed ahead anyway; this "doomed the success of the effort from the start."[1038] It is certainly true that Johnson had provided his Republican opponents with a great deal of "combustible matter."[1039] But that really was the problem; impeachment was "a great act of ill-directed passion and was supported by little else."[1040] Ultimately the effort to remove Johnson fell one vote short of the necessary two-thirds majority in the Senate on May 16, 1868.[1041] The fall-out of this fiasco was mixed but mostly negative. It is true that Johnson "stopped his interference [with Reconstruction] while impeachment proceeded," and he also pledged "good behavior for the rest of his term."[1042] But Johnson himself was no longer a major factor in the resistance of the South to Reconstruction.

The failure to remove Johnson from office had "an electrifying effect upon the South" while at the same time it left Southern Unionists, black and white, "deeply depressed."[1043] Violence in the South was reaching "staggering proportions."[1044] Johnson had been presiding over "a slow-motion

---

[1037] The high bar was an effort to avoid precisely the Republican use of impeachment as a political vendetta by limiting it to the strict standard of "high crimes and misdemeanors."

[1038] Gordon-Reed, *Andrew Johnson*, 137. The "vast majority of historians and legal authorities" have agreed that Stanton should not have been removed from office. Castel, *Andrew Johnson*, 164–65.

[1039] McKitrick, *Andrew Johnson*, 505–6.

[1040] McKitrick, *Andrew Johnson*, 506.

[1041] Thirty-five for and nineteen against; seven of the nineteen no votes were from Republicans.

[1042] Benedict, *Impeachment*, 138–39. Benedict observes that Johnson "honored his pledge" and did not renew "intense strife" (180).

[1043] Trefousee, *Andrew Johnson*, 332–33.

[1044] Gordon-Reed, *Andrew Johnson*, 117.

genocide."[1045] Even so, despite their failure to remove Johnson, it was still possible for Republicans to feel optimistic. They were, for the most part, united; Johnson was on his way out, and their political prospects in 1868 seemed excellent.

Grant was the clear Republican choice. He had strong credentials as an opponent of Andrew Johnson who had been untainted by the impeachment fiasco and who was a committed supporter of Reconstruction and racial justice.[1046] Grant was unanimously nominated by the Republican convention. He concluded his acceptance letter by saying, "Let us have peace."[1047] The Democrats countered ineffectually with the "frail and colorless" Horatio Seymour of New York, who reduced the entire campaign to the single issue of opposition to Reconstruction.[1048] Opposition to Reconstruction was predicated on an equally strong opposition to racial justice and an affirmation of white supremacy. The Democratic Party platform of 1868 demanded "an immediate restoration of all States" along with "amnesty for all past political offenses."[1049] The platform denounced "the Radical party" [i.e., Republicans] for "the unparalleled oppression and tyranny which have marked its career." This party "in time of profound peace" has subjected ten states to "military despotism and Negro supremacy." The platform concluded with extravagant praise for Andrew Johnson's "patriotic efforts" to uphold constitutional rights. The party platform concluded by asking all people to join "the present great struggle for the liberties of the people." This platform was the prelude to a racist campaign which played out against an outbreak of violence in the South which "directly entered electoral politics."[1050]

The Republican Party platform praised the new constitutions of Southern states for "securing equal civil and political rights to all," including "equal suffrage to loyal men at the South."[1051] The platform, however, waffled on the issue of black suffrage in Northern states. While calling for equal suffrage

---

[1045] Gordon-Reed, *Andrew Johnson*, 118. Hans Trefousee asserts that he "had made any effective Reconstruction impossible." Trefousee, *Andrew Johnson*, 233. But white supremacist Southern Democrats did not need Johnson to foment their resistance. One estimate is that around fifty thousand Southern blacks were killed between 1865 and 1887 in addition to an indeterminate number of whites. Downs, *After Appomattox*, 247.

[1046] Grant has been put near the bottom of presidential rankings, largely because of the serious scandals which plagued his administrations. However, his firm commitment to racial justice for both blacks and Indians has elevated his reputation.

[1047] Smith, *Grant*, 457.

[1048] Smith, *Grant*, 458. During the murderous New York City draft riots of 1863, Seymour had addressed rioters as "my friends." Foner, *Reconstruction*, 340.

[1049] This and the following quotations are from the Democratic Party platform of 1868; see https://www.presidency.ucsb.edu/documents/1868-democratic-party-platform.

[1050] Foner, *Reconstruction*, 342.

[1051] This and the following quotations are from the Republican Party platform of 1868; see https://www.presidency.ucsb.edu/documents/republican-party-platform-1868.

in the South, it asserted that the question of suffrage "in all the loyal States properly belongs to the people of those States."[1052] Some Republican moderates believed that they had to be cautious on this issue. Connecticut, Minnesota, and Wisconsin narrowly defeated black suffrage measures. Democrats "mounted an anti-suffrage campaign that exploited race prejudice in the usual manner," while "a large majority of Republicans" supported black suffrage.[1053] Despite this ambivalence, the Republican Party platform did affirm "the great principles in the immortal Declaration of Independence as the true foundation of Democratic government" and praised efforts to make these principles "a living reality on every inch of American soil."[1054] The result was that "blacks now found the North's public life open to them in ways inconceivable before the War."[1055] The contrast of party platforms carried over into the campaign itself. Republicans continued to affirm that the principles of Reconstruction embodied the idealism of the Declaration of Independence. For Democrats, "white supremacy was the cornerstone" of their strategy in waging "one of the most explicitly racist campaigns in American history."[1056] This extended even to the denunciation of Grant himself as a "black Republican" and "nigger lover."[1057] The *New York Herald* insisted that "Universal Nigger Suffrage is the Great Issue of the Campaign."[1058]

The election of 1868 was a Republican landslide. The party won the electoral vote 214-80, while controlling the Senate with a four-fifths majority and the House with a two-thirds majority. The election of 1868 represents the high-water mark of the Republican Party during the Reconstruction era. And yet not far beneath the surface, there were significant reasons for uneasiness. Grant won the popular vote by only 306,000 out of 5.7 million cast, while the Democrats gained twenty-five seats in the House.[1059] The fragile Southern state Reconstruction governments were at their peak in producing black and white Republican votes with elections protected by the army.[1060]

[1052] The Fifteenth Amendment was proposed in Congress with strong Republican support in early 1869.

[1053] McPherson, *Ordeal by Fire*, 499. McPherson calculates that Republicans actually approved black suffrage by 85 percent, 75 percent, and 80 percent in Connecticut, Minnesota, and Wisconsin respectively. Democrats were able to exploit "nervous Negrophobia" to a degree which alarmed even some nervous Republicans. Hyman, *A More Perfect Union*, 519.

[1054] Republican Party platform, 1868.

[1055] Foner, *Reconstruction*, 472.

[1056] Blight, *Race and Reunion*, 101. But even this was only "a harbinger of things to come" (104), and an integral part of the Democratic playbook until well into the twentieth century.

[1057] White, *Grant*, 466.

[1058] Witcover, *Party of the People*, 236.

[1059] See White, *Grant*, 468.

[1060] The Reconstruction state governments across the South "could not survive without outside protection." Fitzgerald, *Splendid Failure*, 97.

Grant's inaugural speech of March 4, 1869, represented the high point of presidential support for Reconstruction policies. With the Republican Reconstruction policies securely in place in the South, Grant held out the hope for peace expressed in accepting the Republican nomination. He also showed strong support for black suffrage which he thought would be secured by "ratification of the Fifteenth Amendment to the Constitution."[1061] He also urged "proper treatment of the original occupants of the land." He favored "any course toward them which tends to their civilization and ultimate citizenship."[1062] Therefore, it was possible to regard Grant's victory and his demonstrated commitment to racial justice as showing that "the path of Reconstruction" would be "one that reflected the Republican vision of a harmonious free-labor world."[1063]

The passage and ratification of the Fifteenth Amendment also served to encourage optimism. It passed Congress on February 27, 1869, and was ratified by the states at the end of March 1870.[1064] Its passage seduced many Republicans into a "sense of Reconstruction completed," the definitive conclusion of "the great antislavery struggle."[1065] However, there were at least two powerful reasons why this optimism was unwarranted. The amendment sailed through Congress, but the ratification by the states was messy. It required approval by twenty-eight of the existing thirty-seven states. Those Southern states with Reconstruction governments approved it, but the others resisted. Finally, in April and again in December 1869 Congress passed legislation requiring that four Southern states —Georgia, Mississippi, Texas, and Virginia—ratify it as a condition of readmittance to the Union. Eventually the amendment passed in Southern states still under control of Republican governments and was imposed on the rest of the South.

The reluctance of Southern states to support black suffrage—and civil rights for blacks in general—should have tempered any optimism resulting from ratification of the amendment. Another reason for caution is simply that it lacked all "but the vaguest enforcement provisions."[1066] Despite these reasons for caution, the amendment was depicted as the "great panacea of the age."[1067] The result of this optimism is the emergence of what may be

---

[1061] Smith, *Grant*, 467.

[1062] White, *Grant*, 472.

[1063] Heather Cox Richardson, *The Death of Reconstruction: Race, Labor, and Politics in the Post-Civil War South* (2001), 75.

[1064] Democrats continued their strong opposition to any civil-rights legislation. Seventy-seven percent of Democratic senators voted against the amendment, while 70 percent of Republican senators supported it. Linden, *Politics or Principle*, 11.

[1065] Hyman, *More Perfect Union*, 525; Fitzgerald, *Splendid Failure*, 132.

[1066] Hyman, *More Perfect Union*, 523.

[1067] Rable, *But There Was No Peace*, 191.

called legislative animism, the idea that laws have a life of their own, so mere passage is all that is necessary. Events would soon provide a dramatic refutation.

The pivotal year 1868 was paradoxical. It was the year when "Reconstruction had succeeded," but it was also the year in which "its eventual failure became clear." [1068] This paradoxical juxtaposition of success and failure was made against the backdrop of "an onslaught of violence and harmfulness" which bombarded Northern newspapers.[1069] Northern political candidates "could beg for peace, but there would be no peace."[1070] The central political reality of the period was the growth, spread, and mounting intensity of the violent resistance. It would be easy enough to move from one atrocity to another, a grim narrative of constant violence. Historians who confront this reality throw up their hands with a confession of literary insufficiency. It is simply too much to deal with except when painted with the broadest of brushes.[1071] This pervasive violence was unfolding in an American society traditionally suspicious of military force and standing armies. But the Reconstruction state governments owed their tenuous existence to the shrinking presence of the army scattered throughout the South.[1072] The result is that by mid-1871, "white insurgents" controlled much of the South and the role of the army "was reduced to that of a bystander."[1073]

The "conquered provinces" approach advocated by a small group of Radicals was unachievable. Even if the resources had been available, the political will did not exist. But if the political will to succeed by force was lacking, even the maintenance of anything like the status quo became problematic given the clamor of other issues for attention. The Republican Party had launched what is arguably the greatest reform effort in American history, including three constitutional amendments, civil rights acts, and the establishment of reform state governments with black suffrage and participation. But reforming zeal weakens over time, so rationalizations for satisfaction with the status quo become powerful. Enough eventually seems to be enough. While the Union had "ended the largest and most powerful system

---

[1068] Summers, *Ordeal of the Reunion*, 152. It succeeded only in the legislative animism sense.

[1069] Summers, *Ordeal of the Reunion*, 152. In passing, Summers dispatches the myth that it took "Radical Reconstruction to set off the savagery" (173) by simply citing the example of border state Kentucky which had never experienced Reconstruction.

[1070] Summers, *Ordeal of the Reunion*, 152.

[1071] See especially the authors of specialized monographs cited here. Mainstream textbooks and popular histories rarely deal with the violent aspects of Reconstruction in connection with the Democratic Party, North and South.

[1072] Army strength declined from 48,000 in September 1868 to 30,000 in July 1871. Downs, *After Appomattox*, 233.

[1073] Downs, *After Appomattox*, 232.

of slavery in the modern world in just four years," many Northerners came to believe that "was enough for one generation."[1074]

From 1868 onward, there was an irreversible weakening of the Reconstruction effort. Stock-market turbulence, the money question, and the onset of the Grant scandals sapped Republican strength, and in the off-year elections of 1870 the Republicans "lost much of their House majority."[1075] At almost the very time when support for Reconstruction was weakening in the North, Southern defiance became even more intense with the emergence of the Ku Klux Klan, an openly terrorist organization.[1076] The Ku Klux Klan was first organized as a sort of fraternal group for ex-Confederate soldiers.[1077] But after the election of Confederate general Nathan Bedford Forrest as leader, the original concept of the group "was quickly overtaken by a maelstrom of physical bullying and violence against blacks."[1078] The problem posed by Klan activists dominated the Reconstruction issue during Grant's first term. This era of mass violence was "certainly one of the most ignoble chapters in all of American history"[1079] It was rendered even more ignoble because Klan membership was "synonymous with Democratic voters and activists."[1080] The deadly efficiency of the Klan terror was augmented by the presence of many ex-Confederate soldiers, giving it the character of a "guerrilla military force."[1081]

The Federal government had to take action or lose all credibility, so Congress passed an anti-Klan enforcement act in May 1870, followed by another measure which Grant signed on April 20, 1871. The response of the Democrats was vitriolic. Grant was denounced as "Kaiser Grant."[1082] Opposition to the Klan met with "nearly hysterical condemnations."[1083] The effect of these anti-Klan enforcement measures was mixed. The act of 1871 did have a good effect; it resulted in "a dramatic decline in violence throughout the South."[1084] But the problem was that the anti-Klan activity in 1870–71 produced "only temporary peace and order."[1085] The good effects of the anti-

---

[1074] Edward Ayers, quoted in Greg Toppo, "Park System Deconstructs Reconstruction," *USA Today*, February 1, 2016.

[1075] Fitzgerald, *Splendid Failure*, 132.

[1076] Eric Foner calls it "an American al-Qaeda." Teppo, "Park System."

[1077] White, *Grant*, 519. The Greek word for circle, "kuklos," was extended alliteratively to Ku Klux Klan.

[1078] White, *Grant*, 519.

[1079] Foner, *Reconstruction*, 459.

[1080] Egerton, *Wars of Reconstruction*, 289.

[1081] McPherson, *Ordeal by Fire*, 539.

[1082] Egerton, *Wars of Reconstruction*, 300.

[1083] Hyman, *More Perfect Union*, 530.

[1084] Foner, *Reconstruction*, 458–59.

[1085] McPherson, *Ordeal by Fire*, 560.

Klan measures demonstrated that only by "steady unswerving power from without" could peace and racial justice be ensured.[1086]

But how would the Republicans stay firmly on course? By attempting to provide civil rights for individuals, Congress "moved tentatively into modern times."[1087] But this act also "pushed Republicans to the outer limits of constitutional change."[1088] For some Republicans, the Klan act seemed to be an overreach. Carl Schurz and the emerging faction of Liberal Republicans were growing weary of what they saw as a hopeless quagmire and were beginning to finesse out of Reconstruction by the route of "widespread amnesty."[1089] A temporary lessening of Klan violence did not indicate any weakening of the Southern Democrats' determination to resist Reconstruction. In fact, the Klan was "only one of many such [white supremacist] organizations" which continued their violent resistance.[1090] The trend lines regarding Reconstruction were not favorable at the end of Grant's first term.

This downturn became even more pronounced as the presidential election of 1872 loomed; it was conducted under significantly changed conditions in the South. On February 1, 1870, the Senate voted to readmit Georgia to the Union; this meant that "no rebel state remained under military control," and the army "had to abide by its normal peacetime regulations."[1091] Republicans "lost much of their majority" in the off-year elections of the same year.[1092] At the Republican Party convention on June 12, 1872, Grant was unanimously nominated. His running-mate was Henry Wilson, a Radical Republican, replacing Schuyler Colfax who had become lukewarm on Reconstruction. The Republican Party platform concentrated on "the problem of racial equality in the South."[1093] It also called for vigorous enforcement of the Fourteenth and Fifteenth Amendments which, as a concession to Liberal Republicans, was linked to a general amnesty for almost all ex-Confederates.[1094]

But there was division in the Republican Party. In Cincinnati, Charles Sumner and Carl Schurz led a rump convention of Liberal Republicans along with a "fluttering of East Coast intellectuals who had tired of cigar smoke

---

[1086] Foner, *Reconstruction*, 459.

[1087] Hyman, *A More Perfect Union*, 529–30.

[1088] Foner, *Reconstruction*, 455.

[1089] On racial issues, there was little about them that was liberal. Summers, *Ordeal of the Reunion*, 271.

[1090] Stampp, *Era of Reconstruction*, 199. There was a veritable witches' brew of such groups. Egerton, *Wars of Reconstruction*, 304.

[1091] Downs, *After Appomattox*, 236.

[1092] Fitzgerald, *Splendid Failure*, 132.

[1093] Smith, *Grant*, 549.

[1094] Hyman, *More Perfect Union*, 533.

in the White House."[1095] They supported several laudable reforms, including tariff reform, civil-service reform, and good government generally.[1096] But they also believed that the Reconstruction governments "underscored the dangers of unbridled democracy and the political incapacity of the lower orders."[1097] They united behind Horace Greeley, founder and editor of the *New York Tribune*. His political positions had fluctuated over the years. By 1872, however, he had settled on the standard Liberal-Republican reform proposals, while calling for amnesty "for all former Confederates" as well as "local self-government," which was code for home rule which was code for white supremacy.[1098]

The Democrats once again demonstrated their "uncanny talent for survival."[1099] The party "fell in behind Greeley without a whimper."[1100] While clearly benefitting from Liberal-Republican support, it remained "eagerly determined to support white supremacy."[1101] The Democrats backed away from "explicit appeals to race."[1102] Instead, they tried to make Grant's treatment of the South "the central issue of the campaign" while complaining about "bayonet rule."[1103] Frederick Douglass was not fooled by the Liberal-Republican smokescreen. For blacks, he insisted, "the Republican Party is the ship and all else is the sea."[1104] Benjamin F. Butler, with his take-no-prisoners rhetoric, exclaimed: "Go vote to burn schoolhouses, desecrate churches, and violate women, or vote for Horace Greeley which means the same thing."[1105]

Despite all of the Liberal Republican–Democratic Party blandishments, Grant strolled to a landslide victory. He won 56 percent of the popular vote and also won the electoral vote 286-66. He carried every Northern state and ten of the sixteen Southern and border states. The Republican Party also maintained its two-thirds majorities in both houses of Congress.[1106] But the election of 1872 was another example of pride preceding a fall. Beyond "the hubris [that] led to mistakes" there was "a perfect storm of poor adminis-

---

[1095] Smith, *Grant*, 548.
[1096] Foner, *Reconstruction*, 497.
[1097] Foner, *Reconstruction*, 497.
[1098] Smith, *Grant*, 548.
[1099] Foner, *Reconstruction*, 510.
[1100] Smith, *Grant*, 549.
[1101] Smith, *Grant*, 545.
[1102] Foner, *Reconstruction*, 511.
[1103] Smith, *Grant*, 549–50.
[1104] Smith, *Grant*, 535.
[1105] White, *Grant*, 535.
[1106] McPherson, *Ordeal by Fire*, 565. Because the Reconstruction state governments, though growing weaker, were still in control, this election was probably the fairest and most democratic until the election of 1968.

tration, corruption, and scandal."[1107] More fundamentally, Grant's election only temporarily masked the growing divisions within the Republican Party and its diminished commitment to Reconstruction policies. The charges of "bayonet rule," resonated with many Northern voters, including some Republicans. the election marked the "high point of Grant's presidency."[1108] It was all downhill thereafter.

The major blow to Grant's presidency was the Panic of 1873 which "ushered in the longest hard times in living memory."[1109] The political fallout was catastrophic. The off-year election of 1874 was "one of the great election reversals in American history."[1110] The Republicans lost more than ninety seats in the House, leading to Democratic control. Some Republicans blamed Reconstruction policy as the "most expedient interpretation."[1111] The passage in February of the Civil Rights Act of 1875 was a Republican success, but it had major flaws. Although it granted blacks access to all public places, it did not mandate school desegregation which Democrats "opposed . . with a fervor that had marked their antebellum defense of slavery."[1112] The act lacked any enforcement provisions. Without the army and the police, the act simply could not be enforced, and there was "no prospect of either one."[1113] The Justice Department made "little effort to enforce the law."[1114] The act was "the nation's final chance" for many years, to "learn how to transform the Declaration of Independence into 'the practice of everyday living.'"[1115]

As Republican strength weakened, Southern Democrats responded in two different ways. A new generation of Southern leaders appeared who called themselves "Redeemers," a term that conveyed both propaganda and euphemism. Outwardly respectable and willing to eschew harsh racial rhetoric, they expressed support for the Fourteenth and Fifteenth Amendments. But the reality behind the façade was a different thing entirely. Their actions "showed the hollowness of their words."[1116] Blacks in the "Redeemers' New

---

[1107] Smith, *Grant*, 552.

[1108] Smith, *Grant*, 552.

[1109] Summers, *Ordeal of the Reunion*, 238. It lasted at least five years.

[1110] Fitzgerald, *Splendid Failure*, 187.

[1111] Fitzgerald, *Splendid Failure*, 187.

[1112] Kirk H. Wilson, *The Reconstruction Desegregation Debates: The Politics of Equality and the Rhetoric of Place, 1870–1875* (2002), 15.

[1113] Summers, *Ordeal of the Reunion*, 309.

[1114] McPherson, *Ordeal by Fire*, 570.

[1115] Wilson, *Reconstruction–Desegregation Debates*, 16. Wilson argues that the act was "extremely important" because it had "a powerful symbolic presence within the African American community" (45). But even this lasted only until its overturn by the Supreme Court in the *Civil Rights Cases* (1883).

[1116] Summers, *Ordeal of the Reunion*, 352.

South found themselves enmeshed in a seamless web of oppression, whose interwoven economic, political, and social strands reinforced one another."[1117]

Behind the bland rhetoric of the Redeemers there was the reality of ongoing violence. The massacre at Colfax, Louisiana, on April 13, 1873, may have been "the deadliest incident of racial violence in the history of the United States."[1118] Although Grant was "personally appalled by the violence," he backed away from any attempt at intervention.[1119] Then, two years later, violence flared up in Mississippi. During an election in September, Democrats abandoned even the benevolent façade of the Redeemers, engaging in the "relentless intimidation of black voters."[1120] So Mississippi was "redeemed" by open violence and election interference. Grant initially planned to intervene but reluctantly abandoned the idea because of a lack of political support. In the absence of Federal assistance, Republicans lost control of the state.[1121] A powerful Democratic counterrevolution swept across the South. Grant in the annual messages of his second term referred "only infrequently to Southern developments."[1122] Republicans found it "impossible to devise a coherent policy for the South," so there was "a broad retreat from the politics of Reconstruction."[1123] During Grant's second term, Democrats across the South were returning to power by appealing to "white supremacy, low taxes, and control of the black labor force."[1124]

The election of 1876 has been depicted as leading directly to the end of Reconstruction. Although the election is indeed significant, it is best understood as "merely . . . the culmination of the counterrevolution and the completion of redemption."[1125] Southern Democrats used "intimidation and force in a way carefully calculated to sap the strength of their enemies without provoking federal intervention."[1126] As the election of 1876 approached, the Democratic Party maintained its unity. Northern Democrats continued enabling Southern Democratic racial hatred and ongoing violence. Northern

---

[1117] Foner, *Reconstruction*, 598.

[1118] Keith, *Colfax Massacre*, xviii. It left 150 blacks and three whites dead, including fifty-nine members of a black militia unit (xi).

[1119] Keith, *Colfax Massacre*, 151.

[1120] McPherson, *Ordeal by Fire*, 584.

[1121] Adelburt Ames, the Republican governor, blamed the failure of Reconstruction on the racial inferiority of blacks. Rable, *But There Was No Peace*, 162.

[1122] Hyman, *More Perfect Union*, 525.

[1123] Foner, *Reconstruction*, 528.

[1124] Foner, *Reconstruction*, 551. It was fueled by a Herrenvolk democracy in which "equality of whites depended on the subjugation of black men." Rable, *But There Was No Peace*, 64.

[1125] Rable, *But There Was No Peace*, 185.

[1126] Rable, *But There Was No Peace*, 189.

Democrats were, in effect, continuing their support of the Confederacy, which had "never surrendered beyond the mere laying down of arms."[1127]

The Republican Party, however, was deeply divided. The growing disenchantment with Reconstruction policies, at least in part, reflected an uneasy sense that the task was a hopeless one. Southern resistance was too strong for the relatively weak remedies a democracy historically suspicious of the military could bring to bear. After the fact, Grant recalled that the problem was that Reconstruction depended ultimately on the army but "our people did not like it [military rule]. It was not in accordance with our institutions."[1128] The older idealists of the Civil War era were passing from the scene. For those who remained committed to Reconstruction policies, the signs were ominous. There was a growing, broader pro-business convergence because the so-called Redeemers "had much in common" with Northern Republicans who sought to "further the ends of commerce and thwart labor activism."[1129] While these issues simmered significantly below the surface, outwardly the issues of the campaign of 1876 and, for the most part, the candidates themselves represented business as usual.

For Grant, a third term was unthinkable. In June 1876, a divided Republican convention nominated Rutherford B. Hayes. He had had a distinguished Civil War military career, had served in Congress and as a three-time governor of Ohio. A Washington outsider, he was untouched by the bruising nature of Washington politics. He represented the emerging Republican exclusively pro-business mainstream. He was accused of surrendering to "Southern whites and the Democrats."[1130] While this seems overly harsh, it is true that, while saying the right things in public regarding black rights, he also seemed "privately at odds with his party's Reconstruction policy."[1131] To be sure, he did occasionally invoke the memory of the Union war dead as well as the victims of Southern violence, a tactic ridiculed by the Democratic press as "waving the bloody shirt."[1132] He believed that the best way to help blacks was "by trusting the honorable and influential Southern whites."[1133]

[1127] Rable, *But There Was No Peace*, 188.

[1128] Quoted in Downs, *After Appomattox*, 253, from John Young Russell, *Around the World with General Grant* (2 vols.; 1879), 2: 362–63. This is the best, classically succinct, explanation.

[1129] Blight, *Race and Reunion*, 138.

[1130] Smith, *Grant*, 566.

[1131] C. Vann Woodward, *Reunion and Reaction: The Compromise of 1877 and the End of Reconstruction* (1991), 24.

[1132] Summers, *Ordeal of the Reunion*, 4. Summers observes that, "The Republican tactic of waving the bloody shirt gets greater play than how the blood speckled it in the first place." See his review of Roy Morris Jr., *Fraud of the Century: Rutherford B. Hayes, Samuel Tilden, and the Stolen Election of 1876* in the *Register of the Kentucky Society* 101 (2003): 158.

[1133] Woodward, *Reunion and Reaction*, 25. Is this naivete or a case of making a virtue of necessity?

Perhaps the best interpretation is to say that Hayes did not "consciously betray black rights; he instead indulged in an optimistic scenario to ease retreat from an impossible situation."[1134] Hayes delivered a significant speech at the Hampton Institute in May 1877, using the analogy of separate fingers working for the common good, an analogy that Booker T. Washington was to use fifteen years later in his Atlanta Exposition speech.[1135] The separation of the races became the escape hatch for racial harmony in the South.

For Democrats, nothing had changed. The Democratic nominee in 1876, Samuel J. Tilden, former governor of New York, said all the right, predictable things. In contrast to Hayes's Civil War service, Tilden had worked for George McClellan in 1864. He parroted the unthinking Democratic racism, speaking against black suffrage and urging unwavering commitment to "a white republic."[1136] Blacks were "incurably deficient citizens." He offered a toast to "the light of other days when liberty wore a white face and America wasn't a Negro."[1137] So Tilden entered the presidential contest of 1876 firmly in the Democratic racist tradition. He explicitly repudiated Reconstruction by denouncing "the systematic and insupportable misgovernment imposed on the States of the South."[1138]

The outcome and resolution of the election of 1876 has received voluminous attention. The razor-thin margin of the outcome reflects resurgent Democratic strength stemming dramatically from the "redeemed" South as well as the continued ebbing of Republican strength in the North. The resulting deadlock had Republicans claiming electoral votes in three doubtful Southern states.[1139] Republicans charged, no doubt rightly, that they had been robbed of black votes "in all Southern states."[1140] When this is taken into account, the election was indeed a stolen election, stolen by the Southern Democratic redeemers. But when Democrats refused to accept the results in the openly disputed states, the result was a volatile situation heightened by talk of armed resistance to a Hayes victory.

[1134] Fitzgerald, *Splendid Failure*, 207. Southern Republicans, however, knew that "white supremacy remained the overriding issue" (208).

[1135] Wilson, *Reconstruction–Desegregation Debate*, 190.

[1136] Baker, *Affairs of Party*, 257.

[1137] Baker, *Affairs of Party*, 257.

[1138] Morris, *Fraud of the Century*, 135. He quotes a letter of Tilden's of August 4, 1876. Morris's indignation over the "stolen election" does not extend to the racial violence of the South. The violence was the work of "defiant Southerners" and was not "officially condoned by the Democratic Party" (33).

[1139] Florida, Louisiana, and South Carolina. "Fraud and violence" plagued the voting in each of these states. Egerton, *Wars of Reconstruction*, 315–16.

[1140] McPherson argues that the Republicans would probably have won Florida, Louisiana, and South Carolina in a truly fair election. McPherson, *Ordeal by Fire*, 589.

Cooler heads on both sides ultimately prevailed. Conventional accounts have cited the settlement reached at a conference at Wormley's Hotel in Washington, D.C., in February 1877.[1141] By its terms, the Democrats would end opposition to Hayes's election in exchange for the withdrawal of all Federal troops from the South and a final end of Reconstruction. The old-line anti-slavery Republicans opposed the deal. The fiery abolitionist Wendell Phillips asserted that "the whole soil of the South is hidden by successive layers of broken promises. To trust a Southern promise would be fair evidence of insanity."[1142] But, insane or not, the deal was done. Hayes was president. Long in dying, Reconstruction expelled its last feeble breath. W. E. B. Du Bois put it best: "The slave went free; stood a brief moment in the sun; then moved back again toward slavery."[1143]

[1141] In addition to the political compromises reached, there was the convergence of probusiness Republicans and their emerging Southern counterparts—the Redeemers who sought to create, with Northern help, a new industrialized South. The hotel was owned by James Wormley, "a worthy black businessman." It was here that the fate of Southern blacks for the next hundred years was determined. A. J. Langguth, *After Lincoln: How the North Won the War and Lost the Peace* (2015), 351.

[1142] McPherson, *Ordeal by Fire*, 593.

[1143] Quoted in Foner, *Reconstruction*, 301 from Du Bois, *Black Reconstruction in America* (1935). After the promises of Reconstruction, blacks were abandoned to "a condition more resembling serfdom than freedom." Rable, *But There Was No Peace*, 185.

Chapter Twelve: Ongoing Follies—To the Urban Plantation

We can imagine Democratic loyalists exclaim that all this was regrettable but a long time ago. But the Democratic Party kept blacks on Southern plantations as long as possible, well into the twentieth century. Then, at the moment of apparent victory, the flawed policies of the Great Society consigned many blacks to the misery of burgeoning urban plantations of social dissolution, dependency, and crime. Democrats have never abandoned their politics of exploitation.

The New South was a racist nightmare, dominated by demagogues like Ben Tillman, Eugene Talmadge, James Vardaman, and Theodore Bilbo, among many others.[1144] The consistent goal of the entire Democratic Party, North and South, had been the defeat of Reconstruction. This led to a one-hundred-year wasteland in which the slightest concession to black rights was ruthlessly punished at the polls. Democrat apologists have resorted to the "it's only in the South" rationalization. The Democratic Party as a whole was enlightened, progressive, and reformist, but it was saddled, unfortunately, with Southern racists.[1145] The problem was regional, not national.

But there is a two-word refutation: Woodrow Wilson. He was a Southerner, but his influence, particularly while president, was broadly national in

---

[1144] "New South" is essentially a slogan adopted by postwar Southerners supporting the idea of a modern South of industry and commerce as well as agriculture. It was led by such men as Henry W. Grady, editor of the *Atlanta Constitution*. While new in economic aspiration, it was all too old in racial attitudes.

[1145] Allen J. Matusow has given us an unsparing overview: "Until the Great Depression, the South dominated the Democratic Party on behalf of states' rights and white supremacy." See his *The Unraveling of America: A History of Liberalism in the 1960s* (2009; first ed., 1984), xi.

scope and impact. He had a PhD in political science but was also a ruthless authoritarian and a white supremacist. He is out of favor now, "disowned by the left for his racial bias and by the right for his concentration of power in Washington."[1146] He was not even willing to follow the enlightened policies of his Progressive predecessor Theodore Roosevelt. One of Roosevelt's first acts upon becoming president after William McKinley's assassination was to invite Booker T. Washington to dinner at the White House. This invitation triggered "an orgy of hysteria" in the Southern press.[1147] During his presidency, Roosevelt made efforts to appoint black Republicans to various Federal positions throughout the South, though usually without much success.[1148]

Wilson made few concessions to racial justice. For blacks, Wilson's administration in 1912 began on a note of betrayal. Wilson had appealed for their support and had received "an unprecedented number" of black votes.[1149] Yet his administration was "a bitter blow to [black] hope of advancement."[1150] Wilson was a committed Southerner. His father, Joseph Ruggles Wilson, defended slavery on Biblical grounds.[1151] In 1896, when Wilson spoke at a meeting of the American Historical Association, he asserted that "there was nothing, absolutely nothing, for which to apologize in the history of the South."[1152]

From the outset, the Wilson administration pursued segregationist policies for Federal employees; he "did not hesitate to sacrifice vital Negro interests on the altar of politics."[1153] Even after major reforms had been achieved, he remained influenced "by social prejudices, however much he may have struggled against them."[1154] His policy of segregation brought him into conflict with Oswald Garrison Villard, one of his strongest supporters,

---

[1146] Richard Norton Smith, review of Patricia O'Toole, *The Moralist: Woodrow Wilson and the World He Made* (2018), *Wall Street Journal*, April 21/22, 2018.

[1147] Dewey W. Grantham Jr., "Dinner at the White House: Theodore Roosevelt, Booker T. Washington, and the South," *Tennessee Historical Quarterly* 17 (1958): 116.

[1148] Grantham, "Dinner," 130.

[1149] Kathleen L. Wolgemuth, "Woodrow Wilson and Federal Segregation," *Journal of Negro History* 44 (1959): 158.

[1150] Wolgemuth, "Woodrow Wilson," 158. The segregation policy was pervasive. See also Eric S. Yellin, *Racism in the Nation's Service: Government Workers and the Color Line in Woodrow Wilson's America* (2013).

[1151] Arthur L. Link, "Woodrow Wilson: The American as Southerner," *Journal of Southern History* 36 (1970): 5.

[1152] *AHA Annual Report, 1896* (1897), 295, quoted in Link, "Woodrow Wilson," 14.

[1153] Henry Blumenthal, "Woodrow Wilson and the Race Question," *Journal of Negro History*, 48 (1963): 20.

[1154] Blumenthal, "Woodrow Wilson," 21.

who was a grandson of William Lloyd Garrison, a pioneering abolitionist.[1155] There was great pressure from Villard and other white reformers as well as mass protests by blacks. This pressure led to some moderation of Wilson's segregationist policy.[1156] But despite various efforts at rationalization, there is no evidence that Wilson ever invested any real effort in securing racial justice. He was "on matters of race, a true son of the South."[1157]

A dramatic racially-charged event during Wilson's presidency occurred when he agreed to a showing of D. W. Griffith's *Birth of a Nation* at the White House on February 2, 1915. The film was based on the work of Thomas Dixon, author of *The Clansman* (1905). Dixon believed that "a unified country of white supremacists had emerged from the ashes of Reconstruction."[1158] Griffith was the son of a Confederate cavalry officer. Griffith and Dixon formed a white-supremacist alliance. Dixon was Wilson's friend; he persuaded Wilson to view the film. Wilson was reported to have said that the film was "like writing history with lightning. And my only regret is that it is all so terribly true."[1159] However, there is good reason to attribute the remark instead to the highly effective Dixon–Griffith publicity machine.[1160] Even so, when all the extenuating circumstances have been cited, this is a very public, racially charged incident. The contrast with Roosevelt is stark. Roosevelt's White House dinner with Booker T. Washington preceded Wilson watching the most racist film in American history. The social consequences of the film were appalling, and Wilson's approval enhanced the impact of the film, leading many viewers to cheer "as violent barbaric white conduct toward blacks became heroism in defense of civilization."[1161]

This was the low point of Wilson's relationship with black Americans because of his full embrace of the hyper-Confederate view of American history from one who was uniquely qualified to have known better. The first Democratic president since Grover Cleveland, and a Progressive as well, set the clock backward. The Wilson presidency ended in disarray and defeat on all counts, offering a parallel to the sad state of Wilson's health. World War I did not make the world safe for democracy, and the overreach of the

---

[1155] Wilson attempted to justify the policy by citing the need to avoid friction between the races and keep blacks "more safe in their possession of office." Wolgemuth, "Woodrow Wilson," 163–64.

[1156] Wolgemuth, "Woodrow Wilson," 171.

[1157] H. W. Brands, *Woodrow Wilson* (2003), 133. John M. Cooper cites Wilson's "permissiveness" towards his Southern Cabinet members as an explanation. John M. Cooper, *Woodrow Wilson: A Biography* (2009), 204–5.

[1158] Egerton, *Wars of Reconstruction*, 331.

[1159] Egerton, *Wars of Reconstruction*, 331.

[1160] Cooper, *Woodrow Wilson*, 272. Cooper is persuasive on this point, but he goes too far in arguing that Wilson, an innocent with a PhD, "fell into a trap" (272).

[1161] Lawrence J. Friedman, *The White Savage: Racial Fantasies in the Postbellum South* (1970), 122.

Versailles Treaty and the League of Nations cleared the way for a period of Republican ascendency from 1920 to 1933. Wilson could not even make the American South safe for democracy.

In an ideal world, the return of the Republicans to power should have led to a renewed, focused effort to remain true to their idealistic origins by working for racial justice. Unfortunately, the ineffectiveness of Republican racial policies from Reconstruction through Theodore Roosevelt's administration continued during the 1920s. Southern blacks continued to endure ongoing subjugation typified by segregation, disenfranchisement, and lynching. The Republican response was hopelessly inadequate. Charles Evans Hughes, the Republican candidate in 1916, did not address these issues at all. Only the black "disgust" with Democrats kept most of them reluctantly in the Republican camp.[1162] But still there are significant contrasts. Even in the face of such Republican fecklessness, Democrats continued to exploit the race issue. In the election of 1920, Harding was accused of having "Negro ancestry" by Democrats who also published such hysterical pamphlets as *The Threat of Negro Domination* (1920).[1163]

The Republican Party of the 1920s had abandoned virtually all its earlier commitment to racial justice. It was pursuing the near-impossible task of reconciling "the demands of both the white South and the Negro."[1164] The aspirations of Southern Republicans who sought success by a "lily-white" policy clashed with black expectations in both the North and the South. Throughout the early twentieth century, Republicans had "dropped their insistence on the enforcement of the Fourteenth and Fifteenth Amendments and instead had mildly and vaguely favored equal rights for the Negro."[1165] Republican policy reflected the general indifference of white Americans to the plight of blacks. Despite the draining away of Republican idealism, the contrast with the Democrats remained strong for the simple reason that Democratic racism remained unabated. Southern Democrats were in a kind of time warp; their behavior in the early twentieth century showed "an amazing parallel with proslavery ideology."[1166] This contrast between the parties in the 1920s was most clear with regard to lynching.[1167]

[1162] Richard B. Sherman, *The Republican Party and Black Americans: From McKinley to Hoover, 1896–1933* (1973), 121–22.

[1163] Sherman, *Republican Party*, 141–42.

[1164] Sherman, *Republican Party*, 144.

[1165] Vincent de Santis, "The Republican Party and the Southern Negro, 1877–1897," *Journal of Negro History* 45 (1960): 87.

[1166] George W. Rable, "The South and the Politics of Antilynching Legislation," *Journal of Southern History* 51 (1985): 219–20.

[1167] Between 1889 and 1941, almost four thousand blacks were lynched. Kenneth O'Reilly, *Nixon's Piano: Presidents and Racial Politics from Washington to Nixon* (1997), 122. Rable reports

Republican efforts to pass an anti-lynching bill lacked the commitment of their earlier efforts at Reconstruction, but even these almost perfunctory efforts produced strong Southern resistance. Generally, the whole process settled into a predictable pattern. Southerners, usually with little provocation, fell back on the Southern phobia of black men raping white women. The result was that even half-hearted Republican anti-lynching efforts met with determined resistance by Southern Democrats, often culminating in filibusters or the threat of filibusters, in effect paralyzing Congress. This pattern was repeated throughout the 1920s, down to the passage of the Civil Rights Act of 1964.[1168]

Hoover demonstrated little understanding or sympathy for blacks; for him nonwhites generally constituted "the lower races."[1169] He was firmly committed to the Southern Republican "lily-white" policy. Hoover's easy victory over Al Smith in 1928 did not motivate him to alter his attitude to blacks, even though the returns showed the growing importance of their vote in Northern cities. For shortsighted Republicans, the returns "provided no incentive for Republicans to attempt to strengthen the ties of Negroes to the party."[1170] Hoover's performance in office was equally dismal. He made "fewer public statements on racial issues than any president in the twentieth century."[1171] Yet even in this environment of Republican indifference, the intensity of Democratic racism could be activated over trifles. One such incident occurred when the wife of black Republican congressman Oscar de Priest of Chicago attended a series of teas given for the wives of congressmen and Cabinet officers. The result was that the "cries of outrage" throughout the South were nearly as strident as those generated by the Roosevelt–Washington dinner.[1172]

Things never improved for blacks during Hoover's administration. In 1932, the Republican platform had only "a vague and meaningless Negro plank," while Hoover paid only "perfunctory attention to the black voter."[1173] Nevertheless, most blacks, North and South, stayed with the Republicans; indifference is preferable to open hostility. Hoover's shattering defeat in 1932

---

that between 1881 and 1901, there were almost always more than one hundred a year and at least sixty a year even during the Progressive era. Rable, "Politics of Antilynching," 202. See also Sherman, *Republican Party*, 176, for more statistical analysis.

[1168] For an overview, see Rable, "Antilynching Legislation," 202–8, and Sherman, *Republican Party*, 174–223.

[1169] Sherman, *Republican Party*, 225.

[1170] Sherman, *Republican Party*, 233.

[1171] Sherman, *Republican Party*, 233.

[1172] Sherman, *Republican Party*, 233. De Priest was the first black elected to Congress since Reconstruction and "the first ever from a northern district." David M. Kennedy, *Freedom from Fear: The American People in Depression and War, 1929–1945* (1999), 18.

[1173] Sherman, *Republican Party*, 253.

began a twenty-year era of Democratic dominance which spanned the Great Depression, World War II, and the onset of the Cold War. Although Roosevelt and the New Deal have generally basked in the warm glow of historiographical approval, the actual accomplishments in terms of civil rights were surprisingly modest.[1174] Cautionary signs were evident at the outset. Neither Hoover nor Roosevelt responded to an NAACP questionnaire on specific racial issues. The Democratic Party platform in 1932 was "entirely silent on racial problems."[1175] Blacks could hardly be reassured by the party's vice-presidential nominee, the unreconstructed John Nance Garner of Texas. Even so, the New Deal era did see a shift in black loyalty from Republicans to Democrats. This shift did not reflect a fundamental change in the racial stance of the Democratic Party. The reason for the shift is that the New Deal helped blacks economically. Bread-and-butter issues, especially in hard times, trump everything else. But even this initially tentative shift posed difficulties for Democrats. They did not need the Southern black vote, but the black vote in Northern cities was becoming increasingly significant.[1176]

But this process confronted Democrats with a problem more daunting than the "lily-white" policy of Republicans. The political realities of the Solid South meant that Southern congressmen and senators enjoyed seniority which enabled them to dominate key Congressional committees. An essentially unreconstructed, racist South controlled Congress, and there was nothing that Roosevelt could do about it. But what did he want to do? Schlesinger provides the best clue in his *Age of Roosevelt* by observing that Roosevelt was "fairly conventional in his racial attitudes." This tepid observation does not even rise to the level of a mild compliment.[1177]

The White House was segregated, as was Hyde Park.[1178] Roosevelt had served complacently under Josephus Daniels, a full-blown racist, in Wilson's Department of the Navy and was complicit in the Democratic race-baiting

---

[1174] Uncritical adulation is most clearly seen in Arthur M. Schlesinger Jr.'s three-volume *Age of Roosevelt* (1957–60). Subsequent works have been more balanced but still are generally favorable.

[1175] Sherman, *Republican Party*, 355.

[1176] The push of Southern racism and the pull of Northern economic opportunity resulted in the increase of the black population percentage in the North and West from 11 percent to 21.3 percent from 1910 to 1930. Sherman, *Republican Party*, 125. Later, the lure of defense industry jobs triggered another "enormous black exodus from the South." Kennedy, *Freedom from Fear*, 768.

[1177] Bartlett, *Wrong on Race*, 111. The quote is from *The Politics of Upheaval* (1960), 430, the third volume of *The Age of Roosevelt*. Bartlett's chapter on Roosevelt is entitled "Franklin D. Roosevelt: Insensitive Liberal."

[1178] Bartlett, *Wrong on Race*, 111. Evidently, he used the word "nigger" casually in private conversation, a fact carefully hidden in most standard biographies, although it is acknowledged in Geoffrey C. Ward's *A First-Class Temperament: The Emergence of Franklin D. Roosevelt, 1905–1928* (1989), 173.

in the election campaign of 1920, running as the party's vice-presidential nominee.[1179] He became "a self-proclaimed son of the cracker state" at his Warm Springs, Georgia, retreat where he "listened to the darkies sing" in a segregated environment.[1180] Roosevelt even failed the anti-lynching test by showing "utter cowardice" in refusing to support an anti-lynching bill.[1181] He was publicly rebuked for this by Oswald Garrison Villard in an article in the *Nation* magazine, June 5, 1935. Roosevelt's many defenders plead political necessity, given the reality of Southern Democratic Congressional dominance.

But this is a defense which proves the larger point. Roosevelt acquiesced on lynching in deference to the racism of his own political party. There is a second observation, admittedly more speculative. Once the ameliorative effects of the New Deal had become apparent in the mid-1930s, would Southern politicians have risked political suicide by thwarting beneficial economic policy over lynching? This is uncertain, but Roosevelt never even made the effort. The New Deal era also saw the rise of Democrats of enduring stature whose racist history has been ignored by historians. The roll of dishonor, with at least two Klan members—Hugo Black and Robert Byrd—includes Sam Ervin of Watergate fame, James F. Byrnes, and Richard B. Russell. Perhaps the most egregious example of this is Hugo Black of Alabama whom Roosevelt nominated for the Supreme Court in 1937. It turned out that he had joined the Klan in 1923, embracing its program, marching, giving speeches, and glibly referring to "niggers" in court trials.[1182]

Despite his Klan membership being public knowledge, the Democratic Party "quickly circled the wagons around him."[1183] Although Roosevelt denied any knowledge of Black's Klan membership, Black himself admitted that Roosevelt had known of his membership, saying that "some of his best friends and supporters in the state of Georgia were strong members of that organization."[1184] William Leuchtenburg, author of one of the standard New Deal monographs, argues that Black's subsequent career "more than vindicated" those who supported him. Black had to survive "an ugly episode"

[1179] Bartlett, *Wrong on Race*, 112.

[1180] O'Reilly, *Nixon's Piano*, 144. Young black polio victims were treated at the Tuskegee Institute, not Warm Springs.

[1181] Bartlett, *Wrong on Race*, 127. At one point, Eleanor Roosevelt told Walter White of the NAACP that her husband thought that lynching was "a question of education in the states . . . so that localities themselves will wipe it out." O'Reilly, *Nixon's Piano*, 121.

[1182] He had served as U.S. senator from 1927 to 1937. Bartlett, *Wrong on Race*, 120–21. He had also attacked Al Smith in 1928 because he was a Catholic.

[1183] Bartlett, *Wrong on Race*, 122.

[1184] Bartlett, *Wrong on Race*, 122. It is hardly surprising, therefore, that Roosevelt's Warm Springs facility was segregated.

when his Klan membership was revealed.[1185] The phrase "more than vindi-cated" indicates what might be called the Schlesinger defense by which the stature of Democrats is actually enhanced by their earlier misdeeds. Schlesinger argued that "those who thought about the drowning of Mary Jo Kopechne in just the right way" would see in it "one more reason to vote for Ted Kennedy" because his subsequent career was a heroic effort to redeem himself by constant devotion to the public good.[1186] By some strange alchemy, misdeeds by Democrats become resume-enhancers.

The New Deal was a vast, variegated reform movement. Some high-ranking New Deal officials were sympathetic to blacks and worked as best as they could under the circumstances. Such New Dealers as Harry Hopkins, Aubrey Williams, and Harold Ickes did try to help blacks.[1187] Eleanor Roosevelt was a steady and ardent supporter for blacks.[1188] The creation of the Fair Employment Practices Committee in 1941 was the most important civil rights initiative since Reconstruction.[1189] But in the South, time stood still. Southerners made every effort to ensure that New Deal measures did not benefit blacks. They resented Federal relief workers "mistering the Niggers."[1190] The New Deal operation in the South "exposed the depths of the region's economic backwardness as the difficulties that attended any policy that might perturb the tense membrane of class and race relations in the South."[1191] It seems that the Jim Crow system actually "reached its perfec-tion in the 1930s."[1192]

One of the greatest reform movements in American history made only modest progress in civil rights. The Democratic Party bears direct responsi-

---

[1185] William E. Leuchtenburg, *Franklin D. Roosevelt and the New Deal, 1933–1945* (1993), 238. There is no index entry in Leuchtenburg's book for lynching.

[1186] William Voegeli, "He's History," *Claremont Review of Books*, Spring 2018, 52.

[1187] Harold Ickes had been a lifelong Republican. Some other Republican progressives, such as George Norris and Henry A. Wallace, were also important allies of the New Deal.

[1188] Yet she had to overcome what one of her biographers characterized as "flip, class-bound arrogance and egregious racism." Quoted in Kennedy, *Freedom from Fear*, 97. She was even "occasionally infected with caution on lynching and other questions of race." O'Reilly, *Nixon's Piano*, 120.

[1189] O'Reilly, *Nixon's Piano*, 142.

[1190] Kennedy, *Freedom from Fear*, 194.

[1191] Kennedy, *Freedom from Fear*, 194.

[1192] C. Vann Woodward, *Thinking Back: The Peril of Writing History* (1986), quoted in Kennedy, *Freedom from Fear*, 19. The process of disenfranchisement had reached such a point that by 1940 only about 5 percent of eligible blacks were even registered to vote. They were tied to the land "by debt, ignorance, and intimidation as they had been by slavery itself" (19). Even during the liberal Democratic heyday of the New Deal, the condition of Southern blacks did not improve. The socialist Norman Thomas was forced off a speaker's plat-form in Arkansas in 1934 by a sheriff's deputy: "We don't need some Gawd-damned Yankee Bastard to tell us what to do with our niggers." David M. Kennedy, *Freedom from Fear*, 209. There was no freedom from fear in the New Deal New South.

bility for this. It was almost totally in control. Having thwarted civil rights during and after Reconstruction, the Democratic Party thwarted it again during its era of maximum political strength. Over fifty years after the end of Reconstruction, the South remained a white man's country and the growing black voting strength in the North had not yet translated into significant civil-rights achievements. Democratic apologists, however, generally avert their gaze from this depressing reality.[1193] The party had devoted itself, largely unchallenged, to racism until the New Deal era. The twenty-five-year period up to the Great Society saw only fitful efforts by the party to secure racial justice.

The primary architect of the New Deal was Roosevelt himself, and its legislative foundation and implementation were largely achieved in the face of the powerful opposition of some Democrats, particularly Southern Democrats.[1194] Roosevelt once responded to a query about his philosophy somewhat dismissively: "Philosophy? Philosophy? I am a Christian and a Democrat—that's all."[1195] Nevertheless, one of his core convictions with vast political implications was his powerful opposition to what was then called the dole. Often waffling and chameleon-like, he was uncharacteristically firm on this point. He wanted work relief, not mere relief, whenever possible, saying that "the Federal Government must and shall quit this business of relief." He went on to say, "in words that might have been uttered by Herbert Hoover," that relief alone "induced a spiritual and moral disintegration fundamentally destructive to the nation's fiber." The result was "to administer a narcotic, a subtle destroyer of the human spirit." So the government had an indispensable role, but it was to provide the work necessary to nurture "self-respect . . . self-reliance and courage and self-determination."[1196] Later Democratic reformers, particularly in the Great Society era, while claiming Roosevelt's

---

[1193] When the South began a shift toward the Republican Party, there was an obsession with those racist Republicans. A classic example is Joan Cashin's review of Edward H. Peeples' autobiography *Scalawag: A White Southerner's Journey through Segregation to Human Rights Activism* (2018). In her overview of Peeples' bitter experience of growing up in the Jim Crow South of the 1930–40s, there is no mention of political parties. But in the 1960s and 1970s, it was the Republican Party which "embraced the racism he had grown up with a generation earlier," complete with "code words to oppose racial equality." *Ohio Valley History* 18 (2018): 100–2 (102). Liberal historians have ignored the lynchings and the Klan of the Democratic South only to wax indignant over the South of Barry Goldwater and Richard Nixon.

[1194] Most Republicans opposed it, although Roosevelt did have the support of some Progressive Republicans.

[1195] Quoted in Kennedy, *Freedom from Fear*, 131.

[1196] Quoted in Kennedy, *Freedom from Fear*, 250–51. Elizabeth Perkins, Roosevelt's secretary of labor, recalled his objection to an early draft of the Social Security Act of 1935: "Ah, but this is the old dole under another name." Quoted in Amity Shlaes, *Great Society: A New History* (2019), 336.

---

mantle, ignored this core conviction. In doing so, they laid the foundation for an ongoing social catastrophe.

Progress in civil rights in these years was real but often discouragingly slow throughout the administrations of Truman, Eisenhower, and Kennedy. The biggest early breakthrough in these years occurred outside the direct realm of politics in the *Brown v. Board of Education* decision in 1954 which mandated school desegregation. The Democratic Party did not emerge from the Great Depression and New Deal with a strong commitment to civil rights even though the voting strength of Northern blacks continued its steady increase. The strongest commitment to civil rights in this period came from an unlikely source—the unprepossessing Harry Truman, who became president in April 1945. He was an "unsung civil rights hero."[1197] Truman demonstrated a courageous belief in civil rights early in his career when he refused to join the Klan in Missouri in 1924, at a time when it was near the peak of its strength; the courthouse in Jackson County, Missouri, built under his supervision, did not have segregated restrooms.[1198]

Although Southern Democrats initially welcomed a fellow Southerner to the White House, they were quickly chagrined by his request in July 1945 to continue funding the Fair Employment Practices Commission and to make it a permanent Federal agency. In January 1946, Truman made a national appeal to this effect, an action which triggered the time-honored Democratic resistance tactic of filibustering which proved successful once again.[1199] The effort was led by some powerful Democratic leaders of national stature, including James Eastland and Richard B. Russell. Some liberals were disappointed that Truman "did not denounce the filibusterers against the FEPC."[1200]

Nevertheless, Truman continued to frustrate Democrats with his "dogged pursuit of civil rights for blacks."[1201] He did this even though he passed through a difficult period politically, including the disastrous midterm elections of 1946. He established a Presidential Committee on Civil Rights in December 1946. He spoke to the NAACP in June 1947; in October 1947 he received a comprehensive response from it, entitled "To Secure These Rights," giving specific recommendations which he promptly submitted to

---

[1197] Bartlett's chapter on him is entitled "Harry Truman: Unsung Civil Rights Hero." Bartlett, *Wrong on Race*, 131–49.

[1198] Bartlett, *Wrong on Race*, 131–32. The ethical anomaly of Truman's career was his lifelong loyalty to the Thomas J. Pendergast machine in Kansas City; Pendergast was "perhaps the most corrupt big city boss of his era" (132). But through it all, Truman "kept his hands clean," remarking at one point, "It looks like everybody got rich in Jackson County but me." Patterson, *Freedom from Fear*, 790.

[1199] Bartlett, *Wrong on Race*, 137.

[1200] James T. Patterson, *Grand Expectations: The United States, 1945–1974* (1991), 144.

[1201] Bartlett, *Wrong on Race*, 139.

Congress. The Democratic response was overwhelmingly negative. Lyndon Johnson denounced the report as "a farce and a sham—an effort to set up a police state in the guise of liberty."[1202] The report went nowhere in Congress.

Truman continued his civil-rights efforts, even in the face of the Dixie-crat revolt which seemed to make his election campaign in 1948 appear hopeless.[1203] But against all apparent odds, he defeated Thomas Dewey, who seems to have taken the black vote for granted. But the fact is that the Demo-crats were able to kill "every item on his [civil rights] agenda for the balance of his presidency."[1204] Therefore, Truman turned increasingly to executive orders to bypass Congressional resistance. These orders were to offer more Federal jobs to blacks and to integrate the armed forces. Whatever he was able to do, he did "on his own."[1205] He was thwarted not by the Republicans but by members of his own party.[1206]

In an odd parallel to Roosevelt's presidency, which transitioned from "Dr. New Deal" to "Dr. Win-the-War," Truman's second term was domi-nated by Communism and Korea. Even so, among other initiatives, he did move to eliminate racially restricted covenants in the housing industry, and his Justice Department was "very active in filing court cases and friend-of-the-court briefs on civil rights issues."[1207] All in all, Truman does deserve praise for the courage he demonstrated on behalf of civil rights in the face of powerful resistance, a courage much greater than that ever shown by the much-praised liberal icon, Franklin Roosevelt.

The election of Eisenhower in 1952 broke a twenty-year Democratic stranglehold on the presidency. But the election itself had a largely unac-knowledged ironic aspect. Truman was "dismayed" at the nomination of Adlai Stevenson, who had opposed the Fair Employment Practices Commis-sion.[1208] Stevenson has enjoyed generally uncritical acceptance as a liberal,

---

[1202] Bartlett, *Wrong on Race*, 141. LBJ's speech was delivered on May 22, 1948, in Austin, Texas.

[1203] Bartlett, *Wrong on Race*, 141–45. The Dixiecrat revolt was triggered by the adoption of a stronger civil-rights plank in the party platform in 1948. Some Southern delegates "marched out of the hall waving battle flags of the Confederacy." Patterson, *Grand Expectations*, 151. The Republican civil-rights plank in 1948 was "very progressive" (158).

[1204] Bartlett, *Wrong on Race*, 147.

[1205] Bartlett, *Wrong on Race*, 147. Bartlett notes that a number of historians, including Kenneth O'Reilly, Barton Bernstein, and William Berman, tend to belittle his civil-rights accomplishments (148).

[1206] While O'Reilly acknowledges that Truman did more "than Franklin Roosevelt or any twentieth-century president who came before him," he does not deal with the magnitude of the Democratic opposition. O'Reilly, *Nixon's Piano*, 165. O'Reilly's book is full of subtle and not-so-subtle bias. Strom Thurmond is a "rabid segregationist," while Robert Byrd is merely a "former Klansman" (239, 191).

[1207] Bartlett, *Wrong on Race*, 148.

[1208] O'Reilly, *Nixon's Piano*, 165.

but on racial issues, he was "hardly much of a liberal."[1209] His running-mate in 1952 was John Sparkman, "an Alabama segregationist."[1210] He ran against Eisenhower again in 1956, suffering another landslide defeat.[1211] Neither Eisenhower nor Stevenson "paid attention to civil rights" during the campaign.[1212]

Despite this neglect and the superficially placid surface of the 1950s, civil-rights issues were fermenting with the rise of the modern civil-rights movement. Eisenhower enjoyed a generally high level of popularity during the eight years of his presidency, but clearly the greatest and most divisive domestic issue he confronted was civil rights, particularly as it focused on the vexing question of school desegregation in the South.[1213] Eisenhower's leadership on civil-rights issues was certainly limited. He was "was overly cautious in deploying his immense personal popularity and leadership in addressing civil rights." [1214] This reflects a general consensus among Eisenhower scholars.[1215] Yet even one of his toughest critics concedes that "progress, no matter how fitful, was made."[1216] Even this had to be achieved in the face of fierce Democratic resistance.

Eisenhower's description of the Democratic Party seems pertinent: "Extremes on the left, extremes on the right with political chicanery and corruption shot through the whole business."[1217] A major part of the problem was that the Van Buren coalition, though weakened at times, endured through the Civil War, after Reconstruction, and well into the twentieth century. In addition, Eisenhower also had to deal with "both the rising

---

[1209] Patterson, *Grand Expectations*, 253.

[1210] O'Reilly, *Nixon's Piano*, 165.

[1211] Bartlett, *Wrong on Race*, 165. His running-mate in 1956 was another Southerner, the relatively more liberal Estes Kefauver of Tennessee. Meanwhile, Truman's opinion of Stevenson had not changed; he endorsed Averell Harriman.

[1212] Patterson, *Grand Expectations*, 406. Nevertheless, Eisenhower's support among black voters increased from 21 percent in 1952 to 39 percent in 1956. Nixon received 32% of the black vote in 1960. See Theodore Johnson, "What Nixon Can Teach the GOP About Courting Black Voters"; https://www.politico.com/magazine/story/2015/08/what-nixon-can-teach-the-gop-about-courting-black-voters-121392).

[1213] Patterson, *Grand Expectations*, 383–84. There was widespread de facto school segregation in the North which reflected equally widespread segregated housing. But resistance in the North was neither as widespread nor as violent as that in the South.

[1214] Paul Lettow, review of William I. Hitchcock's *The Age of Eisenhower: America and the World in the 1950s* (2018), *National Review* (May 26, 2018), 38.

[1215] Patterson notes that he has, nevertheless, risen in presidential polls from being ranked number twenty-one of thirty-four presidents in 1962 to ninth among the ten best in 1982. Patterson, *Grand Expectations*, 243.

[1216] O'Reilly, *Nixon's Piano*, 186. Nevertheless, some black Republicans received high-ranking appointments and influential positions, and even the moderate approach to desegregation and civil rights was preferable to the racist hysteria of Southern Democrats. Joshua D. Farrington, *Black Republicans and the Transformation of the GOP* (2016), 38.

[1217] Quoted by Conrad Black in "Avenue to Renovation," *New Criterion* (May 20, 2017), 8.

expectations and increasing impatience of blacks, which at the same time hardened the opposition of white supremacists in the South."[1218] Southern Democrats presented "a near-united front" against school desegregation and other civil-rights issues.[1219] The Jim Crow system of segregation "remained more systematically oppressive than anything experienced by other racial groups . . . and that changed very little over time." It is small wonder, then, that blacks continued to flee the South "in unprecedented numbers."[1220]

In the face of fierce Democratic resistance, Eisenhower used executive orders to desegregate federally run hospitals and shipyards.[1221] He also appointed Earl Warren, a well-known Republican liberal, to the Supreme Court.[1222] His efforts at passing civil-rights bills best demonstrate his belief in racial justice. He called for a civil-rights bill in his first State of the Union address. In mid-1957, it was introduced to Congress by Attorney-General Herbert Brownell, one of the powerful advocates for civil rights in the administration. It passed the House by a heavily partisan vote 285–126.[1223] In the Senate, even the weakened bill faced the threat of a filibuster. Senate Majority Leader Lyndon Johnson secured passage by ensuring that those accused of violating voting rights would have a trial by jury. The amendment passed 51–42; then the bill itself passed 72–14. Eisenhower had "wanted a much stronger bill," but he signed it on September 9, 1957.[1224] This was a historic occasion because it was the first civil-rights bill passed by Congress since Reconstruction. Yet the trial-by-jury provision was an open door for blatant jury nullification. Johnson and his fellow Democrats had "gutted the bill of any practical impact."[1225]

Another civil-rights bill at the end of Eisenhower's presidency suffered a similar fate. He took the initiative in proposing a bill to protect black voting rights in a special message to Congress on February 5, 1959.[1226] The history of the bill followed the familiar trajectory. Democrats delayed it throughout

---

[1218] Bartlett, *Wrong on Race*, 152.

[1219] Patterson, *Grand Expectations*, 397.

[1220] Patterson, *Grand Expectations*, 380. By 1970, over 47 percent of blacks were living outside the South.

[1221] Patterson, *Grand Expectations*, 393.

[1222] He later regretted this nomination as the "biggest damn-fool mistake" he ever made because he did not realize how quickly Warren would force the school desegregation issue to the forefront. See Patterson, *Grand Expectations*, 399.

[1223] Republicans supported it 167–19 and Democrats opposed it 118–107.

[1224] O'Reilly, *Nixon's Piano*, 179.

[1225] Patterson, *Grand Expectations*, 413.

[1226] Eisenhower denounced mob violence; he also requested equal protection under the law and stricter laws against any violent resistance to school desegregation. Bartlett, *Wrong on Race*, 159.

1959. It was finally passed by the House 311–109.[1227] The bill was then delayed by a Democratic filibuster which Johnson failed to prevent. Then Johnson once again "compromised on the substance of the bill" just to get something, however meaningless, passed.[1228] So, like the Civil Rights Act of 1957, this bill also lacked significant enforcement provisions. Eisenhower was defeated twice in his second term by Democratic resistance to effective civil-rights legislation. He later recalled that he wanted a stronger bill but "the Democrats, including Mr. Johnson, wouldn't let me have it."[1229] Even so, Johnson, his finger ever in the wind and eyeing a presidential run in 1960, was reinventing himself by a transition from white supremacist to civil-rights advocate.

The most dramatic domestic crisis Eisenhower faced during his presidency was violent resistance to school desegregation. He did not disagree with the intent of the 1954 *Brown* decision, but he feared the social consequences of moving "with all deliberate speed."[1230] Eisenhower had tried to prepare the South for racial reform in ways consistent with his political philosophy. He appointed Federal judges in the South who "did yeoman work insisting on desegregation."[1231] Southern Democrats moved to resist the *Brown* decision. The Southern Manifesto, issued in March 1956, denounced it as a "clear abuse of judicial power."[1232] This set the stage for the violent explosion in Little Rock, Arkansas, in September 1957 which was his "worst nightmare."[1233] His top aide, Sherman Adams, later observed that calling out the troops to resist the resistance was "the most repugnant to him of all his acts in his eight years at the White House."[1234] But he did it in fidelity to what he saw as his constitutional duty. During his administration, the cause of civil rights advanced with little thanks to Democrats generally and no thanks whatever to Southern Democrats. In 1960, nearly one hundred years after the outbreak of the Civil War, large segments of the Democratic Party continued their resistance to the principles for which it had been fought.[1235]

[1227] Democrats supported it 179–93; Republicans supported it 132–15.

[1228] Bartlett, *Wrong on Race*, 160.

[1229] O'Reilly, *Nixon's Piano*, 179.

[1230] The phrase was used in the Supreme Court case called "Brown II" (1955).

[1231] Michael Barone, review of James F. Simon, *Eisenhower v. Warren: The Battle for Civil Rights and Liberties* (2018), *Wall Street Journal*, April 10, 2018.

[1232] Patterson, *Grand Expectations*, 398. It was signed by twenty-two senators and eighty-two congressmen. Johnson, Albert Gore, and Kefauver, with their eyes on the White House, did not sign it.

[1233] O'Reilly, *Nixon's Piano*, 180.

[1234] Patterson, *Grand Expectations*, 415.

[1235] Senator Richard B. Russell denounced Eisenhower for using the tactics of "Hitler's storm troopers." In 1972, the old Senate Office Building was renamed the Richard B. Russell Senate Office Building. Bartlett, *Wrong on Race*, 159, 75.

The election of the youthful, dynamic John F. Kennedy in 1960 aroused fresh hopes for progress in civil rights. Yet despite his glowing rhetoric, he did little to further the cause, even when one allows for his tragically fore-shortened presidency. The Republican Party platform was much stronger on civil rights than its Democratic counterpart.[1236] Both Kennedy and his brother Robert "believed abstractly" in civil rights, but they "felt no passionate attachment to the cause."[1237] Both Kennedys "remained civil rights minimal-ists for the whole thousand days."[1238] They wanted to do as little as possible and still get the black vote. Kennedy did have to deal with an increasingly activist approach by civil-rights advocates, requiring difficult choices no matter who occupied the White House. Freedom-riders provoked horri-fying violence by a resurgent Ku Klux Klan. Kennedy did offer some helpful initiatives. The Interstate Commerce Commission pledged to litigate inter-ference with black rights in interstate travel. He established a Committee on Equal Employment Opportunities, nominated blacks to judgeships, and directed the Justice Department to intervene as needed to ensure voting rights. Even so, the dominant approach was one hedged with caution. There was no national groundswell for civil rights. Powerful Southern Democrats, especially James Eastland of Mississippi, still controlled key Congressional committees.[1239] So the Kennedys tried "deal-making with Southern politi-cians" with predictably mixed results.[1240]

There is also the J. Edgar Hoover factor. While in the White House, Kennedy was sharing his mistress Judith Campbell with mobster Sam Gian-cana. She had visited Kennedy twenty times and was in frequent telephone contact with him.[1241] The phone calls had been "logged and made known to the FBI."[1242] Kennedy severed his ties with Campbell after J. Edgar Hoover warned him about her in March 1962.[1243] Hoover detested Martin Luther King, Jr., as "a tom cat with obsessive degenerate sexual urges" who harbored

---

[1236] It supported voting rights and school desegregation, and it expressed opposition to filibusters. Bartlett, *Wrong on Race*, 161–62. The Democratic Party platform did contain the promise of a civil-rights act, but Kennedy even backed away from that. Patterson, *Grand Expectations*, 474

[1237] Patterson, *Grand Expectations*, 475.

[1238] O'Reilly, *Nixon's Piano*, 236. O'Reilly reports that "even Arthur Schlesinger" had to admit that the Kennedys had no real civil-rights program.

[1239] To placate Eastland, Kennedy appointed "four ardently segregationist men" to Federal district courts. Patterson, *Grand Expectations*, 474.

[1240] Patterson, *Grand Expectations*, 477.

[1241] Giancana had worked with the FBI on plots to assassinate Castro. Ultimately Robert Kennedy did prosecute him. Patterson, *Grand Expectations*, 476.

[1242] Patterson, *Grand Expectations*, 476.

[1243] Patterson, *Grand Expectations*, 476.

Communists in his inner circle.[1244] Kennedy had put himself in a blackmail situation with Hoover, and he was compelled to give Hoover "wide leeway in handling racial confrontation in the South."[1245] In addition to Kennedy's own reluctance to engage fully in the cause of civil rights, he was inhibited from protecting the movement from Hoover's malevolence. In addition to the surveillance, Hoover "was spreading rumors about King throughout Washington."[1246] It is impossible to determine how King and his civil-rights movement suffered because of Kennedy's moral dereliction.[1247]

Kennedy's primary stance throughout the various civil-rights crises was that of damage control. He rationalized minimal activity by adopting the position that local affairs should be handled locally with Federal intervention appropriate "only when local officials have completely lost control."[1248] This was the stance he adopted with regard to the violence at the University of Mississippi in September 1962, the upheavals in Birmingham in April 1963, and the march on Washington in August 1963. Kennedy's last major response to the civil-rights issue was to call for another civil-rights bill in June 1963. This bill has been called "an important turning point in the history of the civil rights movement."[1249] But progress in Congress was painfully slow; by November 1963, it was "snarled" in the House and certain to face yet another filibuster in the Senate.[1250] At the time of Kennedy's assassination, a badly divided Democratic Party and an irresolute and compromised president impeded progress on the increasingly urgent issue of civil rights.[1251]

Kennedy may well have served the civil-rights movement more effectively by the manner of his death than by his policies in life. The assassination made him an instant martyr for the cause. The time was ripe for a civil-rights breakthrough which was fueled by a number of factors. There was the perennial struggle since Reconstruction which had quickened signifi-

---

[1244] Patterson, *Grand Expectations*, 475–76.

[1245] Patterson, *Grand Expectations*, 476. King was under intense FBI scrutiny, wiretaps and all, for the rest of his life. Robert Kennedy had "no problem with Hoover's wiretapping King." O'Reilly, *Nixon's Piano*, 232–33.

[1246] Patterson, *Grand Expectations*, 476.

[1247] Patterson does acknowledge Kennedy's "reckless and irresponsible sex life" by which he "exposed himself to blackmail and disgrace." However, he devotes less than one page of text and one footnote to the subject. He devotes over ten pages of analysis to Watergate. Patterson, *Grand Expectations*, 416, 476, 767, 769, 771-82.

[1248] Patterson, *Grand Expectations*, 477. It is hard to differentiate this position from that of Eisenhower. When African ambassadors complained of not being served meals on Route 40 from New York City to Washington, D.C., Kennedy's response was to suggest that they fly instead. Patterson, *Grand Expectations*, 475.

[1249] Patterson, *Grand Expectations*, 481. The original version was weak on voting rights, particularly in state and local elections, and dealt only with de jure school segregation.

[1250] Patterson, *Grand Expectations*, 484–85.

[1251] Patterson, *Grand Expectations*, 485.

---

cantly by the rise of the civil-rights movement of the 1960s. This movement, in turn, was strengthened by the political effects of massive black migration to the North and the relative weakening of the hardline segregationists in the South.[1252] But the Kennedy assassination was the catalyst which magnified the strength of the other factors. Lyndon B. Johnson and some Democratic liberals seized the moment to link the cause of civil rights with Kennedy's martyrdom, taking full advantage of the outpouring of emotion by the American people who "had been touched as they had never been before."[1253]

The first major result was the resurrection of the long-stalled civil rights bill of 1963 and its eventual passage as the Civil Rights Act of 1964. Despite the Kennedy martyrdom, there was still strong resistance. The inevitable filibuster was launched in the Senate on March 30, 1964. After fifty-four days of frustration, a compromise bill was introduced.[1254] On June 10, Robert Byrd completed a fourteen-hour filibuster speech. Finally, the Senate voted for cloture, so the bill passed on June 19; Johnson signed it into law on July 2.

This was a landmark piece of legislation which the Democrats have been taking credit for ever since after having delayed such a measure for over one hundred years. Therefore, it is important to note that a higher percentage of Republicans supported the measure than Democrats. In the House, the Republican vote was 138–34 (80 percent), the Democrats 152–96 (61 percent). In the Senate, the tally was Republicans 27-6 (82 percent) and Democrats 47–23 (67 percent).[1255]

The Kennedy assassination also had a profound impact on the evolving nature of liberalism. Kennedy had espoused a "brand of pragmatic liberalism" which could be "tough and realistic" in the Franklin Roosevelt–Harry Truman mold.[1256] However, the interpretation of Kennedy's assassination had the effect of undermining this New Deal–postwar liberalism which peaked in 1964–65. Afterwards, the dramatic emergence of the McGovern/ New Left pulled the Democratic Party steadily leftward. It all began with the primal lie to obscure an inconvenient truth. For Democrats, the worst thing about the Kennedy assassination, besides the death of the president,

---

[1252] The South was moving forward sociologically and economically. Hardline segregationists had always been linked to an overwhelmingly agricultural economy. But a truly new New South was emerging in the 1960s.

[1253] Patterson, *Grand Expectations*, 531.

[1254] The main thrust of the bill was preserved, but the power to regulate private businesses was weakened.

[1255] See https://freedomsjournalinstitute.org/uncategorized/urban-legend-goldwater-against-civil-rights/. This source also reports that since 1933, 96 percent of Republicans supported civil-rights legislation in twenty-six major votes, while 80 percent of Democrats were opposed.

[1256] James S. Pierson, *Camelot and the Cultural Revolution: How the Assassination of John F. Kennedy Shattered American Liberalism* (2007), xix.

was that he had been killed by a Communist. For decades, many Democrats, swaggering around as proud anti-anti-Communists, had been minimizing the threat of Communism and accusing Republicans of paranoia. Jackie Kennedy gave the earliest, most revealing insight into the damage control by saying that her husband "didn't even have the satisfaction of being killed for civil rights. It had to be some silly little Communist. It even robs his death of any meaning."[1257] It was not possible to deny that Oswald was a Communist but subsequent Democratic historiography continues to marginalize the significance of the assassination as the actions of "a highly unstable individual."[1258] Psychopathology trumps political conviction.[1259] The tragic death of a shining Democratic icon must never be permitted to vindicate the anti-Communist strictures of Republicans.

The assassination was a turning point by which the pragmatic liberalism of the Roosevelt–Truman tradition began giving way to the "cultural liberals and radicals who gained influence following Kennedy's death."[1260] The first and most dramatic symptom of the change was that Kennedy's assassination was America's fault. Somehow, we had killed Kennedy. The popular columnist Drew Pearson made it explicit––Kennedy "was felled by a climate of hate especially in Texas but also in the nation at large."[1261] Robert Rutland observes that Kennedy had been under increasing "verbal assault" by "conservative and reactionary groups." The November 22, 1963, edition of the *Dallas Morning News* had carried "full-page advertisement" denouncing him. Rutland then informs his readers that the president was shot "on a Dallas street by a sniper." Lee Harvey Oswald is nowhere to be found either in the text or the index of his book.[1262]

The tragedy of the Kennedy assassination was a crisis too good to waste. The only way America could redeem itself for the crime of permitting a president to be shot by a Communist would be by an unquestioning adherence to every article of an increasingly leftist program. This reflects a Manichaean worldview which has grown ever stronger down to the present. Lyndon

---

[1257] Quoted in Pierson, *Camelot*, 59.

[1258] Patterson, *Grand Expectations*, 519. Patterson also describes Oswald as "a self-styled Marxist" whose actions "reflected the super-frigid context of the Cold War" (519–20). Arthur M. Schlesinger Jr. did not mention Oswald in his massive Kennedy biography *A Thousand Days: John F. Kennedy in the White House* (1965). He implies that somehow in a way never specified right-wingers were responsible. Pierson, *Camelot*, 98.

[1259] Oswald identified "with the virtues of Castro's regime in Cuba." Patterson, *Grand Expectations*, 519. But in a "bizarre paradox," Castro was "turned into a hero in the late 1960s by many of those who had mourned Kennedy's death in 1963." Pierson, *Camelot*, 107.

[1260] Pierson, *Camelot*, 53. Kennedy's sudden death, "left a void that could not be filled by programmatic liberalism" of the FDR–New Deal tradition.

[1261] Quoted in Pierson, *Camelot*, 95.

[1262] Robert A. Rutland, *The Newsmongers: Journalism in the Life of the Nation* (1973), 377.

Johnson had been an old-style liberal.[1263] He immediately linked the passage of the civil-rights bill with the honoring of Kennedy's memory, so his assassination "was being used to promote an agenda that was disconnected from the actual facts of the case."[1264] Johnson's Great Society program unfolded within the context of New Deal liberalism even as the ground was shifting ominously toward a far more radical variety.[1265]

But none of this was apparent in 1964 when Johnson seemed invincible. Riding the crest of the Kennedy martyrdom, he swept to a laughably easy victory over Barry Goldwater in the 1964 election. A sinister indication of the dark side of Johnson's character is the extent of his reliance on FBI spying. He "planted FBI informants" to spy on his opponents at the Democratic National Convention, then spied on Goldwater during the campaign itself.[1266] This was in addition to spying on Martin Luther King and other civil-rights leaders.[1267] There was "a degeneration of Johnson's Great Society into the seedy reality of a surveillance state."[1268] But at the time, people saw only a man poised to do great things. This was Johnson's unique opportunity to seize the Kennedy mantle of reform, thus securing his own place in history as a reformer on the scale of Franklin Roosevelt.[1269] His reforms would create a Great Society.[1270] Like the New Deal, the Great Society was a vast, complicated, multifaceted endeavor. It also embodied Johnson's euphoric grandiosity: "Hell, we are the richest country in the world, the most powerful country in the world. We can do it all."[1271]

The Great Society began with the unquestioned assumption that all social problems stemmed ultimately from a lack of economic opportunity. Therefore, the idea that poor people needed governmental assistance and guidance "lay at the heart of subsequent liberal efforts in the 1960s to fight

---

[1263] Until the late 1950s, Johnson's record of "opposition to all civil rights initiatives was spotless." Bartlett, *Wrong on Race*, 156. He had supported the New Deal "bread and butter" liberalism. Patterson, *Grand Expectations*, 530.

[1264] Pierson, *Camelot*, 94.

[1265] He would "have to deal with forces that were on their way to fragmenting the United States." Patterson, *Grand Expectations*, 525.

[1266] Patterson, *Grand Expectations*, 555. Lee Edwards, "The FBI Spied for LBJ's Campaign," *Wall Street Journal*, May 25, 2018.

[1267] O'Reilly, *Nixon's Piano*, 252.

[1268] O'Reilly, *Nixon's Piano*, 275.

[1269] The night before the Kennedy assassination, Robert Kennedy described Johnson as "mean, bitter, vicious—an animal in many ways." O'Reilly, *Nixon's Piano*, 228. Johnson was well aware of this attitude which made him even more eager to surpass the Kennedys as the great reformer.

[1270] Johnson first used the phrase in a speech to the graduating class of the University of Michigan in May 1964. Patterson, *Grand Expectations*, 561.

[1271] Patterson, *Grand Expectations*, 531.

poverty."[1272] This idea is not entirely wrong, but it is certainly insufficient. The basic problem, which the Great Society and all subsequent antipoverty legislation never solved, was simply how to help people without hurting them.[1273] To be sure, the initial intent of at least some of the Great Society leaders was to avoid welfare, "a dirty word in the lexicon of liberals as well as conservatives."[1274] But welfare in various forms incrementally became an essential aspect of Great Society programs. The Democrats of the Great Society era and beyond systematically repudiated Franklin Roosevelt's deeply felt and effectively expressed fear of the "dole" with all its pernicious effects on the human spirit. They thought they knew more about social and economic reform than the architect of the New Deal.

There is abundant evidence of these negative outcomes, but out of the welter of Great Society programs two indicators stand out. The Aid to Families of Dependent Children (AFDC) program increased dramatically in the 1960s; "the upward course of welfare rolls seemed both rapid and escalatory."[1275] The number of recipients nearly doubled from 1960 to 1968.[1276] The perverse incentives of the program greatly contributed to spiking divorce rates, fatherlessness, and single-parent families (almost all female). The Great Society programs of the 1960s have set an enduring pattern for inner-city social dysfunction with its attendant human misery.[1277]

The response to Daniel Patrick Moynihan's report *The Negro Family: The Case for National Action* (1965) demonstrates another aspect of the problem. In a remarkably prescient analysis, Moynihan identified the breakup of the black family as central to the plight of blacks in America.[1278] The *Report* embroiled the administration in "furious controversy."[1279] Black leaders "responded with outrage." This totally negative reaction by many liberals, both black and white, introduces the "blaming the victim" mantra by which any analysis including the issue of personal responsibility is preemptively

---

[1272] Patterson, *Grand Expectations*, 533.

[1273] Jason Riley, *Please Stop Helping Us: How Liberals Make It Harder for Blacks to Succeed* (2015).

[1274] Patterson, *Grand Expectations*, 535.

[1275] Patterson, *Grand Expectations*, 672.

[1276] 1960–3.1 million; 1968–6.1 million. Patterson, *Grand Expectations*, 672.

[1277] Patterson, *Grand Expectations*, 672–77. Patterson's own perspective on this issue is generally balanced, though he hints that some of the backlash may have reflected racial prejudice. It is also true that the immiseration is not confined to the inner city but is very much present in rural Appalachia as well with its overwhelmingly white population where the same perverse incentives are present.

[1278] He was an assistant secretary of labor in the Johnson administration. Family breakup was linked to both a "rapidly increased rate of unemployment" and "welfare dependency." Patterson, *Grand Expectations*, 586.

[1279] Patterson, *Grand Expectations*, 586. The report was considered "so divisive, so controversial" that the Johnson administration "shut Moynihan out," and "the taint never seemed to fade." Shlaes, *Great Society*, 316.

rejected. The resulting putative compassion conceals a crippling dehumanization. The overall thrust of the Great Society programs was to set the country on the fundamentally wrong path to the unsustainable entitlement culture of today.[1280]

This evolution was embedded in a synergy of cause and effect. According to James T. Patterson, the whole era of 1945 to 1971 was an era of Grand Expectations which emerged from the prosperity engendered by the economic stimulus of World War II and continued into the 1950s and early 1960s. However, this did not bode well because the exuberant optimism of the social programs set the stage for a socially destructive long-term outcome. To this mix must be added the effect of what Patterson calls the Rights Revolution. The rise of Grand Expectations stimulated "a Rights Revolution that reverberated long afterwards."[1281]

The end result of the Great Society is the present reality of an unsustainable entitlement society where continuing grand expectations are totally detached from personal responsibility. What makes this dystopian reality intractable is the persistent investment of the Democratic Party in exploiting the resultant human misery, seen most graphically in the festering inner-cities of twenty-first-century America.[1282] The Democratic Party has engaged in a long-term repudiation of the wisdom of the Founders with increasingly

---

[1280] Allen J. Matusow *The Unraveling of America: A History of Liberalism in the 1960s* (2009; first ed., 1984). Matusow subjects the Great Society programs to detailed analysis. He is certainly far from dismissing them entirely—some programs helped sometimes. However, in the first edition, he nevertheless accepted the "conventional wisdom" that "the liberal effort to improve America [was] a failure" (xx). In the 2009 edition, he still maintained that liberalism failed because "its ideas and programs . . were too often flawed" (ix). The most recent extended analysis is even harsher. For Amity Shlaes, it seems clear that "the government lost the War on Poverty." Its programs "established a new kind of poverty, a permanent sense of downtroddeness" which "fostered a new sense of hopelessness and disenfranchisement." Shlaes, *Great Society*, 11.

[1281] There is no end in sight as Patterson indirectly acknowledges by admitting that while the liberalism of the 1960s was "both attractive and well meaning," it was nevertheless "destined for serious trouble ahead." Patterson, *Grand Expectations*, 592. The "Rights Revolution" does not always look so good to ground-level observers. J. D. Vance recalled noticing the deductions for state and federal income taxes from his small paycheck, while also noticing that his "drug-addict neighbor would buy T-bone steaks which I was too poor to buy for myself but was forced by Uncle Sam to buy for someone else." J. D. Vance, *Hillbilly Elegy: A Memoir of a Family and Culture in Crisis* (2016), 139.

[1282] Who is more likely to vote Democratic—an inner-city welfare mother or a middle-class black professional in the suburbs? Central to the hope for the long-term success of the War on Poverty was the promise of education reform, particularly in the success of compensatory-education programs to close racial education gaps. Since 1980, we have spent almost $500 billion (in 2017 dollars) without any significant success. The gaps have persisted. It is evident that "what America has been doing, at a cost of hundreds of billions of dollars, hasn't worked." Eric A. Hanushek and Paul E. Peterson, "The War on Poverty Remains a Stalemate," *Wall Street Journal*, March 18, 2019.

---

pernicious results.[1283] Today, we are at a tipping point for the sustainability of our society. For black Americans, the saga has been played out by the transition from the cotton plantation to the urban plantation. Even the political eccentrics among us get it right occasionally. The black rapper Kanye West certainly did when he said: "All blacks gotta be Democratic? Man, we ain't made it off the plantation."[1284] Not yet, Kanye, not yet— and not ever, if the Democrats can help it, regardless of the cost to blacks and to the American experiment in democracy.

The gloomy but perceptive John Adams asserted that "democracy never lasts long. It soon wastes, exhausts, and murders itself. There never was a democracy yet that did not commit suicide."[1285] One wonders even if a John Adams could have foreseen the prescription for social and political suicide proposed by the contemporary Democratic Party.

[1283] Evidence continues to accumulate that the Great Society's War on Poverty was "causing irreparable damage to the very communities it was designed to help." Indeed, an "institutional sclerosis" inexorably "corrodes and corrupts the ever-enlarging welfare state." Charles Krauthammer, *Things that Matter: Three Decades of Passions, Pastimes, and Politics* 2013), 13. See also Charles Murray, *Losing Ground: American Social Policy, 1950–1980* (2015) and Mancur Olson, *The Rise and Decline of Nations: Economic Growth, Stagflation, and Social Rigidities* (2008).

[1284] www.hotair.com/archives/2018/04/29. See also Jason Whitlock, "Kanye Had One of the Best Tweets of All Time," *Wall Street Journal*, May 8, 2018. Liberalism, Whitlock observes, is the "black people's cigarette" and "the welfare check, the replacement of black fathers, is liberalism's nicotine."

[1285] John Adams to John Taylor, December 17, 1814, https://founders.archives.gov/documents/Adams/000-02-02-6371.This observation, first cited in the introduction, seems also a fitting conclusion in light of our perilous, uncertain future.

SELECTED BIBLIOGRAPHY

Alden, John R. *The American Revolution, 1775-1783* (1962).

Alexander, Gerard. "The Myth of the Racist Republicans," *Claremont Review of Books*, Spring 2004.

Allen, Danielle. *Our Declaration: A Reading of the Declaration of Independence in Defense of Equality* (2014).

Ammon, Harry. *James Monroe: The Quest for National Identity* (1971).

Ayers, Edward L. *The Promise of the New South: Life after Reconstruction* (1992).

Bailyn, Bernard. *Ideological Origins of the American Revolution* (1967).

Baker, Jean H. *Affairs of Party: The Political Culture of the Democratic Party in the Mid-Nineteenth Century* (1998).

Bancroft, George. *A History of the United States from the Discovery of the American Continent* (1888).

Banning, Lance. *The Sacred Fire of Liberty: James Madison & the Founding of the Federal Republic* (1995).

————. *The Jeffersonian Persuasion: Evolution of a Party Ideology* (1978).

Bartlett, Bruce. *Wrong on Race: The Democratic Party's Buried Past* (2007).

Barnet, Randy E., "Free at Last," *Claremont Review of Books*, Winter 2015/16.

Bauer, Jack K. *The Mexican War, 1846-1848* (1974).

Beard, Charles. *An Economic Interpretation of the Constitution* (1913).

Becker, Carl L. *The Declaration of Independence: A Study in the History of Political Ideas* (1958).

————. *The Heavenly City of the Eighteenth-Century Philosophers* (2003).

Belz, Herman. "The Legend of Sally Hemings." *Academic Questions*, Summer 2012, 218-27.

Bemis, Samuel Flagg. *John Quincy Adams and the Union* (1956).

Benedict, Michael L. *The Impeachment and Trial of Andrew Johnson* (1999).

Bennett, Lerone. *Forced into Glory: Abraham Lincoln's White Dream* (2007).

Bergeron, Paul H. *The Presidency of James K. Polk* (1986).

Blight, David W. *Race and Reunion: The Civil War in American Memory* (2001).

Bordewich, Fergus M. *Congress at War: How Republican Reformers Fought the Civil War, Defied Lincoln, Ended Slavery, and Remade America* (2020).

Borritt, Gabor S. *Lincoln and the Economics of the American Dream* (1978).

Brinton, Crane. *The Anatomy of Revolution* (1965).

Buel, Richard Jr. *America on the Brink: How the Political Struggle over the War of 1812 almost Destroyed the Young Republic* (2005).

Burstein, Andrew. *The Passions of Andrew Jackson* (2003).

Carter, Dan T. *When the War was Over: The Failure of Self-Reconstruction in the South, 1865-1867* (1985).

Castel, Albert. *The Presidency of Andrew Johnson* (1979).

Charles, Joseph. *The Origins of the American Party System* (1956).

Chernow, Ron. *Alexander Hamilton* (2003).

Cole, Donald B. *The Presidency of Andrew Jackson* (1993).

Crofts, Daniel W. *Lincoln & the Politics of Slavery: The Other Thirteenth Amendment and the Struggle to Save the Union* (2016).

Cunningham, Nobel E. *The Presidency of James Monroe* (1996).

————. *The Jeffersonian Republicans: The Formation of a Party Organization, 1789-1801* (1957).

Curry, Leonard P. *Blueprint for Modern America: Non-Military Legislation of the First Civil War Congress* (1968).

Dangerfield, George. *The Era of Good Feelings* (1952).

————. *The Awakening of American Nationalism, 1815-1828* (1965).

Dattel, Gene. "The Untold Story of Reconstruction." *New Criterion*, September 2015, 12-18.

Dell, Christopher. *Lincoln and the War Democrats* (1975).

Downs, Gregory P. *After Appomattox* (2015).

Dusinberre, William. *Slavemaster President: The Double Career of James K. Polk* (2003).

Egerton, Douglas R. *The Wars of Reconstruction* (2013).

Eisenhower, John S. D. "The Election of James K. Polk, 1844," *Tennessee Historical Quarterly* 53 (1994): 74-87.

Ellis, Joseph J. *American Creation: Triumphs and Tragedies at the Founding of the Republic* (2007).

———. *Passionate Sage: The Character and Legacy of John Adams* (1976).

———. *Founding Brothers: The Revolutionary Generation* (2000).

———. *The American Sphinx: The Character of Thomas Jefferson* (1997).

———. *The Quartet.* (2015).

Emberton, Carole. *Beyond Redemption: Race, Violence, and the American South after the Civil War* (2014).

Escott, Paul. *"What Shall We Do with the Negro? Lincoln, White Racism, and Civil War America* (2009).

Estes, Todd. *The Jay Treaty Debate: Public Opinion and the Evolution of American Political Culture* (2006).

Feldberg, Michael. *The Turbulent Era: Riot and Disorder in Jacksonian America* (1980).

Fehrenbacher, Don E. *The Dred Scott Case: Its Significance on American Law and Politics* (1978).

Fischer, David Hackett. *The Revolution of American Conservatism: The Federalist Party in the Age of Jeffersonian Democracy* (1965).

Fitzgerald, Michael W. *Splendid Failure: Postwar Reconstruction in the American South* (2008).

Foner, Eric. *Forever Free: The Story of Emancipation and Reconstruction* (2005).

———. *Reconstruction: America's Unfinished Revolution, 1863-1877* (1988).

Fornieri, Joseph R. *Abraham Lincoln's Political Faith* (2004).

Frederickson, George M. *The Inner Civil War: Northern Intellectuals and the Crisis of the Union* (1965).

Friedman, Lawrence J. *The White Savage: Racial Fantasies in the Postbellum South* (1970).

Gallagher, Gary W. *The Union War* (2011).

Grantham, Dewey W. Jr. "Dinner at the White House: Theodore Roosevelt, Booker T. Washington, and the South," *Tennessee Historical Quarterly* 17 (1958): 12-30.

Gray, Wood. *The Hidden Civil War: The Story of the Copperheads* (1942).

Greenburg, Amy S. *A Wicked War: Polk, Clay, Lincoln, and the 1846 Invasion of Mexico* (2012).

Grimsted, David. "Rioting in Its Jacksonian Setting." *American Historical Review* (1972): 361-97.

————. *American Mobbing, 1828-1861: Toward the Civil War* (1998).

Guelzo, Allen C. "Gettysburg and the Eternal Battle for a 'New Birth of Freedom'" *Wall Street Journal*, 7-1-13.

————. *Fateful Lightning: A New History of the Civil War and Reconstruction* (2012).

————. "Defending Reconstruction." *Claremont Review of Books*, Spring 2017, 77-80.

Hargreaves, Mary. *The Presidency of John Quincy Adams* (1985).

Haynes, Sam W. *James K. Polk and the Expansionist Impulse* (1997).

Hickey, Donald R. *The War of 1812: A Forgotten Conflict* (1989).

Hicks, John D. *Republican Ascendency: 1921-1933* (1960).

Hietala, Thomas R. *Manifest Design: Anxious Aggrandizement in Late Jacksonian America* (1985).

Hoadley, John F. *Origins of American Political Parties, 1789-1803* (1986).

————. *The Idea of a Party System: The Rise of Legitimate Opposition in the United States, 1780-1840* (1969).

Hoftstadter, Richard. *The Paranoid Style in American Politics and Other Essays* (1948).

Holt, Michael F. *The Rise and Fall of the American Whig Party: Jacksonian Politics and the Onset of the Civil War* (1999).

————. *Political Parties and the American Political Tradition: From the Age of Jackson to the Age of Lincoln* (1992).

Howe, Daniel Walker. *The Political Culture of the American Whigs* (1979).

———. *What Hath God Wrought: The Transformation of America, 1815-1848* (2007).

Isenberg, Nancy, and Andrew Burstein, *The Problem of Democracy: The Presidents Adams Confront the Cult of Personality* (2019).

Jameson, J. Franklin. *The American Revolution Considered as a Social Movement* (1967).

Jensen, Merrill. *The New Nation: A History of the United States during the Confederation, 1781-1789* (1950).

Keehn, David C. *Knights of the Golden Circle: Secret Empire, Southern Secession, Civil War* (2013).

Keith, Lee Anna. *The Colfax Massacre: The Untold Story of Black Power, White Violence, and the Death of Reconstruction* (2008).

Kennedy, David M. *Freedom from Fear: The American People in Depression and War* (1999).

Klement, Frank L. *Dark Lanterns: Secret Political Societies, Conspiracies, and Treason Trials in the Civil War* (1984).

Kranish, Michael. *Flight from Monticello: Thomas Jefferson at War* (2010).

Langguth, A. J. *After Lincoln: How the North Won the Civil War and Lost the Peace* (2015).

Lefer, David. *The Founding Conservatives: How a Group of Unsung Heroes Saved the American Revolution* (2013).

Leonard, Elizabeth D. *Lincoln's Forgotten Ally: Judge Advocate General Joseph Holt of Kentucky* (2011).

Leuchtenberg, William E. *Franklin D. Roosevelt and the New Deal, 1933-1940* (1993).

Levy, Leonard. *Jefferson and Civil Liberties: The Darker Side* (1963).

Linden, Glenn. *Politics or Principle: Congressional Voting on Civil War Amendments and Pro-Negro Measures, 1838-1869* (1976).

Link, Arthur S. "Woodrow Wilson: The American as Southerner," *Journal of Southern History* 36 (1970): 3-17.

McKitrick, Eric L. *Andrew Johnson and Reconstruction* (1960).

Magnet, Myron. *The Founders at Home: The Building of America, 1735-1817* (2014).

Masur, Louis P. *Lincoln's Hundred Days: The Emancipation Proclamation and the War for Union* (2012).

Matusow, Allen J. *The Unraveling of America: A History of Liberalism in the 1960s* (1984).

May, Robert E. *The Southern Dream of Caribbean Empire, 1854-1861* (1973).

Mayfield, John. *Rehearsal for Republicanism: Free Soil and the Politics of Antislavery* (1980).

McDonald, Forrest. *The Presidency of Thomas Jefferson* (1976).

————. *We the People: The Economic Origins of the Constitution* (1958).

————. *Novus Ordo Seclorum: The Intellectual Origins of the Constitution* (1985).

Meacham, Jon. *Thomas Jefferson: The Art of Power* (2012).

————. *American Lion: Andrew Jackson in the White House* (2008).

————. *American Gospel: God, the Founding Fathers, and the Making of a Nation* (2008).

Meyers, Marvin. *The Jacksonian Persuasion: Politics and Belief* (1957).

Middlekauff, Robert. *The Glorious Cause: The American Revolution, 1763-1789* (1982).

Miller, John C. *The Federalist Era, 1789-1801* (1960).

Milton, George Fort. *The Age of Hate: Andrew Johnson and the Radicals* (1965).

Morison, Samuel Eliot. *The Conservative American Revolution* (1976).

Morris, Richard B. *The Forging of the Union, 1781-1789* (1987).

Morris, Roy Jr. *Fraud of the Century: Rutherford B. Hayes, Samuel Tilden, and the Stolen Election of 1876* (2003).

Nagel, Paul C. *John Quincy Adams: A Public Life, A Private Life* (1997).

Neely, Mark E. Jr. *Lincoln and the Democrats: The Politics of Opposition in the Civil War* (2017).

Oakes, James. *Freedom National: The Destruction of Slavery in the United States, 1861-1865* (2013).

O'Reilly, Kenneth. *Nixon's Piano: Presidents and Racial Politics from Washington to Clinton* (1997).

Patterson, James T. *Grand Expectations: The United States, 1945-1974* (2009).

Paulsen, Michael Stokes and Luke Paulsen. *The Constitution: An Introduction* (2015).

Pessen, Eward. *Jacksonian America: Society, Personality, and Politics* (1978).

Perman, Michael. *The Road to Redemption: Southern Politics, 1869-1879* (1984).

———. *Reunion without Compromise: The South and Reconstruction, 1865-1869* (1973).

Pestritto, Ronald J. *Woodrow Wilson and the Roots of Modern Liberalism* (2005).

Peterson, Norma Lois. *The Presidencies of William Henry Harrison and John Tyler* (1989).

Piereson, James. *Camelot and the Cultural Revolution: How the Assassination of John F. Kennedy Shattered American Liberalism* (2007).

Rable, George C. *But There Was No Peace: The Role of Violence in the Politics of Reconstruction* (2007).

Rakove, Jack N. *Original Meanings: Politics and Ideas in the Making of the Constitution* (1996).

Remini, Robert V. *Life of Andrew Jackson* (2010).

———. *John Quincy Adams* (2002).

———. *Martin Van Buren and the Making of the Democratic Party* (1959).

———. *Henry Clay: Statesman of the Union* (1991).

Richards, Leonard L. *"Gentlemen of Property and Standing": Anti-Abolition Mobs in Jacksonian America* (1970).

Richardson, Heather Cox. *The Death of Reconstruction: Race, Labor, and Politics in the Post-Civil War North, 1865-1901* (2001).

Rogin, Michael Paul. *Andrew Jackson and the Subjugation of the American Indian* (1975).

Rutland, Robert A., *The Democrats: From Jefferson to Clinton* (1979).

———. *The Republicans: From Lincoln to Bush* (1996).

———. *The Presidency of James Madison* (1990).

Saxton, Alexander. *The Rise and Fall of the White Republic: Class Politics and Mass Culture in Nineteenth-Century America* (1990).

Schlesinger, Arthur M. Jr. *The Age of Jackson* (1945).

———. *The Age of Roosevelt* (1965).

Schroeder, John H. *Mr. Polk's War: American Opposition and Dissent, 1846-1848* (1973).

Schweikart, Larry and Michael Allen. *A Patriot's History of the United States.* (2004).

Shlaes, Amity. *Great Society: A New History* (2019).

Silbey, Joel. *A Respectable Minority: The Democratic Party in the Civil War Era, 1860-1868* (1977).

Smelser, Marshall. *The Democratic Republic, 1801-1815* (1968).

Smith, Elbert B. *The Presidency of James Buchanan* (1975).

Smith, James Morton. *Freedom's Fetters: The Alien and Sedition Laws and American Civil Liberties* (1956).

Stampp, Kenneth M. *The Era of Reconstruction, 1865-1877* (1965).

Stewart, David O. *Impeached: The Trial of Andrew Johnson and the Fight for Lincoln's Legacy* (2009).

Summers, Mark Wahlgren. *The Ordeal of the Reunion: A New History of Reconstruction* (2014).

———. *Party Games: Getting, Keeping, and Using Power in Gilded Age Politics* (2004).

———. "What Fresh Hell is This? Revisiting Reconstruction," *Register of the Kentucky Historical Society* 110 (2012): 559-74.

Towne, Stephen E. *Surveillance and Spies in the Civil War: Exposing Confederate Conspiracies in America's Heartland* (2015).

Trefousse, Hans L. *Rutherford B. Hayes* (2002).

———. *Andrew Johnson: A Biography* 1989).

———. *The Radical Republicans: Lincoln's Vanguard for Racial Justice* (1975).

Trelease, Allen. *White Terror: The Ku Klux Klan Conspiracy and Southern Recon-struction* (1971).

Vorenberg, Michael. *Final Freedom: The Civil War, the Abolition of Slavery, and the Thirteenth Amendment* (2004).

Ward, John W. *Andrew Jackson: Symbol for an Age* (1955).

Weber, Jennifer L. *Copperheads: The Rise and Fall of Lincoln's Opponents in the North* (2006).

White, Ronald C. Jr. *American Ulysses: A Life of Ulysses S. Grant* (2016).

Widmer, Edward L. *Martin Van Buren* (2005).

Wiencek, Henry. *Master of the Mountain: Thomas Jefferson and His Slaves* (2012).

Wilentz, Sean. *The Rise of American Democracy: Jefferson to Lincoln* (2005).

Wills, Garry. *"Negro President": Jefferson and the Slave Power* (2003).

Wilson, Kirt H. *The Reconstruction Desegregation Debates: The Politics of Equality and the Rhetoric of Place, 1870-1875* (2002).

Wilson, Major L. *The Presidency of Martin Van Buren* (1984).

Witcover, Jules. *The Party of the People: A History of the Democrats* (2003).

Wolgemuth, Kathleen L. "Woodrow Wilson and Federal Segregation," *Journal of Negro History* 44 (1959): 158-73.

Wood, Gordon S. *Revolutionary Characters: What Made the Founders Different* (2006).

———. *Empire of Liberty: A History of the Early Republic, 1789-1815* (2009).

———. *The Radicalism of the American Revolution* (1992).

———. *The Creation of the American Republic, 1776-1787* (1969).

Woodward, C. Vann. *The Strange Career of Jim Crow* (1979).

———. *The Burden of Southern History* (1968).

Woodworth, Steven. *The Great Struggle: America's Civil War* (2012).

Zinn, Howard. *A People's History of the United States, 1492–Present* (2003).

Index

Printed in the United States
By Bookmasters